P9-DMG-709

JX
1905.5
.M48
1988

Meyer, Robert S.,
1915–

Peace organizations,
past and present

DATE DUE

JX
1905.5
.M48
*1988

Meyer, Robert S.,
1915–
Peace
organizations, past
and present

LIBRARY/LRC
OUACHITA TECHNICAL COLLEGE
P.O. BOX 816
MALVERN, ARKANSAS 72104

OUACHITA TECHNICAL COLLEGE

*Peace Organizations Past and Present*

# Peace Organizations Past and Present

## *A Survey and Directory*

*by*

## Robert S. Meyer

**With a foreword by**
JOSEPH W. ELDER

McFarland & Company, Inc., Publishers
*Jefferson, North Carolina, and London*

OUACHITA TECHNICAL COLLEGE

**Library of Congress Cataloguing-in-Publication Data**

Meyer, Robert S., 1915–
 *Peace organizations, past and present.*

 Bibliography: p. 257.
 Includes index.
 1. Peace — Societies, etc. — Directories. I. Title.
JX1905.5.M48   1988       327.1′72′06       88-42515

ISBN 0-89950-340-3 (60# acid-free natural paper) ∞

© 1988 Robert S. Meyer. All rights reserved.

Printed in the United States of America.

McFarland & Company, Inc., Publishers
 Box 611, Jefferson, North Carolina 28640

f
05,5
m48
988

*This book is dedicated to all persons and organizations*
*engaged in positive efforts to promote world peace.*

# Acknowledgments

First of all, I wish to acknowledge the inspiration for this study received from Sister Anna, an Anglican nun from Northern Ireland.

Also, without the cooperation of the many respondents to our survey of positive efforts to promote peace, this compilation would not have been possible. We acknowledge with gratitude their important contributions, including their descriptive brochures, fact sheets, newsletters, reports, and other materials about their respective organizations.

I also wish to thank those who provided assistance and encouragement in this project, including Dr. Joseph W. Elder, Professor of Sociology and South Asian Studies, University of Wisconsin–Madison; Dr. Everett Refior, retired Professor of Economics, University of Wisconsin–Whitewater; Dr. Michael Hartoonian, Social Studies Consultant, Wisconsin Department of Public Instruction; Eric Liljequist, President of Madison's chapter of Educators for Social Responsibility; and Theodore Page, Secretary-Treasurer for Wisconsin's Dane County chapter of the World Federalist Association.

Finally, I wish to thank the Reverend Doctor Ralph Ley and his wife, Ruth, for their encouragement and helping me catch my typing errors in the manuscript; and my wife, Doris, for her assistance in proofreading the proofs sent us by the publisher.

*Robert S. Meyer*

# Table of Contents

# Foreword

*by Joseph W. Elder, Ph.D., Professor of Sociology
and South Asian Studies, University of Wisconsin*

In a day when the media are filled with accounts of international disputes, weapons in outer space, "terrorist" attacks on civilian populations, and national recriminations and counter-recriminations, Robert S. Meyer's book comes as a breath of fresh air. In this book he takes a look at a different dimension of the international scene — a dimension filled with ordinary people who are concerned about the levels of violence on which our world is poised, and who have done something about their concerns.

These "ordinary people" have organized scores of different groups, each group having as a common thread the promoting of peace. Some groups focus on personal approaches to world peace; others on instructional approaches to world peace; and still others on structural approaches to world peace. Within these three categories, defined by Mr. Meyer, lie scores of further sub-categories in which people have identified specific steps they believe they and their colleagues can take to reduce the chances of war and enhance the chances of peace. Readers of these pages will be astounded at the varieties and degrees of commitment represented in the 92 peace groups identified by the writer and tabulated into his analyses.

Meyer's findings give one cause for both encouragement and discouragement. It is encouraging that tens of thousands of citizens throughout the world are saying "no" to war. In many cases they are rejecting war in spite of the pressures brought upon them by their fellow citizens to follow their national leaders and to lend their efforts to military solutions. It is discouraging that, despite the fact that tens of thousands of citizens — perhaps even millions of citizens — around the world are saying "no" to war, wars continue, and national leaders promote and glorify wars. In his last chapter, the author addresses this problem directly, and invites his readers as well to address this problem.

Those of us interested in the promotion of peace owe a debt of gratitude to Robert S. Meyer. Thanks to his patient hours of letter-writing and archival digging, we now have in easily accessible form thumbnail sketches of scores of peace activist groups. Each reader is bound to find a few surprises — if only at the ingenuity of people committed to ending war.

Each reader, I dare say, will also be a little encouraged at the efforts of the human race to end one of our time-honored scourges. With so many people trying to solve the problems of war, can the solutions remain forever elusive?

# Preface

*The What, Why, and How of an Investigation Concerning Positive Efforts to Promote Peace*

In August of 1983, my wife, Doris, and I had the pleasure of having an Anglican nun, Sister Anna, from Northern Ireland, stay in our home for two nights during her fund-raising visit to the United States of America. Throughout her trip she lectured on peace education, and enthusiastically told her audiences of the success they were having in educating Catholic and Protestant boys and girls (ages 11–17) together in an integrated school in Belfast, Northern Ireland.

Sister Anna explained that while the Catholics and Protestants in Northern Ireland "did business" with each other, they almost never met socially. But, at her school, Lagan College, young people from both groups were studying and playing together and learning about each other and their families. This practical approach to developing mutual appreciation and understanding among the youth in both groups was first initiated due to pressure from concerned parents. Also, these Catholic and Protestant pupils and their parents are often brought together in family weekend retreats. (See Chapter 2 for an update.)

In our conversations, some of Sister Anna's enthusiasm rubbed off onto me, and I shared my reaction with her: "What a great idea!" This positive approach to solving the problem of misunderstanding and distrust between two groups for generation upon generation led me to wonder, "How many other such positive approaches to promoting peace are going on today? What other efforts to promote peace among groups of people have been successful in the past? Can we learn from them?"

As a result of my talk with Sister Anna, I was moved to investigate other positive efforts to promote peace from ancient to current times, and to share whatever I could learn with others.

For the next five months, I procrastinated, rationalizing that I should postpone my research until my obligation as chairperson for a community organization committee expired at the end of the year. However, I was now on the alert for materials related to peace efforts. For example, our daily newspaper, the *Wisconsin State Journal,* had a story from the *New York Times* News Service entitled, "Arabs, Jews Combat Enmity." It told about positive efforts to promote peace and understanding between these traditional enemies.

1

Another feature story from the Associated Press told of the Armand Hammer United World College of the American West near Montezuma, New Mexico. This is one of six United World Colleges. The others are located in Canada, Italy, Singapore, Swaziland, and Wales. The United World Colleges have two main goals: to promote international understanding through education, and to provide a pattern of education adapted to meet the special needs of our time. (For more information on UWCS, see Chapter 3.)

Once started, I have been gathering materials ever since. Also, knowing of our interest, some of our friends have been sending us clippings. A recent "find" was a quote from an undelivered 1945 speech by President Franklin D. Roosevelt inscribed in marble in the museum at the foot of the St. Louis Gateway Arch. It reads:

> Today, we are faced with the preeminent fact that, if civilization is to survive, we must cultivate the science of human relationships — the ability of all peoples, of all kinds, to live together and work together in the same world, at peace.

Several other statements such as the following helped to motivate me to get started with my study.

> War in our time has become an anachronism. Whatever the case in the past, war in the future can serve no useful purpose. A war which becomes general, as any limited action might, could only result in virtual destruction of mankind.
>
> President Dwight Eisenhower
> *Speech in July 1957*

> The threat of the atom bomb cannot be met by removing the bomb alone. It can only be met by removing war, by establishing world peace. ... If a new world war comes, atom bombs are sure to fall. If an atomic holocaust is to be averted, no world war must break out. Every little war threatens to set off a world war. So there must be no more war.
>
> Karl Jaspers, German Philosopher
> *The Future of Mankind,* 1958

> Unconditional war can no longer lead to unconditional victory. It can no longer serve to settle disputes. It can no longer be of concern to great powers alone. For a nuclear disaster, spread by winds and waters and fear, could well engulf the great and small, the rich and the poor, the committed and the uncommitted alike. Mankind must put an end to war or war will put an end to mankind.
>
> John F. Kennedy
> *1961 Address to the UN*

> ... we are led to wonder why it should be necessary to seek safety in terror, survival in annihilation, existence in nothingness, and to wonder

why we shouldn't resort to the more straightforward measure of disarmament: of seeking survival by banning the instruments of death.

> Jonathan Schell
> *The Fate of the Earth,* 1982

With thousands of nuclear explosives in the world everyone must come to understand that a military solution of any kind is not a solution at all.

> Victor Weisskopf, Physicist
> Professor Emeritus, MIT
> *Physics Today,* March 1983

In January of 1984 I enrolled as a guest student at the University of Wisconsin for the purpose of reading and research on positive efforts to promote peace. I was assigned to Dr. Joseph W. Elder, Professor of Sociology and South Asian Studies, and he and I arranged to meet approximately every three weeks to discuss findings.

In answer to one of my inquiries, Dr. Elder referred me to a colleague, Dr. Vincent Kavalosky, a Philosophy professor at the University of Wisconsin–Richland Center. He, in turn, invited me to sit in on a ten-week colloquium on peace education for area teachers that he and Dr. Jane Ragsdale of the Department of International Studies and Programs at the UW–Madison campus were going to conduct.

Among the educators enrolled in the colloquium was Ms. Ruth Gudinas from the Department of Human Relations, Madison (Wisconsin) Metropolitan School District. A Native American herself, she told us about the Iroquois Great League of Peace — of which I had never learned in my "education."

Also, in my discussions with Dr. Elder, I learned of Link House in Madison, Wisconsin. Its director, Sister Betty Richardson, brings together representatives from more than 60 local organizations in the Madison Justice and Peace Network; and she and her volunteers publish a monthly bulletin, *Linkage,* which lists all the peace activities scheduled for the coming month. They are also in the process of developing a peace resource center.

Through Link House I learned about the local chapter of Educators for Social Responsibility and contacted its president, Eric Liljequist, an elementary school teacher for the Madison schools. He was most helpful in lending me materials, including his curriculum guides for peace education. One guide listed a brief but excellent reference book entitled *Peace and War: Man-Made,* by Tom Galt (Boston: Beacon, 1962). It included information on both the Greek Achaean League and the Iroquois League. I found Galt's parallel approach to man's progress in both war and peace to be a good foundation for my study.

Other activities which have helped to broaden my awareness of peace organizations have been attendance at state conventions of the Educators for Social Responsibility, regular meetings of local chapters of UNA-USA

(United Nations Association of the United States of America) and WFA (World Federalist Association). At a monthly study group of the latter, our Secretary-Treasurer, Ted Page, gave a book report on *A Common Sense Guide to World Peace* by Benjamin B. Ferencz (New York: Oceana, 1985). We are indebted to Dr. Ferencz for much of the historical background shared in this publication.

In the fall of 1984, our area World Federalist Association sponsored a luncheon meeting at which we heard Franklin Stark, national president of the Campaign for UN Reform. He urged us to inform our senators and representatives in Congress that their constituents want United States support in making the UN more effective.

At this same luncheon, I met Dr. Everett Refior, Professor of Economics at the University of Wisconsin–Whitewater. He told me about the *American Peace Directory* published by the Institute for Defense and Disarmament Studies. Although I had already started to send a survey instrument to a selected sampling of peace organizations from a mailing list I had developed myself from sources in the UW Reference Library, Dr. Refior's specific directory of peace organizations was of great help. (See Appendix A for survey cover letter.)

Most of those contacted were quick to respond, enabling us to get a good feel for the large amount and variety of grass roots efforts in progress. Of the 133 surveys mailed, three were returned by the post office; there were 96 responses to the 130 delivered surveys — 73.85 percent rate of return. (See Appendix B for listing of 92 respondents whose materials were used in this publication. Four were not used.)

The responses from the various peace organizations were most heartening. Surely, with all these groups working for peace, something good must result! How could our national leaders ignore them? Could some of these groups get through to the "powers-that-be" more effectively if they combined their efforts?

As responses came in, they seemed naturally to group themselves into three categories: (1) organizations using *personal approaches* in promoting peace, (2) those using *instructional approaches,* and (3) those advocating *structural approaches.* The first were promoting world peace primarily through positive pacifism, assistance programs, and the development of friendships, understanding, and an awareness of "oneness." The second group was promoting peace primarily through research, publications, and education. The third category included those promoting peace primarily through reform of the United Nations to make it more effective, or through some form of world federation of nations.

The first chapter of this publication will summarize the historical background of the peace movement primarily as outlined in the two previously mentioned books by Benjamin B. Ferencz and Tom Galt. The next three chapters will share the information received within the three categories of responses to our survey of positive efforts to promote peace. The fifth and last chapter will recap project findings and their possible impacts and implications for the future. Humanity has been engaged in an ageless contest between war and peace, and we are rapidly approaching a "showdown" in which one will surely overcome the other. On this "final approach," we will either commit global suicide by nuclear war, or we will abolish war and establish structures which will enable us to resolve conflicts, manage global affairs, and share a brighter future in a world of peace and justice.

With the help and encouragement of many interested individuals and the cooperation of many peace organizations, I have produced this compilation of materials sent me, provided some historical background, and added a discussion of findings. It is hoped that this information being brought together under one cover will:

• Help various peace organizations become aware of ways in which they could support and strengthen each other in developing successful programs for moving world leaders to more actively work for peace.

• Help highlight recommendations of various peace organizations for serious consideration by world leaders in positions enabling them to support and implement practical steps toward world peace.

• Help those involved in peace education.

• Provide encouragement to those already active in peace organizations by helping them become aware of the magnitude of the peace movement of which they are a part.

• Provide motivation to readers to become active in promoting peace through one or more of the wide variety of organizations in operation.

• Motivate individuals, foundations, and others to provide financial support for peace organizations of their choice.

It is also hoped that this compilation of positive efforts to promote peace will provide food for thought on possible methods for bringing all of these diverse groups into a viable coalition for a peaceful world. This coalition could encompass all the world's people, their thousands of peace organizations, the world's parliamentarians, and the national executives with their foreign relations staffs. In its thirty-ninth session, the UN General Assembly passed a Declaration on the Rights of Peoples to Peace. We must have it!

# 1. Historical Approaches

*The Evolution of Social and Political Units; and a
Review of Efforts to Promote Peace Before and
Since 1788*

In considering how best to share what I learned in my investigation of positive efforts to promote peace, it seemed most logical to provide a brief historical review of the peace movement leading up to the current organizations responding to my survey. (See Preface and Appendices A and B.)

Thus, the first chapter will provide a brief review of the evolution of human relationships including the development and implementation of:
- Social and political units.
- Positive efforts to improve international relations, through 1788.
- Accelerating cooperative efforts among nation-states, since 1788.
- The League of Nations.
- The United Nations.

Hopefully, this historical review will help to assure us that we have been moving slowly in the right direction and provide encouragement to continue and accelerate our efforts in promoting world peace. The next three chapters will share information about the work of a broad sampling of current peace organizations.

## Evolution of Social and Political Units

There is evidence that prehistoric peoples lived in peaceful and cooperative relationships. However, fighting between families, clans, and tribes eventually began over the need for sources of food and water.

Fighting between families and clans stopped only when they learned to live together in tribes. Then tribes began to fight each other, especially in times of scarcity. Sometimes tribal chiefs encouraged war with other tribes to unite their people and help them forget problems within their tribes by fighting a common enemy. Intertribal wars decreased only when tribes merged into larger legal/polical systems such as city-states, republics, principalities, or feudal villages under noblemen. These units also fought each other until they were consolidated into still larger governmental systems such as kingdoms or empires. Thus, these political units evolved

7

into our nation-states that are still threatening or fighting each other. Now, we are in the midst of regionalization and cooperation for various common interests, and are gradually moving toward world organization.

Under the feudal system in Europe during the Middle Ages (approximately 476–1492), people lived in small villages under the protection of nobles who lived in medieval castles. The nobles usually had a baron or duke over them; and they, in turn, may have had a king above them. It was a time of "personal wars."

In 1066, *William the Conqueror* forced all of England to become one nation. The various parts of Spain became one nation in 1492.

*The Thirty Years War* (1618–1648) between the Catholics and the Protestants reduced the German population by a third. It ended with the *Treaty of Westphalia,* which realigned Europe into several sovereign and independent states defined by precise borders. The Westphalian system became the model for territorial organization of the entire world as we know it today.

Throughout history, peace between groups of people with conflicting interests has never been possible, and wars continued until some source of law and power was established over and above the clashing social units, integrating them with a higher sovereignty. People have learned to live in peace within ever larger "communities" by developing laws and governments for these expanded communities. Now that the community has come to include the whole world, today's world anarchy requires a global solution, in the development of universal laws, administered and enforced by a democratic federal world government.

## Positive Efforts to Improve International Relations, Through 1788

When groups of prehistoric peoples began to fight each other, it started with hand-to-hand fighting augmented with sticks, stones, slingshots, and cunning. Over the years, they developed weapons of increasing efficiency. By 500 B.C., Greeks, Persians, and Egyptians were fighting with arrows, swords and spears. Between 359 and 325 B.C., King Philip of Macedonia and his son, Alexander the Great, developed disciplines, techniques, and strategies of warfare far beyond previous levels. Through the ages, each war has brought "improvements" in modes of fighting and weapons, such as armor, catapults, towers, gunpowder, guns, bayonets, rifles, cannons, machine guns, grenades, airplanes, bombs, submarines, missiles, chemicals, and now nuclear and computer controlled weapons for the mass destruction of civilians along with military forces. With more complicated weapons have come more sophisticated training and preparation for warfare. Also, along with each increase in national ability to wage war has come an increase in the cost of war.

Let us take time to review some of the important statements and events in the evolving peace movement both before and since 1788 (the year the United States Constitution became official with the ratification by the required number of states); i.e., efforts to counteract the evolution of weapons and warfare.

The world's first known pacifist was the *Egyptian Pharaoh Akhenaton,* father of Tutankhamen. Akhnaten was pharaoh from 1375 to 1356 B.C. He worshipped one god, the Sun god, and he refused to fight battles. He turned his back on martial pomp and preached frankness, honesty, peace, simplicity, and sincerity from his throne.

*Isaiah* advised Hezekiah to use passive resistance against the Assyrian conqueror Sennacherib. Two centuries later, *Jeremiah* advised people to use a nonviolent approach when dealing with Nebuchadnezzar and his Babylonian armies.

In India, 500 B.C., Gautama, the Enlightened One, the *Buddha,* preached purity, renunciation, harmlessness, and nonviolence. He preached: "Only by love doth hatred cease"; "Overcome anger by love"; "Overcome evil with good, meanness with gifts, and lies with truth."

About 500 B.C. in China, *Confucius* taught conduct in which violence was depreciated. *Lao Tie,* exponent of Taoism, also advocated nonviolence and deflating war in favor of repose, calm, and unruffled, serene nobility.

While King Philip and his son, Alexander, were improving their techniques of warfare, the Ancient Greeks came up with an idea for keeping peace. Upon Alexander's death, they formed the *Achaean League,* consisting of twelve city-states. Voters elected ten councilors from each city. These 120 men formed the League Council. The League also had a popular assembly twice a year. As many as could attend formed the League's parliament. It made laws, levied taxes, managed the League's army, and established common money for the whole League.

When disputes between city-states arose, councilors and fact-finding lawyers asked questions and voted decisions. If a city disobeyed a decision, the army of the League as a whole, led by its president, marched on the city and arrested its officials, tried them in court, and punished those found guilty.

The Achaean League worked well among the twelve city-states for about 130 years, but it found it necessary to fight outsiders. After fighting another league, the Aetolian League, they were both so weakened that the Romans conquered both in 146 B.C.

In Palestine, *Jesus* was a true pacifist, and his early followers were opposed to war. "I am a Christian and therefore I cannot fight," was repeated over and over. Christianity became the "state religion" of Rome in 312 A.D. *St. Francis of Assisi* was a true believer in nonviolence.

Other individuals and groups have continued through the centuries to promote peace as a way of life. For example, *Baha'u'llah* (1817–92), founder of the Baha'i faith in Persia (now Iran) taught the oneness of God, oneness of religion, oneness of humanity, independent investigation of truth, elimination of prejudice, universal auxiliary language, equality of men and women, universal education, harmony of science and religion, elimination of extremes of wealth and poverty, world peace through world government and protection of cultural diversity.

Throughout history, humanity has sought ways to settle differences peacefully through law and order. Early tables of law were often attributed to divine origin and inspiration. They were introduced by men such as *Menes,* ruler of Egypt about 3,000 B.C., *Hammurabi,* ruler of Babylonia about 2,000 B.C., and by *Moses* en route to the promised land in the thirteenth century B.C. A few centuries later, *Manu* of India and *Mencius* and *Confucius* in China introduced divine tables of law which also influenced national and international laws centuries later.

Roman rules for waging war became the foundation for international law; and Roman law and justice helped to maintain peace (its Pax Romana) throughout the Roman Empire for 200 years.

In 1215, the *Magna Carta* prepared by English nobles reduced the power of King John. This "great charter" stated that every freeman has a right to a trial before being imprisoned or executed, that property could not be taken or destroyed without legal proceedings, and that justice must not be sold, denied, or delayed. The Magna Carta established that the law was greater than any single person, even a king.

The feudal system was replaced by mercantilism, with its maritime councils and guilds which developed rules for the regulation of international commerce. By 1219, the guilds were joining together to form hanses, and cities joined to form the *Hanseatic League.* Its purpose was to keep peace, to protect business from brigands and pirates, to address common problems such as high custom duties, and to improve commerce. It was successful through the sixteenth century.

Carved boldly into the ancient grey stones just above the arched entryway into the medieval city of Lubeck are the words, "Concordia Demi Foris Pax," which translate roughly into "harmony at home, peace abroad." This slogan represented the Hanseatic League's founding principle.

Disputes between members were settled by appeal to reason and law rather than arms. An ingenious system of mediation and arbitration functioned for over 200 years to prevent war between member cities.

Scholars in the Middle Ages studied history, including the Greek leagues of city-states, and began proposing European Leagues. The French lawyer *Pierre Dubois* developed a plan in 1306 which would unite Europe into a federation and make the Pope the head of its council. *George Podiebrad,* king of Bohemia (Czechoslovakia), tried to resurrect the good parts of Dubois' plan in 1464. He asked all kings to send ambassadors to meet together as a council to appoint judges for an international court. Unfortunately, the Pope did not like the plan, which did not include him, and he excommunicated Podiebrad two years later.

In 1310, an Italian scholar, *Dante Alighieri,* proposed one king for all of Europe for the sake of peace.

While scholars in Europe were searching for a peaceful society, the Iroquois in North America agreed to and implemented their Great Law of Peace and formed the *Iroquois League of Nations* in the mid-fifteenth century. It was managed by a council of representatives from each of the six nations. These male representatives were nominated by the noblest women of each tribe and were elected by their "local" council of chiefs. The council of the League made laws on matters of concern to the whole league, but left local problems for local councils to handle. Although it fought others, the League was very effective in keeping peace within itself. It still exists today.

A Dutch scholar, *Erasmus,* wrote "A Complaint of Peace" in 1514. It stressed the need for an international court to arbitrate disputes between kings.

*Father Franciscus de Victoria* of Spain has been recognized as one of the founders of international law. He was appalled by the genocidal slaughter of the Incas in the New World and was influenced by the writings of Cicero. He taught that all wars must be morally justifiable (e.g., to right a wrong); warriors should do as little harm as possible to an enemy, even in self-defense; and no person was bound to serve in an unjust war, even when commanded by his sovereign.

A Dutch jurist, commonly known as *Hugo Grotius,* is usually given credit for being the father of international law. He was jailed in 1619 but escaped to France, where he published his famous *Three Books on the Laws of War and Peace* in 1625. He introduced the idea that "international law" consisted of accepted customs, reasonable conduct, and treaties. According to Grotius, war was unavoidable due to the lack of legal precedents, and inevitable in the absense of an effective court. He espoused the brotherhood of man and the need for fair treatment of all peoples.

Early in the seventeenth century, *Henry IV,* king of France, proposed his "Grand Design," a system of cooperation that called for a union of fifteen European states to maintain order regarding commerce, politics, and religion—the three issues that most frequently led to war.

During the Thirty Years War (1618–48), a Parisian, *Emeric Cruce,* wrote a book, *The New Cineas,* containing advice for kings. Building on ideas from Dubois and Erasmus, he recommended that ambassadors from all nations meet continuously in Vienna. This court would settle disputes by majority vote, after listening to both sides and discussing the dispute. He also pointed out that peace was possible only if improvements were made in agriculture, industry, and science.

In 1662, the memoirs of *Duc de Sully* advocated a federal European union.

In 1693, *William Penn,* the Quaker founder of the Pennsylvania colony in America, wrote an essay, "Toward the Present and Future of Europe." It called for the establishment of a European parliament, improving upon Henry IV's Grand Design by proposing proportional representation. Compliance with its laws was to be enforced by all sovereign members.

Several other "peace plans" were written in the seventeenth century. Most were similar, requiring a council of ambassadors to settle disputes between nations and collective enforcement by all members of any nation refusing to abide by a decision. Most placed emphasis on international law, with some attention to international cooperation.

Another Quaker, *John Bellers* of England, suggested that an annual congress of European states meet to agree on ways to maintain international peace.

Penn's and Beller's ideas were strongly supported in France by *Abbe de Saint Pierre,* who, in addition to serving as a clergyman, was secretary to the French ambassador to the Netherlands. He published "Project for Perpetual Peace in Europe." Under it, anyone refusing to join the proposed union of states would be treated as an enemy of peace. He also rewrote the peace plan of Henry IV in 1713, and it, in turn, was edited by an admirer of the Abbe, the French philosopher *Jean-Jacques Rousseau.* Rousseau's version was published in 1761.

Unfortunately, none of these peace plans took hold in Europe, primarily due to the slow communications of their times.

While scholars in Europe were searching for ways to improve international relations and eliminate wars, their ideas were first implemented in the British Colonies of North America. In 1754, *Benjamin Franklin* proposed his Albany Plan of Union for the colonies. It was based on the Achaean League of Greece and Henry IV's Grand Design. In it, he proposed the colonies join together in one union under one British governor. It was rejected by the colonies because they feared dependence on one another. In 1774, Franklin submitted a second plan almost the same as the Achaean League, and it was also turned down. Finally, in 1776, the colonies did vote to join a league of confederation and declare their independence from Britain.

Influenced by the *Iroquois League* in America as well as the Greek leagues and European scholars, the former British colonies provided a big leap forward in international law through their four basic documents of unity:
- Declaration of Independence (1776).
- Articles of Confederation (1777).
- Northwest Ordinance (1787). (An ordinance for the government of the territory of the United States northwest of the River Ohio, passed by the Continental Congress.)
- Constitution of the United States (1787; ratified by required ninth state in June 1788).

Provisions of the Northwest Ordinance foreshadowed the first ten amendments to the Constitution, which became known as the "Bill of Rights," dated December 15, 1791. (See Appendix C for a Listing of Articles, Sections and Amendments, Constitution of the United States of America.)

Between 1783 (when independence was won) and 1787, the states operated as separate sovereign nations held loosely together by the weak

Articles of Confederation. Concerned about interstate bickering over borders, tariffs, boycotts, and other problems such as lack of uniform money and rebellions of destitute farmers in some areas, the Continental Congress issued a "call" to the thirteen states on February 21, 1787, to send delegates to a convention in Philadelphia to develop proposals for modifying and strengthening the Articles of Confederation. The delegates began work on May 25, 1787, but after due consideration, they agreed to draw up a new constitution rather than trying to amend the Articles of Confederation. They debated and deliberated throughout the summer of that year and completed their task with the approval of all twelve delegates (Rhode Island did not participate) on September 17, 1787. On September 28, the Congress of the Confederation resolved to submit the Constitution to the states for ratification, the document to take effect after nine of the thirteen states approved it. Thus, the Constitution of the United States was ratified when New Hampshire became the ninth state to approve it on June 21, 1788.

The document created was distinctive for its federal principle that government could be divided between different levels—i.e., local, state, and national. Each state retained jurisdiction over its own territory, but yielded authority on all matters concerned with common needs and dangers. Thus, a central authority could speak and act for all the states in their collective relationships to the rest of the world.

Implementation began the following year with the election of George Washington as first President on February 4, 1789, and the convening of the first United States Congress on March 4, 1789.

In celebrating the bicentennial of the United States Constitution, we have been reminded that it is the oldest federal constitution still in existence, and that over the years it has served as a model for many other nations. National federations since 1788 include Argentina, Australia, Brazil, Canada, West Germany, India, Mexico, Nigeria, South Africa, Soviet Union, Switzerland, Yugoslavia, and Venezuela.

## Accelerating Cooperative Efforts Among Nation-states, Since 1788

After the 1788 ratification of the Constitution of the United States of America, progress continued in Europe.

In 1789, the French National Assembly passed its *Declaration of the Rights of Man,* including freedom of speech and religion, and freedom from being imprisoned except when breaking the law.

*Baron de Cloots,* a wealthy Prussian, generously supported the new French Republic and gave a forceful speech, "The Universal Republic," and had it printed. He advocated one government for the whole world, in which people would elect representatives to a world parliament, abolish armies, establish a world peace force, and create one kind of money. From then on, peace plans always included "human rights."

On September 25, 1789, concerned that the United States Constitution was not sufficiently explicit regarding individual and state rights, the First Congress submitted twelve Amendments to the Constitution (known as the Bill of Rights) to the states for ratification. Ten of them were ratified by the required three-fourths of the states with Virginia's ratification on December 15, 1791, and they became a part of the United States Constitution. (See Appendix C for a list of those first ten amendments.)

The term "international law" came into common use when *Jeremy Betham* published his book *Principles of International Law* in 1793. Betham had previously written a peace plan calling for (1) a common legislature of European states, (2) an international court of judicators, (3) disarmament, and (4) the emancipation of colonies.

A German philosopher, *Immanuel Kant,* wrote a pamphlet, "On Perpetual Peace," in 1795. He advocated the abolishment of national armies and claimed that compelling soldiers to kill or be killed was a violation of the "Rights of Man." He proposed a federation of free states under a constitution that would prohibit wars and safeguard human rights.

After Napoleon's defeat at Waterloo, the victorious allies, Austria, Great Britain, Prussia, and Russia, tried to establish a lasting peace with the *Treaty of Vienna* in 1815. They changed the map of Europe to produce a balance of power, with the Netherlands, Switzerland, and Sardinia serving as buffer states between the big nations — Austria, France, Prussia, and Russia.

Soon after the Treaty of Vienna, under the leadership of Austria's Prince Metternich, Austria, Prussia, and Russia formed their so-called "Holy Alliance" for the unholy purpose of destroying democracy. After stopping democracies from forming in Naples, Piedmont, and Spain, they planned to suppress the new democracies in South America. Their efforts caused the United States to declare its Monroe Doctrine, stating that if any foreign armies tried to march into any country in the Americas, the United States would defend that country.

The "Holy Alliance" came to an end with revolutions throughout Europe during 1830–1848. Democracy won out. However, the alliance did demonstrate that nations could cooperate if they wanted to.

Another milestone in promoting peace was reached when *William Ladd* started forming peace societies in the United States, as well as writing another peace plan in 1840.

*The Danube Commission* to facilitate trade up and down the Danube River was initiated in 1846 as another attempt by nations to work together. This international organization was successful for 92 years.

During the American Civil War of 1861–65, the ideas of Cicero, Grotius, and others regarding human behavior even among adversaries began to be codified into law.

In 1872, *David Field,* first president of the unofficial *International Law Association,* wrote his "Outline of an International Code." It required arbitration of disputes and collective enforcement action.

Although there had been many peace plans proposed in prior years, *Tzar Nicholas II* of Russia brought together the first *International Peace Conference at the Hague,* Netherlands, in 1899 due to rising military costs and people going hungry. The purpose of the conference was to stop the bloodshed and expenses of war and to discuss disarmament. Delegates from 26 self-styled civilized nations met at the Hague, and they agreed a third party nation could intervene in asking two fighting nations to sit down to discuss and resolve their problems. The third-party nation would serve as judge. This first Hague Conference not only set up rules to follow in arbitration, it also established a Permanent Court of Arbitration. A Commission of Inquiry was developed by another Russian, Frederic de Marens. This commission, with representatives from both sides, was to investigate to determine what really happened in a dispute and then assess the amount of damage.

A *Second Hague Conference* was convened in 1907 with 44 countries represented.

While scholars and politicians were advocating peace plans and holding peace conferences, others were taking practical steps to manage international affairs. For example, the International Postal Union met in Paris in 1863. It established the General Postal Union in 1874 and changed its name to the *Universal Postal Union* in 1878. It now operates as an affiliate of the United Nations.

In 1865, the International Telegraph Union met in Paris with delegates from 26 nations. As more joined, it changed its name to the *International Telecommunications Union,* and it was enlarged to include trans–Atlantic cable. Today, it includes radio and television and is also a part of the UN.

These two communications unions provided a big step toward international cooperation. Other unions followed, such as the International Bureau of Weights and Measures; the International Union to Protect Patents and Trademarks (and copyrights for books); the International Union of Railway Freight Transportation; the International Sugar Commission of 1902; the International Institute of Agriculture in 1905 (later replaced by the Food and Agriculture Organization of the UN); and the International Office of Public Health in 1907. Many smaller international organizations followed, and by 1914, at least 45 international organizations were in operation.

A *League to Enforce Peace* was founded in 1915 in America, with former United States president William Taft serving as president. Also, in 1915, a group of English scholars started a *League of Nations Society.* Similar groups were started in France and Germany. Many were talking about the peace plans of Dubois, Cruce, and de Cloots. While they talked, 45 international unions were already at work.

In the United States, the League to Enforce Peace, the *Women's Peace Party,* and others persuaded President Woodrow Wilson to work for a League of Nations. Thus, at the end of World War I a covenant for the

*League of Nations* was prepared under Wilson's leadership and signed by 53 nations in 1919. (However, the United States never joined the League.) This was the first time this many nations had joined a league recognizing and confirming the importance of international laws as a vital component of international peace.

Even without an army, the League was successful in settling disputes between small nations simply because they wanted to stay on good terms with the larger powers. The League stopped several quarrels between nations and was especially useful in settling border disputes in its early years.

The League actively addressed a variety of international problems. It called conferences to discuss problems such as fishing rights, passport registration, air traffic, and many others. Many nations began signing agreements about several issues on which they had never before agreed. In addressing one common problem, it created a permanent advisory committee on traffic in opium and other dangerous drugs, and in 1920, it established the International Health Organization.

Its World Court began functioning in 1921. (Even though an American, *Elihu Root,* was one of its creators, the United States never accepted it.)

The League appointed a Committee of Experts for the Progressive Codification of International Law in 1924; and in 1928, the *Kellogg-Briand Pact* renounced war as an instrument of national policy. However, the major powers still reserved the right to decide the difference between "aggression" and "self-defense."

An international teacher exchange program was started by a committee of the League, and several of the international organizations became affiliated with the League, e.g., the International Labor Organization under the leadership of an American by the name of George Gompers.

However, largely due to lack of commitment on the part of member nations and the required unanimity for action in both the assembly and the council, it became evident by 1939 that the goal of collective security through the League of Nations could not be achieved. There was no way to stop World War II.

Many believed lack of United States membership made it difficult for the League to meet world hopes and expectations from the start. In effect, it was the nations that failed the League, rather than the League failing the nations. (See separate summary on the League of Nations in this chapter.)

On August 14, 1941, Prime Minister Winston Churchill of Great Britain and President Franklin D. Roosevelt of the United States signed the *Atlantic Charter* demanding a world organization be established to keep peace; and on December 4, 1941, Premier Joseph Stalin of Russia signed a treaty with the Polish government-in-exile which demanded a union of democratic states to uphold international law and keep peace.

Before the end of World War II, initial plans were drawn up for a

United Nations in 1944. These were formalized the next year when representatives from 50 countries formulated its Charter in San Francisco, California, and it started functioning in January 1946.

The *United Nations* was an improvement over the League of Nations, but it retained many of the League's shortcomings and problems. Whereas the League had four bodies (an Assembly, a Council, a Court, and a Secretariat), the United Nations had six parts (four similar): the General Assembly, the Security Council, the Economic and Social Council, the Trusteeship Council, the International Court of Justice, and the Secretariat.

The new *General Assembly* could make decisions by two-thirds vote rather than requiring unanimity as in the League's Assembly. However, it was still primarily a forum where representatives could voice and discuss their concerns, but with no legislative functions.

The new *Security Council* still included the five "big powers," and six other nations, three of whom were elected each year. Its primary task was to keep the peace, using all methods possible, including using all available armies and navies against an aggressor nation. This function was successfully carried out in some cases, but it has been severely hampered by the veto power held by each of the permanent "big five" members of the Council (China, France, Great Britain, Soviet Union, and the United States).

The new *Economic and Social Council* would assist the General Assembly in its work of health, education, and prosperity for all programs; help coordinate the work of the international agencies affiliated with the UN; and provide technical assistance in agriculture, engineering, and other skilled areas upon request from developing nations.

The *Trusteeship Council* took over the former League of Nation's Mandates as UN Trust Territories until they were ready for full independence.

The *International Court of Justice* continued the work of the Court of the League of Nations. Also, the UN Charter gave the Security Council the power to require a nation to obey decisions of the court. (But it is impossible to require any of the "big powers" on the Council due to their veto power.)

The UNRRA (UN Relief and Rehabilitation Administration) distributed $4 billion worth of food, blankets, beds, and medicine through 1948, mostly in Europe; and its refugee work continues. UNESCO (UN Educational, Scientific, and Cultural Organization) has sent many people to other countries to study and teach improvements in areas such as agriculture, airports, hospitals, irrigation, and schools. The UN Children's Fund (UNICEF) has been successful in bringing food and medical care to children throughout the world.

Along with its many other accomplishments, the UN has also been active in peacekeeping; but, unfortunately, it has failed to convince leaders in the United States and U.S.S.R. that they can be free from fear of an attack by the other.

Overlooking the many successes of the UN, some condemn it for not being able to do more in peacekeeping. Again, the words and machinery are provided in the Charter and Operating Principles. What is needed is stronger commitment to these documents on the part of member nations and a willingness to make needed changes to make the UN even more effective.

The 1945 Charter of the United Nations was in itself an act of codification of international law. However, the nations were still not ready to give the UN legislative authority to enact binding international laws. Yet, the Charter did obligate the General Assembly to encourage the development of international law as started by the League of Nations, and in 1947, the General Assembly of the United Nations established an International Law Commission to continue this work.

The General Assembly of the UN has contributed to the clarification of international law by various resolutions, the best known of which is its *Universal Declaration of Human Rights* of 1948. (See Appendix D for UN-UDHR.)

In 1949 the International Law Commission submitted its draft Declaration of the Rights and Duties of States.

After 50 years of attempts to define the term "aggression," it was finally defined in the UN's Nineteenth Declaration on Principles of International Laws Concerning Friendly Relations and Cooperation Among States.

According to the UN Department of Information, the UN has done more to codify international law in its 40-year history than in all of previous history. Also, according to Professor Louis Sohn of Harvard, more treaties have been concluded since the founding of the UN than in the previous 2,000 years. Each treaty has limited the sovereignty of the signatories to some extent. (See separate summary on the United Nations in this chapter, and a summary of the Campaign for UN Reform organization in Chapter IV.)

The long history of development and clarification of international law provides strong evidence that most members of the global community would like to "replace the law of force with the force of law."

Along with international law, the parallel progress made in international courts, judicial processes, emerging social justice, and arms control are all parts of the evolution of human relations concerning war and peace.

When it became apparent that the Security Plan of the UN could not be implemented due to lack of unanimity among the five permanent members of the Security Council, the United States and the Soviet Union turned to direct bilateral negotiations. Also, many nations began moving toward regional coalitions.

For example, the U.S. and the U.S.S.R. came very close to a treaty based on the *McCloy-Zorin Agreement for Disarmament Negotiations* that could have stopped the arms race back in the 1960s, thus saving both countries billions of dollars and rubles. In 1961, John McCloy, appointed by President John Kennedy, and Valerian Zorin, appointed by Premier Nikita Khrushchev, held three meetings, in Washington, D.C., Moscow, and New York. On September 20, 1961, they signed a Joint Statement of Agreed Principles for Disarmament Negotiations. It was reported by both governments to the UN General Assembly, which unanimously adopted it as the foundation for future negotiations toward general disarmament. It was a breakthrough in international efforts to disarm the world.

Based on this agreement, both countries started to draft a treaty. However, negotiations which could have developed a common treaty came to an abrupt stop with Kennedy's assassination. Both sides were unable to move away from the concept of national security based on military power. Fear and suspicion blocked the way to peace. As a result, both countries are still suffering economically while stockpiling nuclear warheads.

Treaties which have been signed by both super-powers include:
- The Non-Proliferation Treaty of 1968.
- The ABM (Anti-Ballistic Missile) Treaty of 1972.
- The SALT I (Strategic Arms Limitations Talks) of 1972. (SALT II of 1979 was not approved by the United States Senate, but the United States has lived up to it—to date of this writing.)

Examples of regional organizations based on mutual economic, political, religious, or other common interests include:
- The Organization of American States.
- The Organization of African Unity.
- The European Common Market.
- The European Parliament.
- The League of Arab States.
- The South East Asian Nations.
- The Non-Aligned Nations (misnomer).

Also, additional international organizations have been formed in relatively recent years to meet the need for international cooperation. Examples would include:
- The International Atomic Energy Agency.
- An International Maritime Organization.
- The UN Conference on Trade and Development.
- The International Air Transport Association.
- The World Health Organization.
- The UN Environmental Program in Nairobi.
- The World Meteorological Organization.

In looking back over these historical approaches to promoting peace, Benjamin Ferencz pointed out in his book *A Common Sense Guide to World Peace* that

>  ...it was war itself—and the shock of its horrors—that became the principal stimulus for progress. The Thirty-Years War produced the Peace of Westphalia in 1648. The Napoleonic Wars gave birth to the Congress

of Vienna in 1815. . . . The threat of war and the burden of an arms race
produced the Hague Conferences of 1899 and 1907. World War I inspired
the creation of the League of Nations. . . . The Second World War led to
the formation of the United Nations in 1945.

The title of Tom Galt's book *Peace and War: Man-made* describes
the theme of his discussion. Both war and peace require organized effort.
Galt listed four primary causes of war as politics; human feelings, emo-
tions, and excitement; money, business interests, and trade; and clashes
between systems of beliefs. He pointed out that we already know four ways
to settle differences between nations: diplomacy, mediation, commissions
of inquiry, and arbitration. Now, with the advantage of today's
developments in instant communications and jet air travel, we can encourage our national leaders to make the most of these methods as we move
gradually from nationalism to regionalism to (as John Dale would phrase
it) "self-government at the global level," achieved through "people based international law."

The balance of this chapter provides summaries on the League of Nations and the United Nations, before going on to reports from current
peace organizations concerning their efforts to promote peace.

## The League of Nations

President Woodrow Wilson of the United States and many others
believed that World War I could have been avoided if the nations involved
had had an opportunity to talk about their problems in public instead of
in secret. To provide such a place, a League of Nations was established at
the end of the war.

Although President Wilson played a leading role in formulating the
League of Nations, its Covenant was a product of political compromise
with conservative values prevailing. Unfortunately, Wilson neglected to involve and keep his United States Senate informed of progress in forming
the League. As a result of this oversight, partisan politics, and growing
isolationism, the United States never did join the League of Nations.

The League was organized in 1920 with four main bodies: (1) the Council, (2) the Assembly, (3) the Secretariat, and (4) the World Court.
However, neither the Assembly nor the Council could act without a
unanimous vote. War was not outlawed but was only delayed while other
methods of conflict resolution were tried. There was no agreement on disarmament or arms control.

The Council was a small group with one member from each of the
larger and more powerful nations and several representatives from the
smaller nations who took turns on the council. Whenever the League Council decided a nation threatened the peace of the world, it would call the
threatening nation and the others involved before it, listen to their

problems, discuss them, recommend solutions, and, when necessary, issue orders to settle the matter.

The League Assembly included one representative from every member nation. The Assembly could discuss any problem any member thought was important enough to bring before the Assembly. The Assembly could make recommendations, but could not make decisions or pass legislation.

Even so, the League was a significant step in humanity's efforts to create a better structure for an international society.

The League of Nations also had a Permanent Court of International Law, and its judges made decisions on the basis of international law.

Several other branches of the League worked to improve the conditions of peace. For example, the International Labor Organization worked to improve working conditions throughout the world. The Economic and Finance Organization arranged loans of money to developing countries. A Mandate Commission governed areas deemed not ready to govern themselves.

In its early years, the League played an important role in resolving border disputes, but its inadequacies became apparent as member nations hesitated to honor the spirit behind the covenant. The idea of collective security had to be abandoned by 1939.

The League failed primarily because it required unanimous consent for any action. There was no way to stop World War II, since Germany, Italy, and Japan simply resigned from the League when others objected to their war activities.

Despite its shortcomings, the League of Nations was a big step forward in humanity's search for world peace. It demonstrated the positive results that could be accomplished through international cooperation in a wide range of transnational affairs and the need for international laws and regulations.

## The United Nations

Initial plans for the United Nations were made at Dumbarton Oaks, an estate near Washington, D.C., in 1944 (during World War II), and it was formally organized in San Francisco, California, in 1945. There, representatives from 50 countries drew up its Charter, and it began operating in January 1946.

The *Preamble* to the Charter expressed the ideals and common aims of the peoples whose governments joined together to form the United Nations. It follows:

We the peoples of the United Nations, determined:
- to save succeeding generations from the scourge of war which twice in our lifetime has brought untold sorrow to mankind, and
- to reaffirm faith in fundamental human rights, in the dignity and worth

of the human person, in the equal rights of men and women and of nations large and small, and

- to establish conditions under which justice and respect for the obligations arising from treaties and other sources of international law can be maintained, and
- to promote social progress and better standards of life in larger freedom,

and for these ends:

- to practice tolerance and live together in peace with one another as good neighbors, and
- to unite our strength to maintain international peace and security, and
- to ensure, by the acceptance of principles and the institution of methods, that armed force shall not be used, save in the common interest, and
- to employ international machinery for the promotion of the economic and social advancement of all peoples.

have resolved to combine our efforts to accomplish these aims.

Accordingly, our representative Governments, through representatives assembled in the city of San Francisco, who have exhibited their full powers found to be in good and due form, have agreed to the present Charter of the United Nations and do hereby establish an international organization to be known as the United Nations.

The *purposes* of the United Nations as set forth in the Charter are:

1. to maintain international peace and security, and to that end, to take effective collective measures for the prevention and removal of threats to the peace and for the suppression of acts of aggression or other breaches of the peace, and to bring about, by peaceful means, and in conformity with the principles of justice and international law, adjustments or settlements of international disputes or situations which might lead to a breach of the peace.
2. to develop friendly relations among nations based on respect for the principles of equal rights and self-determination of peoples, and to take other appropriate measures to strengthen universal peace.
3. to achieve international cooperation in solving international problems of an economic, social, cultural, or humanitarian character, and in promoting and encouraging respect for human rights and for the fundamental freedoms for all without distinction as to race, sex, language, or religion, and
4. to be a center for harmonizing the actions of nations in the attainment of these common ends.

The Charter stated also that the United Nations would act in accordance with certain *operating principles*. They are:

1. The organization is based on the principle of the sovereign equality of all its members.
2. All members, in order to insure to all of them the rights and benefits resulting from their membership, shall fulfill in good faith the obligations assumed by them in accordance with the present Charter.

3. All members shall settle their international disputes by peaceful means in such a manner that international peace, and security, and justice, are not endangered.
4. All members shall refrain in their international relations from the threat or use of force against the territorial integrity or political independence of any member or state, or in any other manner inconsistent with the purposes of the United Nations.
5. All members shall give the United Nations every assistance in any action it takes in accordance with the provisions of the present Charter, and shall refrain from giving assistance to any state against which the United Nations is taking preventive or enforcement action.
6. The organization shall insure that states not members act in accordance with these principles so far as may be necessary for the maintenance of international peace and security.
7. Nothing contained in the present Charter shall authorize the United Nations to intervene in matters which are essentially within the domestic jurisdiction of any state or shall require the members to submit such matters to settlement under the present Charter; but this principle shall not prejudice the application of enforcement measures under Chapter VII.

The *structure* includes six main bodies of the United Nations: the General Assembly, the Security Council, the Economic and Social Council (UNESCO), the Trusteeship Council, the International Court of Justice (World Court), and the Secretariat.

*General Assembly.* All UN representatives are part of the General Assembly, and each has one vote. The General Assembly controls the UN finances, makes nonbinding recommendations on a variety of issues, and oversees and elects some members of other UN organs. Most business is delegated to the Assembly's committees, which prepare recommendations for the approval of the Assembly. Its main committees are:

- First Com.: for Political and Security (disarmament issues).
- Second Com.: for Economic and Financial issues.
- Third Com.: for Social, Humanitarian and Cultural Affairs.
- Fourth Com.: for Decolonization.
- Fifth Com.: for Administration and Budgetary issues.
- Sixth Com.: for Legal affairs.

Two commissions also report to the Assembly: the International Law Commission, and the UN Commission on International Trade Law.

Other organizations created by and reporting to the Assembly are:

- Office of the United Nations Disaster Relief Coordinator.
- Office of the UN High Commissioner for Refugees.
- UN Center for Human Settlements.
- UN Children's Fund (UNICEF).
- UN Conference on Trade and Development.
- UN Development Program.
- UN Environment Program.
- UN Fund for Population Activities.

- UN Industrial Development Organization.
- UN Institute for Training and Research.
- UN Relief and World Agency for Palestine Refugees in the Near East.
- UN University (in Tokyo).
- World Food Council.
- World Food Program.

*Security Council.* The responsibility for maintaining international peace and security rests with the Security Council of the UN. It has fifteen members, five of whom are the permanent members from China, France, U.S.S.R., United Kingdom, and the United States. The ten non-permanent members are nominated by informal regional caucuses and elected for two-year terms by the General Assembly (five each year). Decisions on substantive matters require nine votes; a negative vote by any permanent member is sufficient to defeat the motion. (Veto Power.)

*Economic and Social Council.* Under the authority of the General Assembly, ECOSOC coordinates the economic and social work of the UN. Its 54 members are elected by the General Assembly for three-year terms, eighteen each year.

*Trusteeship Council.* Originally, the Trusteeship Council administered eleven trust territories, but the number has been reduced to one, the Trust Territory of the Pacific Islands. Membership of the Council is made up of the five permanent members of the Security Council.

*International Court of Justice.* This is the World Court, and it has fifteen judges who are elected by an absolute majority of both the Security Council and the General Assembly for nine-year terms, five judges each year. The court hears cases referred to it by the states involved, and provides advisory opinions to the General Assembly and Security Council at their request.

*Secretariat.* The Secretariat administers the programs and policies established by the other UN organs. It is headed by the *Secretary-General,* who is elected by the General Assembly, on recommendation of the Security Council, for a five-year term. The Secretary-General is authorized by the Charter to bring to the attention of the Security Council any matter he believes may threaten international peace and security, and he may attempt to resolve international disputes. Under the Secretary-General are the Director-General for Development and International Economic Cooperation, 26 under-secretaries-general, and 25 assistant secretaries-general.

In addition to the six main bodies of the UN, there are several *specialized agencies* affiliated with the UN. These intergovernmental agencies administer many global affairs that transcend national boundaries. These specialized agencies are:

- Food and Agriculture Organization of the UN.
- International Civil Aviation Organization.
- International Fund for Agricultural Development.
- International Labor Organization.
- International Maritime Organization.

- International Monetary Fund.
- International Telecommunication Union.
- United Nations Educational, Scientific and Cultural Organization (UNESCO).
- Universal Postal Union.
- The World Bank.
- World Health Organization.
- World Intellectual Property Organization, and
- World Meteorological Organization.

The above specialized agencies are autonomous intergovernmental organizations related to the UN by special agreements. They have earned respect and positive recognition for their invaluable service. Two other autonomous affiliated organizations are the General Agreement on Tariffs and Trade, and the International Atomic Energy Agency.

Important dates, years, and decades established by the United Nations are listed at the top of page 26.

Membership in the UN has tripled from its original 51 member states to 159. In the past decade, most new members have been ministates which have joined as they became independent.

The General Assembly, the Security Council, and the Economic and Social Council all publish educational materials on a variety of subjects related to their functions; and the UN operates two bookstores, one in UN Headquarters in New York and one in Geneva.

Although the UN has been hampered by clashes between the democratic nations and the communist bloc, it has accomplished much in keeping the peace, in improving living conditions, and in promoting international cooperation.

Unfortunately, the operating principles established for the UN have been frequently transgressed. As a result, its ability to maintain peace has been questioned. However, it must be remembered that the UN is not a super-state, but an organization whose full effectiveness depends on the political will of the governments of which it is composed. The Secretary-General, Javier Perez de Cuellar, has emphasized the need for member states to reaffirm their commitment to the principles of the Charter and to make the fullest use of the machinery provided by the UN.

Much progress has been made in UN conflict control mechanisms, and on a large number of occasions, it has come up with a basic formula for solution. It has taken numerous actions to limit and control conflicts whose escalation into global conflict has been avoided.

A booklet from the UN Department of Public Information entitled *United Nations Today—1984* points out, "The critical value of peace-making and peace-keeping efforts would be instantly evident if they were to cease. It is essential, in considering our problems, to remember the positive side of the United Nations' account and to keep in perspective politically-motivated criticism."

Among its many other accomplishments are:

*Important Dates, Years, and Decades*
*Established by the United Nations*

**International Dates**

| | |
|---|---|
| March 8: | International Women's Day (Observed since 1916) |
| March 21: | International Day for the Elimination of Racial Discrimination |
| April 7: | World Health Day (Observes the founding of the World Health Organization, 1948) |
| May 17: | World Communications Day |
| June 5: | World Environment Day |
| June 26: | Charter Day (Anniversary of the signing of the UN Charter, 1945) |
| September 8: | International Literacy Day |
| October 16: | World Food Day (Anniversary of the founding of the UN Food and Agriculture Organization) |
| October 24: | United Nations Day (Official Anniversary of the UN's founding in 1945) |
| October 24–30: | UN Disarmament Week |
| October 31: | UNICEF Day (Observed in the U.S. with the Halloween Trick-or-Treat Program) |
| December 10: | Human Rights Day (Anniversary of the Universal Declaration of Human Rights, 1948) |

**International Years**

| | |
|---|---|
| 1985: | Year of the United Nations |
| 1985: | International Year of the Forest |
| 1985: | International Youth Year |
| 1986: | International Year of Peace |
| 1987: | International Year of Shelter for the Homeless |

**International Decades**

| | |
|---|---|
| 1975–1985: | UN Decade for Women: Equality, Development and Peace |
| 1980–1990: | Third United Nations Development Decade |
| 1980–1990: | International Drinking Water Supply and Sanitation Decade |
| 1980–1990: | Second Disarmament Decade |
| 1982–1992: | UN Decade of Disabled Persons |
| 1983–1993: | Second Decade to Combat Racism and Racial Discrimination |

- Playing an important role in the process of decolonization which brought independence to hundreds of millions of people.
- Bringing life and hope to millions of children and mothers in the world through the UN Childrens' Fund (UNICEF) of the General Assembly.
- Making a major contribution in handling global problems through its specialized agencies in their respective areas of expertise.

• Providing an authentic definition of the fundamental rights and freedoms which all human beings should enjoy. (See UN Declaration of Human Rights in Appendix D.)

• Developing the Convention on the Law of the Seas.

• Doing more to codify international law in the 40-year history of the UN than in all of previous history.

• Assisting and protecting millions of refugees through its instruments and agencies.

• Mobilizing international humanitarian concerns and activity on an unprecedented scale.

Recognizing its major contributions, the UN still has much to accomplish in establishing an accepted system for maintaining peace and security, implementing disarmament and arms limitation, and developing a just and effective system for international economic relations.

As reflected in an open letter from the Planetary Citizens organization, "The UN was never completed. It was purposely left unfinished and inadequate. Now, its peacekeeping and peacemaking capacities — the ability to freeze conflict and to settle disputes, must be gradually and fully developed." The World Citizens Assembly organization states the UN is "still the best hope for humankind."

On August 6–9, 1987, an International Bicentennial Symposium on Strengthening the United Nations was held in Philadelphia, Pennsylvania. Initiating sponsors for this symposium were: Common Heritage Institute of Villanova University, the World Federalist Association (usa), and the World Association of World Federalists. Besides these three initiating sponsors, there were 25 co-sponsors for the event. (For their names and more information on the symposium, see the section for the World Federalist Association in Chapter IV.)

At one of the plenary sessions of the symposium, participants heard Harold Stassen present the highlights of his "1987 Draft Charter for a Better United Nations Organization to Emerge from the Original, to Serve World Peace and Progress for the Next Forty Years!" In the Foreword to his proposal, Mr. Stassen began:

As we enter the 42nd year of the United Nations organization, it is my view that it is very, very urgent that a better United Nations now emerge from the original.

He also stated:

As the only one now living of the eight who were appointed in 1945 by President Franklin D. Roosevelt, and then reappointed by President Harry Truman, to draft and sign the original Charter in 1945, I feel a special responsibility.

# 2.  Personal Approaches

*Examples of Organizations Promoting Peace Primarily Through Friendship, Pacifism, Service, Understanding, and Unity*

There is a firm belief among many that a needed first step in creating a peaceful world is to provide as many opportunities as possible for peoples from different areas of the globe to get to know each other on a personal, private basis at the grass-roots level. They reason that these personal contacts will develop appreciations and understanding which will motivate peoples from different nations to insist on the resolution of problems between their nations in peaceful negotiations rather than by going to war over them.

As indicated in the preface, this chapter will describe several responding organizations (in founding date order) which promote peace primarily through the development of friendships and mutual understanding at the personal level, and through positive pacifism and the provision of assistance wherever needed. As might be expected, there is considerable overlap within organizations, with many promoting peace through education, for example, along with the above approaches.

## The Baha'i International Community

The Baha'is are followers of *Baha'u'llah* and come from a wide variety of backgrounds. Over three million in number, they reside in over 200 countries and territories and represent every race and almost every nationality and tribe. They have become part of one universal family through the unifying influence of Baha'u'llah's teachings.

Baha'u'llah was born in Persia (now Iran) and lived from 1817 to 1892. His teachings include: oneness of God; common foundation of all religion; oneness of humanity; individual search for truth; elimination of prejudice of all kinds; universal auxiliary language; equality of men and women; universal education; harmony of science and religion; elimination of extremes of wealth and poverty; universal peace upheld by world government; and protection of cultural diversity. He sought a fundamental redirection for his followers, and his objectives were the transformation of society; the establishment of world peace and a new civilization through the unity of mankind; and the renewal of individual souls.

In 1867, Baha'u'llah wrote to the kings and rulers of the world, including, among others, Napoleon III, Czar Alexander II, Queen Victoria, Kaiser Wilhelm I, Emperor Francis Joseph, the political leaders of the United States, and Pope Pius IX. In his letter, he outlined the requirements for a binding treaty that could create a lasting peace among nations. He called for an organic change in the structure of society in which nations would relinquish some of their sovereign powers to a federated world government with power to enforce its authority. On the 100th anniversary of this letter, in 1967, these messages were compiled and again presented to all governments by a Baha'i community that had spread throughout the world. Another statement from the Baha'i's Universal House of Justice entitled "The Promise of Peace" was distributed to the heads of all nations in 1985. This "peace plan" was also sent to other government leaders such as secretaries of state, congressmen and parliamentarians, governors and even local mayors.

Baha'u'llah believed when the cause of peace became important enough, or when the horror of war became feared enough, a number of "distinguished and high-minded sovereigns" would "arise with the firm resolve and clear vision to establish the Cause of Universal Peace." He envisioned the conclusion of a binding treaty for collective security which would specify the borders of every nation; determine the principles for relations between governments; limit the quality of arms to those needed to maintain internal order; and create an international governing agency.

In one of the Baha'is' brochures entitled, "Beyond National Sovereignty," they state, "The existing world order, based on the sovereignty of nations, grows increasingly incapable of resolving modern international issues," and "no nation can stand independent of the affairs affecting every other nation."

Today, Baha'is around the world are advocating world government and global economics. They are demonstrating the practicality of building a global society based on a foundation of social justice. To them, world unity is the alternative to nuclear war.

In August 1987, the Baha'i International Community was one of 25 co-sponsors of an International Bicentennial Symposium on Strengthening the United Nations. (For more information on the symposium, see section on the WFA in Chapter IV.)

## Fellowship of Reconciliation

In August of 1914, about 150 Christians met in Switzerland for an international ecumenical conference in an attempt to find a way to head off the threat of war, but the war broke out while they were meeting. On their way home, two of the participants, *Henry Hodgkin,* a British Quaker, and

OUACHITA TECHNICAL COLLEGE

*Friederich Siegmund-Schultze,* a pacifist chaplain for the German Kaiser, vowed to oppose war and violence, and to sow seeds of peace. Out of this vow, the Fellowship of Reconciliation was born four weeks later in Cambridge, England. The German branch came later.

As the first chairperson, Hodgkin went to the United States to help establish the American FOR in 1915. Local FOR groups have been organized across the U.S.A., and the American FOR became affiliated with the International FOR, which was established in 1919.

Fellowship of Reconciliation's *Statement of Purpose* reads:

> The Fellowship of Reconciliation (FOR) is composed of women and men who recognize the essential unity of all humanity and have joined together to explore the power of love and truth for resolving human conflict. While it has always been vigorous in its opposition to war, the Fellowship has insisted equally that this effort must be based on commitment to the achieving of a just and peaceful world community, with full dignity and freedom for every human being.
>
> In working out these objectives, the FOR seeks the company of people of faith who will respond to conflict nonviolently, seeking reconciliation through compassionate action. The Fellowship encourages the integration of faith into the lives of individual members. At the same time, it is a special role of the Fellowship to extend the boundaries of community and to affirm its diversity of religious traditions as it seeks the resolution of conflict by the united efforts of people of many faiths.
>
> In the development of its program, the FOR depends upon persons who seek to apply these principles to every area of life. FOR members:
> * Identify with those of every nation, race, sex and religion who are the victims of injustice and exploitation, and seek to develop resources of active nonviolent intervention with which to help rescue them from such circumstances.
> * Work to abolish war and to create a community of concern transcending national boundaries and selfish interests; they refuse to participate personally in any war, or to give any sanction they can withhold from physical, moral, psychological or financial preparations for war.
> * Strive to build a social order that will utilize the resources of human ingenuity and wisdom for the benefit of all, and in which no individual or group will be exploited or oppressed for the profit or pleasure of others.
> * Advocate fair and compassionate methods of dealing with offenders against society; they also serve as advocates for victims of crime and their families who suffer loss and emotional anguish, recognizing that restitution and reconciliation can help to heal both victims and offenders.
> * Endeavor to show reverence for personality — in the home, in vocational relationships, in school and the processes of education, in association with persons of other racial, sexual, creedal or national backgrounds.
> * Seek to avoid bitterness and contention in dealing with controversy, and to maintain the spirit of self-giving love while engaged in the effort to achieve these purposes.

Highlights in FOR's history include:

**1916.** Organized the National Civil Liberties Bureau (now the ACLU).

**1917.** Supported World War I conscientious objectors and contributed to legal recognition of C.O. rights.

**1918.** Helped found Brookwood Labor College.

**1923.** Helped organize the National Conference of Christians and Jews.

**1931.** Provided leadership for Pennsylvania textile strike.

**1932.** Led a Youth Crusade across Europe in support of the Geneva World Disarmament Conference. (IFOR.)

**1936–40.** Sponsored Ambassadors of Reconciliation to visit world leaders.

**1940–45.** Encouraged nonviolent resistance to war. European FOR members rescued Jews and other political refugees from Nazism.

**1943.** Backed first interracial sit-in. Led national protest against internment of Japanese Americans.

**1944.** Published Vera Brittain's *Massacre By Bombing* on Allied obliteration bombing.

**1947.** Sponsored an interracial team on the first "freedom ride" to test court decision outlawing discrimination in interstate travel.

**1953.** Organized the American Committee on Africa to support movement for African independence.

**1954.** Began six-year Food for China Program in response to Chinese famines.

**1955.** Sent first interracial teams to train Southern civil rights groups in nonviolent action.

**1957.** FOR staff worked with Martin Luther King, Jr., in Montgomery bus boycott.

**1961.** Launched Shelters for the Shelterless, building real shelters for homeless people in response to fallout shelter fad.

**1965.** Made contact with Vietnamese Buddhist pacifist movement. Published national peace statement signed by 3,000 clergy.

**1966.** Formed International Committee of Conscience on Vietnam with 10,000 clergy in 40 countries.

**1967.** Raised funds by "meals of reconciliation" to send medical aid to all areas of Vietnam.

**1968.** Sponsored world tour by Buddhist monk, Thich Nhat Hanh, of nonviolent movement in Vietnam.

**1969.** Reported Saigon government's reliance on torture as documented by FOR study team.

**1970.** Founded Dai Dong, a transnational project linking war, environmental problems and poverty. Members of Mission on Repression took part in first transnational peace demonstration in Saigon.

**1971–72.** 2,200 international biologists signed Dai Dong Environmental Statement featured in UN's publication, *UNESCO Courier*. Dai Dong held alternative to UN Environmental Conference in Stockholm.

**1973.** Released names of Vietnamese political prisoners. Launched amnesty campaign and Vietnamese orphan support program.

**1974.** Launched Key Campaign in continuing effort to free political prisoners in Vietnam.

**1975.** Initiated peacemaking project in United States seminaries. Intensified peace efforts in Middle East.

**1976.** Presented signatures on disarmament petition to the White House and Congress. Co-sponsored Continental Walk for Peace and Justice. Provided leadership for United Farm Workers' work camp.

**1977.** Opposed death penalty in concerted campaign with ACLU. Launched national effort with AFSC to close Rocky Flats Weapons Plant in Colorado.

**1977–78.** Worked to free Adolfo Perez Esquivel from prison in Argentina.

**1978.** Sponsored PLOWSHARE Coffee House/Discussion Center during UN Special Session on Disarmament.

**1979.** Intensified campaign against draft registration. Co-sponsored PLOWSHARE II at MIT during World Council of Churches Conference.

**1980.** Took the lead in initiating Nuclear Freeze Campaign in cooperation with other groups. Helped to organize Peace Sabbath.

**1981.** Helped launch New Abolitionist Covenant. Adolfo Perez Esquivel received Nobel Peace Prize.

**1982.** Played key role in UN Special Session on Disarmament II, including PLOWSHARE III presentation of World Peace Pledge and June disarmament rallies.

**1983.** Initiated new programs on U.S./U.S.S.R. Reconciliation and on Latin America. Helped to organize march on Washington for Jobs, Peace, and Freedom.

**1984.** Sent Nobel Prize Laureates to El Barco de la Pazto, Nicaragua, with humanitarian aid and support for the Contadora proposals for peace in Central America.

Recent activities have included:

• Its National Conference, *Hearts on the Line,* in Asheville, North Carolina, July 30–August 3, 1986.

• Offering of *Deepening the Roots* workshops in nonviolence for local communities.

• Publishing a brochure, *A Hopeful Alternative to Amerika,* pointing out the false assumptions in the TV mini-series and urging us to seize the opportunity to correct these assumptions and help others increase their understanding of the Soviet people.

• Publishing a brochure, *The Window of Opportunity.* It calls attention to the crisis in U.S. foreign policy, and the need to turn it around by challenging obsessive anti-communism, militarization of foreign policy and society, covert activity, and domestic and global injustice.

Over the years, some sixteen religious peace fellowships have affiliated with FOR as an interfaith, international pacifist association with an outstanding record of action since its founding in 1914.

## American Friends Service Committee (AFSC)

The American Friends Service Committee is a good example of a multi-faceted approach to promoting peace. For the purpose of organization, however, AFSC is included in this chapter for those promoting peace *primarily* through friendship, mutual understanding, positive pacifism, and service.

The AFSC had its beginnings during World War I when the draft exempted members of historic peace churches such as the Quakers, Mennonites, and the Brethren from combatant duty but not from the draft. Young Friends (Quakers), both men and women, requested assignments in assisting the victims of war; and a training unit was established at Haverford College in a Philadelphia suburb on July 17, 1917. It included a strenuous program of language studies, lectures, skill training, and physical exercises. Upon completion of its training, the Haverford group joined British Friends in France, and this AFSC group became an integral part of the American Red Cross. Along with operating hospitals, the AFSC concentrated on rebuilding and reconstruction of housing and agriculture.

In Russia, a group of English and American Friends provided relief for refugees in the Buzuluk area just north of the Caspian Sea.

At the end of the war in 1918, AFSC became deeply involved in reconstruction projects in France, in feeding German children, in distributing milk and cod liver oil to Austrian children, in feeding and clothing distribution centers in Poland, and in famine relief in Russia. AFSC also became involved in shorter-term projects in Serbia, Syria, Bulgaria, Albania, and China.

As the needs created by World War I became less, the AFSC established International Service Centers to carry on its work. These were located in Paris, Berlin, Vienna, Geneva, Warsaw, and Moscow. Centers were also established in other parts of the world: in Mexico City, Tokyo, Shanghai, Delhi, Amsterdam, and Washington, D.C.

With its experience from World War I, AFSC continued its work throughout the world wherever it saw need for its services, including the United States. In 1925, AFSC was reorganized into four sections: *Foreign Service, Interracial Service, Home Service,* and *Peace Service.*

In a sixtieth anniversary booklet, the American Friends Service Committee outlined its rich history of service (1917–1977). Presented here are some of the highlights from their account, within the four services.

*Foreign Service.* Brief statements concerning foreign service are listed below, opposite the dates or periods in which they were provided.

**1925.** Helped to build a Friendship Village for working people on the outskirts of the city following the Shanghai riots.

**1925.** Sent new graduates from Penn State's graduate college to Albania to help establish an agriculture college in Kavaja.

**1926.** Conducted refugee relief program in Bulgaria for displaced persons before the Red Cross could begin its relief work.

**1936.** Became involved in assisting victims of Spain's civil war; and as refugees fled to France, AFSC workers went with them.

**1938.** Started making emigration arrangements for German Jewish families.

**1939.** Mexican government invited AFSC to participate in a long range educational, health, and cultural project in the state of Nayarit.

**1939.** American Friends joined the British and Canadian Friends Ambulance Unit and they helped transport medical supplies over the famous Burma Road in West China during the war with Japan. Later, the Friends found they were providing needed services to both sides during the Communist Revolution. Not infrequently a communist soldier and a Kuomintang soldier occupied adjoining beds.

**Mid–1940s.** Provided famine relief in India and stayed on to help with reconstruction.

**1946.** With the advent of the United Nations, opened *Quaker House* to provide hospitality and behind-the-scenes conversation for UN delegates.

**1947.** Anticipated the need for postwar relief and reconstruction. First, needs of France were addressed; and then those of Austria, Finland, Italy, Poland, Hungary, Norway, and Holland. In Germany, AFSC worked with other groups under the CRALOG (Council of Relief Agencies Licensed to Operate in Germany). In Japan, AFSC was affiliated with LARA (Licensed Agencies for Relief in Asia).

**1947.** Began to provide for the affiliation of American schools with their counterparts in France, Germany, England, Japan, Russia, Rhodesia, and Mexico. Provision of materials led to exchange of letters, art projects, and other cultural and curriculum items. Student exchanges began in 1947.

**1947.** Continued to meet new emergencies such as the riots in Punjab and Kashmir after the establishment of Indian independence; and the outbreak of violence that accompanied the partition of Palestine.

**Post–World War II.** Expanded domestic work camp projects into Europe and Mexico. Also, expanded U.S. international seminars into Europe, Asia, East Asia, and Africa. (They found Arabs and Israelis, Indians, and Pakistani, East and West Germans could talk with each other in these seminars.) Reactivated the Quaker International Centers, and they continued to serve as bridge-builders between estranged groups.

**1950s.** Helped Italy's Union for the Struggle Against Illiteracy (UNLA) in setting up a series of adult night schools (Centers for Popular Culture).

**1952.** Launched a successful social and technical assistance program in India. (Turned it over to local control in 1962.)

**1952.** Began an educational, health, and cultural project in El Salvador.

**1953.** Met needs resulting from Korean war for home building and community education.

**1956.** Assisted Hungarian refugees pouring into Austria and Yugoslavia.

**1957.** Assisted Canal Zone refugees and evacuees in Egypt.

**1959.** World Refugee Year! Launched two major refugee programs: (1) helping refugees from Mainland China coming into Hong Kong; and (2) helping refugees from Algeria coming into Morocco and Tunisia.

**1958.** Provided feeding program in Lebanon.

**1960.** Launched social and technical assistance programs stressing self-help in India, Pakistan, Zambia, and Peru.

**1962.** Started teacher exchanges with Russia, which led to teacher exchanges with Europe, Japan, Rhodesia, and Mexico.

**1962.** Began conferences for mid-career diplomats which provided "off-the-record" sessions where they could relax from their "official positions" and enter into the give and take of real discussions.

**1963.** Aided hurricane victims in Cuba.

**1966.** Established a Child Care Center and sewing class as the first stage of a coordinated refugee program in Quang Ngai, South Vietnam.

**1966.** Gave donations to the Canadian Friends Service Committee and the Red Cross for medical supplies for both North and South Vietnam and the National Liberation Front.

**Vietnam War Era.** Provided aid to war victims of both North and South Vietnam. Also provided help in Laos and Cambodia (now Kampuchea).

**1967.** Sent a mission to Israel, Jordan, and Palestine following the Six Days War, and produced a set of proposals for peace which were circulated among Arabs, Jews, and others.

**1968.** Provided medical assistance and food distribution to both sides of the Nigerian/Biafra conflict.

**1970-1975.** Operated a program to feed the children of East Pakistan (now Bangladesh), and expanded into a community development project.

**1972.** Engaged in a rural development program in Guatemala.

**1973.** Helped Zambian government upgrade the area surrounding the capital city (following earlier AFSC community development projects in Zambia).

**1974.** After a long drought in the Schel region of Africa, helped establish a new village on the shores of Lake Pagrubine and taught families how to grow their own vegetables and livestock.

**1974.** Established feeding centers for children, and educational program for pregnant and nursing mothers, and helped with agricultural projects in Chile.

**1974.** Established a Mexican Friends Service Committee to carry on assistance programs in Indian villages.

**1976.** Provided emergency and reconstruction assistance to Guatemala following an earthquake.

**1976.** The AFSC's NARMIC (National Action/Research on the Military Industrial Complex) published a slide program on *Sharing Global Resources.*

**1977.** Sent a fourteen-person delegation to assess situation in southern Africa.

**1977.** Started a program of Women in Development which linked women across national and language lines in the discussion of common problems.

*Interracial Service.* Interracial Service was established in AFSC's reorganization in 1925 as one of its four service divisions. This division and its successor, the Community Relations Division, have provided assistance where needed to Native Americans, black Americans, Mexican-Americans, and more recently to Asian-Americans as well as to emigrants from around the world over the years. A few examples of its activities follow:

**1947.** Helped to persuade employers to hire on the basis of merit rather than race.

**1948.** Helped the Navajo and the Hopi indians during a drought and established an ongoing American Indian Program.

**1951.** Began a program of housing integration following the race riots in Cicero, Illinois. This led to working with fair housing groups in Boston, New York, Pasadena, Seattle, Dayton, Des Moines, and other major cities.

**1951.** Established a program in Washington, D.C., to help teachers and school principals, students, and parents to prepare for desegregation. (Program expanded to North Carolina, Louisiana, and Mississippi.)

**1958.** Began working with Mexican-Americans in Texas and California.

**1965.** The AFSC and NAACP's Legal Defense and Education Fund jointly sponsored a School Desegregation Task Force which helped communities in seven Southern states prepare for open schools.

**1972.** Did a study and report on desegration in Southern schools.

*Home Service.* At the end of World War I, to meet domestic needs and the desire of young Friends for service opportunities, AFSC established its Home Service Program. The following were some of the Home Service activities of AFSC, many of which have become part of the Community Relations Division:

**1920.** Fed children in depressed coal mine areas. This led to several other domestic relief programs such as assistance to striking textile workers.

**1930s.** Helped millions of unemployed during the Great Depression.

**1932.** Began health and education programs in the coal fields. Some adults were retrained for other work.

**1933.** Started to become involved with work camps, cooperatives, home industries, federal homesteads and sharecropping during the Depression.

**1939.** Started to help refugees from Europe get established in their new land, frequently arranging for vocational retraining. (Many of the refugees aided by AFSC were teachers, scholars, or members of other professions.) Summer language camps for refugees were established at Goddard College, at Hidden Ranch in California, and at Stillwater, Minnesota.

**1943.** Started its Children's Program to provide opportunities for American children to share their plenty with victims of World War II.

**World War II.** Administered 20 camps and 30 smaller units in which over 2,400 men participated in the Civilian Public Service Program for conscientious objectors. (Only 25 percent of these men were Quakers.) They worked for the government without pay except for "room and board" plus a $25 monthly allowance. Work included soil conservation, help on farms, fighting forest fires, helping in training schools, mental hospitals, Japanese-American relocation camps, and hostels.

**Post–World War II.** Began to sponsor a series of international seminars in the United States to provide opportunities for young people from many nations to discuss international issues. Continued to provide resettlement programs within the United States for European refugees.

**1955.** Developed cooperative self-help programs for the rural poor in California. Similar programs followed for farm workers in southern New Jersey and West Chester County, Pennsylvania.

**1957.** Established cooperative self-help housing projects to rehabilitate a slum area in Philadelphia. (An example of AFSC's Center City Programs to combat apathy and helplessness.)

**1958.** Established Crenshaw House in Los Angeles, a home for parolees, as a part of its historic interest in prison visitation. This was followed by opening of similar houses in San Francisco in 1965 and in Des Moines, Iowa, in 1967.

**1960s.** Provided refugee resettlement programs for Indonesians and Cubans.

**1960s.** Advocated a worldwide organization for better international laws governing refugees, and United States legislation to permit the entrance of refugees on a more equitable basis.

**1967.** Sponsored a national conference on the draft and continued to train draft counselors.

**1970.** Produced a handbook for citizen action against the abuse of government surveillance of private citizens.

**1970s.** Worked with the United Farm Workers to improve the lives of migrant farm workers, including self-help housing projects.

**1974.** Began an exchange program between Puerto Rican youth and young men and women in the continental United States.

Generally speaking, most community development projects stressed training and self-help (letting people set their own goals and proceed at their own pace), and they stressed family planning assistance.

*Peace Service.* While all AFSC programs have as their central purpose the search for peaceful solutions to conflicts, the Peace Education Division has the specific charge to create an informed public opinion on issues of war and peace. Its peace caravans, international institutes, work camps, speakers' bureau, and peace literature have all contributed to that end.

Peace education of the AFSC has two fundamental and interrelated goals: (1) to encourage and support human survival by the abolition of war, beginning with a reversal of the arms race; and (2) to establish a nonviolent world order based on global justice and more equitable sharing of the world's resources. (In pursuit of this goal, it supports efforts to realize universal human rights.)

The approach by the AFSC to peace education is guided by its commitment to nonviolence and the alleviation of suffering by addressing root causes of situations and offering alternative approaches. Its peace education is community-based and coordinated nationwide; and it aims to empower people through education and nonviolent action toward the goals of global survival and justice.

The AFSC was awarded the Nobel Peace Prize in 1947 for its work in alleviating situations that could lead to further conflicts and for the work of its Peace Service. A few of its efforts are given below with approximate dates:

**1925.** Encouraged Friends to work actively for the abolition of war in times of peace. One successful activity of the Peace Service was its peace caravans, in which student peace volunteers spent their summers traveling in rural America to stimulate thinking about the issues of war and peace. They distributed thousands of brochures and other peace literature.

**1930.** Held its first Institute of International Relations at Haverford College, a two-week study of problems in attaining world peace.

**Since 1948.** Actively engaged in efforts to promote peace in the Middle East. For example, AFSC organized both public and off-the-record meetings between Israelis and Palestinians.

**1950.** Began two new programs in peace education: a national speakers' bureau, and family camps involving peace issues.

**1970.** Published a study, *Search for Peace in the Middle East.*

**1975.** Launched a peace education program concerning the Middle East.

**1977.** Held a national conference in Washington, D.C., to which moderates from Israel and the PLO were invited.

In the decade since its sixtieth anniversary booklet, AFSC has continued its service programs around the world—in Brazil, Cambodia, Cuba, Ethiopia, El Salvador, Israel, Lebanon, Laos, Mali, Mexico, Mozambique, Nicaragua, Sri Lanka, Somalia, Thailand, Zimbabwe—wherever needed. In the past two decades, peace education within the United States has focused on situations in Indochina, the Middle East, and on the draft, amnesty, and disarmament.

A more recent brochure about the work of the AFSC included the following highlights:

**1977.** Expanded work on disarmament and peace conversion in effort to halt the nuclear arms race.

**1978.** Addressed immigration and unemployment on the Mexico-United States border.

**1979.** Sent AFSC delegation to Soviet Union to propose mutually reenforcing disarmament initiatives.

**1980.** Sent aid to postwar Zimbabwe in setting up schools and cooperatives and began a training program for paramedics.

**1980.** Established agricultural training for Mapuche Indian staff in Chile to improve nutrition and income for Mapuche small farmers.

**1980–81.** Sent close to $2 million in relief and rehabilitation supplies to war-stricken Kampuchea.

**1981.** Established a Central America Assistance Fund to aid victims of violence and repression.

**1981.** Initiated a Call to Halt the Arms Race which began the Nuclear Freeze Campaign.

**1982.** Published a Middle East study, *A Compassionate Peace.* Began work in Lebanon on war relief, reconstruction, and agriculture.

**1982.** Released a study on *South Africa in Bondage: Time for Compassion and Action.*

**1983.** Started disarmament campaign in the United States and worked against deployment of missiles in Europe and the Pacific.

**1983.** Continued support for Native Americans as they sought enforcement of fishing and other treaty rights, an end to land and water pollution, better health for their people and more accurate school texts.

**1984.** Challenged growing United States intervention in Central America and called for peaceful resolution of conflict.

**1984.** Expanded food and development assistance in drought-stricken countries of Africa through Africa Hunger and Development Fund.

In addition to its newspaper, *Quaker Service Bulletin,* published in January, April, and October of each year, and a wealth of peace education materials, a sampling of brochures received from AFSC since the initial survey bear the following descriptive titles: *You and the Draft; But What About the Russians? (New Resources on the Soviet Union and United States-Soviet Relations); A Call to Conscience (A Challenge to U.S. Foreign Policy in Southern Africa); Talking Sense About Nicaragua; A Quaker Witness for Peace with Justice in Central America; Deadly Connection — Intervention & Nuclear War* (About a new slide show with 215 slides and a 30-minute tape); *Peace Education Resources.*

In a 1986 brochure entitled *Toward a More Human World,* AFSC described some of the practical, effective ways in which it was helping to "empower people in need to attain the dignity and self-sufficiency that all human beings deserve." In closing, it stated:

> Today, in dozens of ways and hundreds of places, the American Friends Service Committee puts the power of love to work on behalf of those who

need it most: the poor, the hungry, the hopeless victims of violence, discrimination and injustice.

In her 1986 Annual Report, *Seventy Years of Quaker Service,* Asia A. Bennett, Executive Secretary, credits three factors for uniting the efforts of AFSC: (1) their confidence in people's capacities even in the darkest of circumstances, (2) their conviction that all life — that of oppressed and the oppressor — is sacred, and (3) their profound respect for diversity.

In 1969, the AFSC established NARMIC (its National Action/Research on the Military Industrial Complex project). It serves as a source of information for journalists, educators, students, peace organizations, religious groups, and concerned citizens in the United States, Canada, and abroad. The information sheets, reports, slide shows and documentary films of NARMIC provide facts on United States military and economic policies and an analysis of how these policies affect people's lives. Study guides help religious, school, and community groups discuss issues and organize to work on those of special interest to them. As one brochure states, NARMIC is "providing resources for action and change."

## International Friendship League Pen Pals

Since its founding in 1934, the International Friendship League, headquartered in Boston, Massachusetts, has served as a clearing house for individuals from six through 69 years of age who wish a correspondent (or Pen Pal) in another country. Approximately 1,600 links are made each month, bringing together a great many people throughout the world on a person-to-person basis. Most use English, but with the study of foreign languages (including Russian and Mandarin) now being taught in the lower grades of the United States, there are few language barriers.

The League operates in the United States and 129 other countries, and it sponsors International Friendship League Pen Pal Clubs in schools and colleges. IFL believes great benefits can result if individuals can learn to know and appreciate the problems of those in other countries. Students become better informed, and, through them, their parents and teachers.

Its slogan is, "Have a pen pal and see the world!" The success of their program is attributed to the yearning of individuals everywhere for a peaceful world. Using the theme that everyone can afford a postage stamp, the program continues to grow and expand.

## Unitarian Universalist Service Committee

The Unitarian Universalist Service Committee was founded in 1939 as a response by religious liberals to growing fascism in Europe. The UUSC began working with refugees and saved countless numbers from death camps and thousands more from starvation.

After World War II, uusc became involved extensively in reconstruction programs throughout Europe. The Committee then broadened its work to include the poorest countries of the developing world.

The uusc now sponsors a wide variety of self-help health and human justice programs, working with staff and volunteers in Central America, the Caribbean, Africa, India, and in the United States. It is a non-sectarian organization with its world headquarters in Boston.

In *Central America,* the uusc works in villages and neighborhoods to help people work for social change, to end hunger in their lives, and to live in peace. Along with its fact-finding missions and development programs, uusc: (1) sponsors relief programs for refugees throughout Central America, and (2) supports efforts to let refugees already in the United States remain until it is safe for them to return home. uusc is also involved in Central American peace efforts.

In *India,* uusc supports economic and health programs for women and children in urban and rural areas, including: (1) a center to counsel the victims of rape and domestic violence, and (2) projects that enable poor women to earn money through weaving and the sale of handicrafts.

In the Caribbean, uusc has sponsored maternal and child health programs for many years. In its four-year Teenage Family Life Education Project in St. Kitts, many young women have received prenatal care, family planning information, and an opportunity to continue their studies and receive job training. In one of the poorest sections of Port-au-Prince, Haiti, the Committee supports a health program that trains people from the community in providing family planning and health care for mothers and children.

In Africa, uusc helped villagers in the poor and struggling country of Benin, West Africa, to build their own community health center. This Pahou Health Center provides health care by and for people in a region of fourteen villages. Generous contributions from United States supporters are helping construct "Health Huts," one-room health facilities where the villagers live.

In the United States, uusc has pioneered local self-help programs for over four decades, in places as diverse as Indian reservations and urban slums. uusc is now focusing on aging, and works to give older citizens, especially women and minorites, a full choice over where and how they will live. The Committee continues to work for constructive change in the criminal justice system, including a moratorium on prison construction, rehabilitation of criminals, and compensation for the victims of crime.

In a special plea for financial support dated November 1986, Dr. Richard S. Scobie, Executive Director of uusc, told of their efforts to help our Central American neighbors and the growing movement in the United States to provide real, constructive aid to Central America. He also reported that uusc had sponsored twelve congressional tours of the region, bringing United States legislators face-to-face with the results of United States policies in the region, to help them understand that further militarization of Central America is definitely not the solution to their problems. (See Chapter 3 for Unitarian Universalist Peace Network.)

## Jewish Peace Fellowship

The Jewish Peace Fellowship, founded in 1941 on behalf of conscientious objectors, is based on Jewish religious beliefs.

Over the years, the Jewish Peace Fellowship (JPF) has worked to improve the legal rights of conscientious objectors; offered training and information for Jewish draft counselors; referred potential C.O.s to the above counselors; and published its advice and efforts:

• In its newsletters.
• Through its Rabbis and Rabbinical organizations.
• Through the National Inter-Religious Service Board for Conscientious Objectors (NISBCO).
• Through Hillel organizations on campuses.
• Through a list of resource materials available from either its Nyack, N.Y., or Los Angeles, Calif., offices.

The JPF recently co-published *The Call to Conscience: Jews, Judaism, and Conscientious Objection,* a book on Jewish attitudes by Rabbi Albert Axelrad.

Since 1966, the Jewish Peace Fellowship has worked with other groups such as the above NISBCO, the American Friends Service Committee (AFSC), and the Fellowship of Reconciliation (FOR).

Its long-range program includes efforts for disarmament and for a Middle Eastern policy and attitude which would recognize the legitimacy of the state of Israel while admitting the justified rights of the Palestinian people. In addition, it has engaged in many other short-term efforts for peace.

The JPF stands for nonviolent social change and has endorsed the Pledge of Resistance and worked with Witness for Peace; for example, concerning Nicaragua. Jewish Peace Fellowship was also represented at the August 1985 Desert Witness for the fortieth anniversary of the bombing of Hiroshima and helped to plan that event.

In its response to our survey, JPF stated, "We have counseled potential conscientious objectors in three wars and under the present conditions offer pre-registration counseling."

The Jewish Peace Fellowship publishes an excellent quarterly entitled *SHALOM: The Jewish Peace Letter.*

## Baptist Peace Fellowship of North America

The Baptist Peace Fellowship of North America includes peacemakers from both the American Baptist and the Southern Baptist denominations, and they invite other Baptist denominations to join their fellowship.

During the Second World War, a group of American Baptists became convinced that the New Testament of the Bible forbade them to take up arms or kill, and they formed a fellowship of mutual support and encouragement. With the advent of nuclear weapons and cold war tensions, many others joined the Baptist Peace Fellowship to bear witness against the escalation of violence; and the number of members grew to approximately 1,500.

In 1979, a group in a Louisville, Ky., Southern Baptist congregation saw a need for a stronger witness for peace within their denomination. To meet that need, they founded a free quarterly tabloid, the *Baptist Peacemaker*. It goes into more than 15,000 homes throughout the world.

A delegation of 50 peacemakers from the two denominations (American and Southern Baptists) visited Baptist brothers and sisters in the Soviet Union in 1983. Their purpose was to affirm their common faith and the Christian love which "transcends the distrust and suspicion between the two countries."

Upon their return, some members of the delegation met with leaders of the Baptist Peace Fellowship to discuss the possibility of forming a Baptist peacemaking organization representing Baptists of all North America.

The following *statement of purpose* is quoted from a brochure published by the Baptist Peace Fellowship of North America:

> The *purpose* of the Baptist Peace Fellowship of North America is to unite and enable Baptist Christians to make peace in our warring world. We are called by God to witness to the Gospel of Peace.
>
> This calling is rooted in our faith in Jesus Christ, who is our Peace, in whom God is reconciling the world and through whom God calls us to the ministry of peacemaking. Peace is not only our goal, but our means. The foundation of Peace is Justice. The force of Peace is Love.

The following *goals* are also listed in their brochure:

- To establish peace groups at the regional/state, associational and local church levels.
- To nourish such peace groups, facilitate communication among them and bring them together for common purposes.
- To encourage all the Baptist groups and conventions in North America to engage in active peacemaking.
- To communicate regularly with our members and friends receiving and generating ideas and enthusiasm.
- To organize a Baptist peace and justice witness in the public sphere.
- To work cooperatively with other peacemakers.
- To share peace and justice concerns with Baptists internationally.

# National Council of American-Soviet Friendship, Inc.

The National Council of American-Soviet Friendship, Inc. (NCASF), has been working for understanding, peace, and disarmament since its founding in 1943 (during World War II). It celebrated a half-century of diplomatic relations between the two governments in 1983, and it continues to work for their improvement.

The Council is involved, nationally and locally, in major peace coalitions and activities. It pioneered in opposing the use of nuclear weapons after the Hiroshima and Nagasaki raids in 1945. It supported the first and second Special Sessions on Disarmament at the UN and worked for the ratification of the second SALT treaty, a comprehensive nuclear test-ban, and a United States pledge not to be the first to use nuclear weapons, to complement the Soviet pledge in 1982.

In its brochure, the NCASF highlights the following aspects of its program:

*Peace Program.* Involves the production and distribution of publications, materials and releases on peace, international affairs, and current events in the U.S.S.R.

*Educational Materials.* Consist of 16 mm films, books, periodicals, exhibits, slides, and recordings from the Soviet Union, available for loan/rental.

*Cultural Exchange.* Receives Soviet touring groups, lecturers and performing artists; teaching Russian language and sending delegations to the U.S.S.R.

*Friendship News.* A quarterly newsletter of this title is published on peace actions and the work of the local societies.

*Friendship Travel.* Arranges a number of tours in the Soviet Union every year, featuring the special people-to-people contact possible through the local *Houses of Friendship* in each Soviet city.

*Communities Linked for Peace.* Help to create formal relations between United States and Soviet cities too small to qualify for the official program of the International Association of Sister-Cities.

*Camp Artek.* This International Pioneer Camp on the Black Sea receives a group of young Americans between the ages of twelve and fifteen who are invited each year. Sponsored by the NCASF since 1967.

*Local Societies.* Twenty-three local branches have active programs including film showings, lectures, discussions, and other cultural activities coordinated locally and also in cooperation with the national office.

The National Council of American-Soviet Friendship is a part of an international network with like organizations in more than 60 countries which seek to share the similarities of peoples and to provide understanding of cultural differences.

The NCASF believes that detente and peaceful coexistence between the U.S. and the U.S.S.R. are basic to achieving world peace, and that friendship and understanding between their two peoples can form the basis for

U.S.-Soviet cooperation in preventing worldwide nuclear holocaust. The Council is deeply concerned about the consequences to both peoples of continuing arms escalation. It is convinced that serious disarmament has been stalled since 1945 primarily due to lack of trust between the two superpowers; and it is striving to combat this distrust through the programs described above.

## Presbyterian Peace Fellowship

To help certify and support Presbyterian conscientious objectors, the United Presbyterian Church U.S.A. (Northern) formed a Council of Presbyterian C.O.'s in 1944. Over the years, those involved have held annual meal meetings at the time of the denomination's General Assembly, and they changed their name to "Presbyterian Peace Fellowship."

Although a similar organization, formed in 1949 by the Presbyterian Church U.S. (Southern) and the Northern group, had been working together for over 30 years, they formally joined forces when their two denominations voted in 1983 to complete official merger by 1988 as the Presbyterian Church U.S.A.

In a new brochure for the combined Presbyterian Peace Fellowship, their stated purpose reads:

> The purpose of the Presbyterian Peace Fellowship is to support and enlarge the peacemaking witness of the Presbyterian Church, to discern, proclaim, educate, and act for peace in, through and for the church, to support the conscientious concerns of members who make commitments for peace and nonviolence, to be obedient to God's intention for peace in the world and in our personal lives.

Members make this commitment:

> By our faith in Jesus Christ we are called to seek justice, reconciliation, and peace through works of love and to reject war and violence. The Fellowship provides a means of mutual support for those struggling to achieve a nonviolent lifestyle, to advocate the policies of peace and justice, and to express this commitment nationally and locally, and in presbyteries and synods.

In 1983-84, the National Committee of the Presbyterian Peace Fellowship planned to focus on enabling the church to:

- Develop information, support, and assistance across the church where persons are struggling with matters of conscience regarding the draft, vocations, tax resistance, civil disobedience.
- Work for disarmament, a reasonable first step being the Nuclear Freeze.
- Work for better understanding between hostile nations, particularly U.S.S.R./U.S.A. and Cuba/U.S.A.

- Promote justice in Central America, the Middle East, and Southern Africa, particularly in helping the church distinguish between authentic expressions of human aspirations and subversive exploitations.
- Explore the need for national repentance in terms of our involvement in this hemisphere's economic development in the last 100 years.
- Monitor Presbyterian Church U.S.A.'s Peacemaking Program, and offer support, encouragement, and loving criticism where needed. [See Chapter 3 for PCUSA Peacemaking Project.]

The combined Presbyterian Peace Fellowship continues to hold a national breakfast meeting each year at the time of the General Assembly.

Along with its quarterly newsletter, *Briefly,* the fellowship has published *Presbyterians and Military Service* (containing 20 questions and answers), an informative booklet for youth and parents, and other brochures and papers on subjects such as sanctuary and conscientious objection.

## AFS International/Intercultural Programs

The American Field Service (AFS) International/Intercultural Programs are dedicated to peace through the promotion of worldwide intercultural learning and living experiences for secondary school students, young adults, and families from all walks of life. It was established in 1947 by volunteer ambulance drivers of both world wars. After the devastation of these two wars, they felt a great urgency for strengthening the bonds between nations. Toward that end, they established an international exchange program as their peacetime contribution to humanity.

In its first year, AFS established a scholarship program for high school students and brought 52 students from 11 countries to the United States to live with families and attend school. In 1950, the same opportunity to live with a family overseas was offered to American students. Since exchanges began, over 150,000 students have lived with host families in over 70 countries around the world.

In recent years, AFS programs have been expanded to include a wide range of intercultural learning experiences for adult professionals; e.g., educators, economists, public interest lawyers, and social workers.

The AFS is operated by an International Volunteer Network of over 100,000 volunteers engaged in recruiting, selecting, orienting, and counseling families and participants; hosting students; raising money; and bringing AFS to the attention of national and local leaders. Its various programs are implemented through local AFS volunteer chapters. Currently there are over 2,500 communities in the United States with AFS chapters.

The AFS Program Guide gives brief descriptions of the Hosting Program:

> *Hosting* is an opportunity for all kinds of families. Host families vary in age, size and income. While most include two parents with children of

varying ages, single parent families, young parents, single people, and older couples whose children have grown and left home also host AFS students.

The most important criteria for AFS host families are open-mindedness, flexibility, curiosity about others, a sense of humor, and a willingness to share their lives with a student.

AFSers from around the world bring new and fresh perspectives on daily life and global issues to their host families. Hosting a student or young teacher gives your family a chance to explore a new culture in your own home. An AFS experience is a time of growth for family members, as each is brought closer together in a joint project — that of welcoming a new son or daughter.

Hosting an AFSer is an affordable international opportunity. You don't have to be wealthy; AFS host families come from all walks of life and vary widely in their income levels and occupations. You should, however, realistically consider the cost of bed and board. To help offset these expenses, the IRS permits you to deduct up to $50 per month during your hosting experience. A modest monthly allowance is provided by AFS to all-year program students.

Hosts have a choice of hosting a student for a school year or for a short-term home stay of five to eight weeks (usually during summer vacation.) They may also host young instructors of English as a foreign language from countries such as Chile, China, Costa Rica, Peru, or Thailand.

Other programs of the AFS include:

*The AFS Student Year Program.* Offers U.S. high school students the opportunity to attend high school in one of 58 countries while living with a host family. Students are given a choice between summer and winter departures.

*The AFS Summer Program.* (June, July, and August.) Places students with families for eight to ten weeks in one of 58 countries around the world. Approximately one-half of the placements include school attendance, which involves other summer program choices available through AFS, among them language study, outdoor skills, and overseas volunteer work.

*The AFS Language Study Program.* Combines a short-term home stay with language instruction. AFS places eight to ten students and an instructor with individual host families in selected areas of AFS countries. The students meet twice a week for 2½ hours of instruction by a high school language instructor certified by Adelphi University. In addition, language study students participate in AFS activities planned for all other summer students placed in that country. Language instruction can be combined with sports programs. For example, the Latin America Sports Program offers participants the opportunity to live with a host family and ski or play soccer in an exciting and different environment.

*New Zealand Outdoor Skills Program.* Students spend 20 days at an Outdoors Pursuit Center and receive instruction on exciting skills, including kayaking, rafting, and mountaineering. Between two ten-day stays at the Center, there are homestays with New Zealand families near the Center. Students attend schools and integrate themselves into the daily routine of family life. This program is not a vacation, but a true challenge, both physically and culturally.

*AFS Work/Volunteer Programs.* Available each year in some countries. These special alternative programs combine a home stay with work projects or activities in agriculture, conservation, or social welfare work. These programs demand a great deal from all participants and at the same time offer opportunities to combine volunteer work with intercultural adventure. Participants are involved in a group experience by living and working together, and they meet people from many different backgrounds. Working as volunteers, they see parts of the countries not usually visited by tourists.

*The Netherlands Arts Program.* An example of AFS cultural studies. While living with an art-oriented host family, participants become involved in Dutch life through the arts and create their own work of art (painting, drawing, photography, etc.).

*The Visiting Teachers' Program* of AFS sends United States teachers to Asia and Latin America on exchanges ranging in length from six weeks to one year. The semester program in nations such as China and Chile allows teachers from the United States to have actual classroom experience in the schools of those nations. Also, there is an annual exchange of teachers between the U.S. and the U.S.S.R., usually for ten-week periods in the fall of the year.

Other special focus programs of AFS include the *Educators' Program,* the *Young Workers' Program,* and the *Inner City Program.*

Impact studies of the AFS experience offer concrete evidence that young people who participate in AFS programs experience a significantly greater amount of personal change than do those who have not had an international or intercultural learning experience.

An AFS experience is regarded as a definite "plus" by colleges when considering applicants for admission. In 1985, more than 35 internationally minded colleges and universities offered scholarships and grants specifically for United States students who had returned from an AFS experience.

The closing paragraph of a recent *AFS Program Guide* asserted:

> AFS is guided by the principle that individuals and families can leave the world different from the way they found it. AFS acts on the belief that people from diverse cultures and socioeconomic backgrounds discover the richness of their differences and the abundance of their similarities when they live and work together toward common goals.

## United States Servas Committee, Inc.

On the cover of its brochure, the United States Servas Committee "welcomes hosts and travelers to build peace through understanding," and quotes M.K. Gandhi:

... with every true friendship we build more firmly the foundations on which the peace of the whole world rests. Thought by thought and act by act, with every breath we build the kingdom of non-violence that is the true home of the spirit of man.

Servas was first conceived by an international group of youths studying at Askov, Denmark, in 1948, and was originally called "The Open Door System of Work, Study, and Travel." The name "Servas" (the Esperanto word meaning "serve") was later adopted to denote the spirit of international mutual service which characterized the movement.

Servas is an international cooperative system of hosts and travelers established to help build world peace, good will, and understanding by providing opportunities for deeper, more personal contacts among people of diverse cultures and backgrounds. Visitors are invited to share life in the home and in the community, and to share their concerns on social and international problems, and their interest in creative activities and mutual responsibility for their fellow beings.

Servas is a nonprofit, interracial, and interfaith organization. It also has NGO (non-governmental organization) consultive status with the United Nations. There are hosts in every region of the United States who welcome approved travelers of every nationality, race, creed, or vocation. United States Servas also welcomes handicapped travelers. Servas International has hosts or contacts in over 100 countries.

Servas is not a travel agency or a "cheap way to travel." It is for the thoughtful traveler who wants to know individuals by working with them, sharing their activities, entering their homes as one of the family. Servas travelers share their hosts' world, work, and ideas.

Servas travelers plan their own trips, using lists of hosts in the countries where they wish to go. These lists give the hosts' addresses, phone numbers, languages spoken, activities and interests. Travelers share the everyday life of the host. Stays are usually for two or three days and provide rewarding experiences which lead to greater international understanding on a personal level, and a basis for world peace.

For those who cannot travel, Servas brings the world into their living rooms through the visits of friendly, enthusiastic people from every continent. As stated by Servas:

Sharing your life with people from other countries and finding out how the world looks through their eyes brings innumerable exciting experiences. It's a remarkable way to dissolve barriers between people and their countries.

Hosts share their meals with travelers and provide accommodations that will fill simple needs. Servas travelers are not tourists, but instead are interested in opportunities to know their hosts and to become part of their homes. Hosts may invite travelers to stay longer than the usual two or three days. Hosts and travelers are expected to jointly plan the visits in advance by letter or telephone. Hosts are urged to accept travelers only when they have enough time and desire for a sharing visit. Those who cannot open their homes to overnight visitors can still share understanding in day visits.

There is a small contribution per year per traveler to cover Servas expenses; but no money is exchanged between travelers and hosts.

## World Pen Pals

In 1950 a class of ninth grade students in Minneapolis, Minnesota, wrote a letter to the President of the United States and the representatives at the United Nations. Portions of this letter read:

> We are the generation of children who have never known peace. We wish to speak to you for the millions of boys and girls who do not want to see more war.... Please keep talking until you find some way to agree.... Please remember the children everywhere.

The letter brought such widespread and spontaneous positive response that a letter-writing organization developed called *World Pen Pals.* It is now the largest organization in the United States specializing in matching wordwide pen pals, 12–20 years of age.

World Pen Pals is now a project of the International Institute of Minnesota. Each year it links more than 15,000 students from 175 countries and territories all over the world with students in the United States. (It does not link students within the United States.)

Those who apply for a pen pal abroad receive the World Pen Pals' newsletter, *Write in There,* and a valuable suggestion sheet including information, tips, and hints for good letter writing. Tips for teachers and leaders are also provided.

Names of potential pen pals abroad are obtained from well-established pen pal organizations abroad, schools, embassies, United States information agencies and Peace Corps volunteers. Some are also received from other cooperating letter-writing organizations in the United States. Individual requests from abroad are often received as the result of personal contacts, articles in newspapers or magazines, the Voice of America radio program and Radio Free Europe.

Years of correspondence often lead to personal meetings as hosts or visitors.

The friendships and understandings developed through World Pen Pals should and can make a positive impact on future international relations.

## Eisenhower Exchange Fellowships

A group of private American citizens established this program of exchange fellowships in 1953 to honor Dwight D. Eisenhower for his contribution to humanity as a soldier, statesman, and world leader. In response, President Eisenhower stated:

> I am proud that this organization carries my name. I believe we have got to have a better exchange of ideas, and above all, of people. Exchanges bring truth and understanding to people; and understanding, in the long run, means peace.

The Eisenhower Exchange Fellowships are dedicated to furthering international understanding and are unique in several ways:
• Eisenhower Fellowships provide exchanges at the leadership level. Unlike academic and research fellowships, they provide professional contacts, cultural experiences, and observations *for individuals who have already demonstrated outstanding achievement* in their countries and professions.
• Eisenhower Fellowships are privately supported and independent of any government, political, or academic affiliation. Each fellowship is designed jointly by the Fellow and a program officer in a free and non-bureaucratic atmosphere.
• Their purpose is to give the Fellows (from 88 participating countries) a better understanding of the United States, as well as access to the best professional expertise the country has to offer in their respective fields.
• An equally important goal is to give Americans better international understanding. Fellows have opportunities to explain face-to-face the situations, policies, and attitudes of their countries to key decision makers in the United States.

Eisenhower Fellows are men and women between the ages of 35 and 50 who are selected by EEF's final selection committee in the United States. The selection process is initiated by bilateral committees in the countries invited to nominate Fellows for a specific year's program. These committees first determine a professional field (or fields) of current paramount importance. Then candidates are sought in these field(s) and applicants are screened for final selection.

The Fellowships provide two to three months of closely scheduled professional conferences, consultations, social contacts, and visits throughout the United States. All costs of travel within the United States, as well as to and from the United States, are paid by EEF, Inc. In addition, EEF provides an allowance to cover living expenses. Fellows are asked to bring their spouses, provided they can stay in the United States at least six weeks.

A program tailored to individual professional objectives is created and administered for each Fellow by one of EEF's staff of experienced program officers. Arrangements are made for Fellows to meet with educators, executives, government officials, professional leaders, politicians, scientists and technologists. Fellows also visit farms, historic sites, laboratories, marketing centers and other places of professional or general interest. Fellows are also provided opportunities to visit "private" Americans in their homes.

Throughout their experience, Fellows are urged to make extensive inquiries about things that will be of most benefit to their homelands and to themselves personally, and to answer inquiries about their countries by Americans.

Overall, there is an emphasis on providing a broad exposure to the traditional strength of the American political system, private enterprise, local initiatives, and individual freedom.

The Eisenhower Exchange Fellowship is supported by annual contributions from corporations, foundations, and individuals (including former Fellows).

A large number of former Fellows have achieved even higher levels of responsibility in their professions. Many are now serving as ambassadors, cabinet ministers, heads of industry, universities, national and international agencies, or members of parliaments, as well as leaders in a variety of other important fields. Hundreds of influential men and women, aided by their experience as Eisenhower Exchange Fellows, are now in positions where they can foster communications, understanding, and agreement on international issues.

## People to People International

People to People was launched on September 11, 1956, when President Dwight D. Eisenhower invited a nucleus of 35 well-known businessmen to a White House conference to establish an organization composed of citizens dedicated to the pursuit of world peace. At this meeting, he said:

> The purpose of this meeting is the most worthwhile purpose in the world today: to help build the road to peace, to help build the road to an enduring peace. A particular part of the work we expect to do is based upon the assumption that no people, as such, want war, that all people want peace.... If we are going to take advantage of the assumption that all people want peace, then the problem is for people to get together and to leap governments, if necessary, to work out not one method, but thousands of methods by which people can gradually learn a little bit more about each other.... There is no problem before the American people, indeed before the world, that so colors everything we do, so colors our thinking, our actions, as does the problem of preserving the peace and providing for our own security.

Many organizations and persons were already doing many things toward the end sought; but, what was new was that the President and others high in government were now spurring them on. There had been no ban on private citizens making friends abroad; but historically, they had not been urged by government to do so as now envisioned.

President Eisenhower believed that if people — by the millions — could reach out their hands in friendship and communicate directly their warmth of personal interest and respect, it would be a real beginning to the struggle for a peaceful world. The technique was to be direct, people to people, as distinct from official government contacts. In describing People to People in 1963, he explained:

> It is a movement which in time could seep in under the structures of governments and through sheer force of popular opinion, create an international climate in which a genuine neighborliness of nations could thrive.

As his term drew to a close, President Eisenhower asked Joyce Hall, founder of the Hallmark Company and Foundation, to take over the sponsorship of People to People. Mr. Hall generously underwrote People to People activities. He shared the hope of his longtime friend, Dwight Eisenhower, to improve the climate for peacemaking by increasing communication and understanding of the people of the world. He also shared the President's view that People to People's credibility was suspect as long as it was administered by the United States government.

As the organization evolved over the years, the hyphens that had formerly been in the name were deleted and "International" was added. It is now a voluntary effort of private citizens to advance the cause of international friendship. It is a non-political, non-profit organization working outside of governments to establish understanding through personal contacts between Americans and other people of the world. People to People is financed by dues and donations.

Today there is a network of People to People chapters and international committees in more than 156 cities around the world.

People to People International has thirteen projects within three sections: (1) International Contact, (2) Youth and Education, and (3) Community Action. The following descriptive comments are quoted from a recent brochure:

> *International Contact.* The program of International Contact plays a major role in the development and realization of People to People's goals and objectives. As we strive to better understand our neighbors from all parts of the world, it is through three basic programs that help People to People obtain these goals.
>
> *The Civilian Ambassador Program* sponsors special interest groups of U.S. citizens to travel overseas to meet their counterparts in prearranged, meaningful meetings and embassy briefings. Each year, almost 2,000 doctors, lawyers, farmers, and other special interest groups travel to meet their counterparts in cities on five continents of the world.
>
> *The International Visitor Program* brings visitors to the United States for homestay visits. Thousands of homes are opened annually to guests from abroad, leading to many lasting friendships and increased mutual understanding. Many U.S. citizens also travel overseas for homestay visits.

In the field of *International Development,* new chapters and committees are being initiated each year, furthering the scope and influence of
People to People.

Within the *Youth and Education* section:

*The High School Student Ambassador Program* sends approximately
1,000 carefully selected students overseas each summer making contacts
in 30 countries. During an extensive educational travel program, each
student lives 12 to 15 days with families in several countries such as
England, Austria, Germany, Spain, Ireland, France, Japan, Denmark,
Holland or Greece. The students receive 12 hours of orientation in their
hometown and have two days of briefings in Washington, D.C. before
leaving. The ambassadors travel in groups of 30 to 35 with three or more
Teacher Leaders in each group.

*The School and Classroom Program* involves classrooms doing a study
and exchange with a counterpart classroom overseas. Students also are
able to learn about their own communities in order to send information
to their exchange partners overseas.

*The Pen Pal Program* attempts to match the thousands of requests
received annually for pen pals. When unable to meet the requests in this
department, the letters are referred to agencies specifically geared for pen
pals.

*The Magazine Exchange Program* works as a clearinghouse to coordinate names of people wishing to exchange magazines with individuals
from various countries.

Under *Community Action:*

*Local chapters* throughout the United States plan programs to introduce their membership to foreign guests so they may better perpetuate
and follow President Eisenhower's goals.

In addition to local chapters, several *Youth Chapters* have been formed
which function primarily as performing groups and travel overseas during the summer months to play for charity benefits in other countries.

In cities where no local or youth chapter exists, *City Representatives*
help promote PTP activities. Many people also become *Members-at-large*
through their belief in the ideals of the organization.

*Meeting the Americans* brings foreign diplomats, press, United Nations representatives, and businessmen to various parts of the United
States for short homestay visits.

*Awards Programs* also exist to recognize those members or citizens
who have made substantial contributions through their efforts toward
world peace within the Eisenhower concept.

# U.S./U.S.S.R. Church Relations Committee
# of the National Council of Churches

The National Council of Churches of Christ in the U.S.A. (better
known as simply the National Council of Churches) activated its U.S./

U.S.S.R. Church Relations Committee in 1956 when it had an exchange of official delegates at the height of the "cold war."

Following this first exchange, official exchanges were planned for every ten years. However, during the period of growing tension between the two nations, the frequency of meetings was accelerated. Christians in both countries have visited each other as part of a long-range plan to improve understanding and dialogue. In 1979, U.S./U.S.S.R. church leaders issued a joint statement on disarmament called *Choose Life.* Also beginning in 1979, a series of yearly meetings in Geneva was established. In addition, frequent informal meetings took place between leaders of the two groups as they were brought together by other events. In 1985, a joint vigil was held at the Summit Conference in Geneva. In 1984, 1985, and 1986 almost 600 persons took part in NCC Travel Seminars to the U.S.S.R. Soviet church leaders and theological students visited the United States in 1986.

In response to my initial survey, the National Council of Churches of Christ in the U.S.A. (NCCC) sent a booklet entitled *On the Way to Unity and Peace,* a report of the 1984 program of its U.S./U.S.S.R. Church Relations Committee.

1984 was the year when the announcement of American plans to deploy a new generation of missiles in Europe and to consider the militarization of outer space caused the Soviets to walk out of the disarmament talks at Geneva, and the year the Soviet bloc decided to boycott the Olympic Games. It was a year when relations between the United States and the Soviet Union were lower than at any time since the Cuban missile crisis.

Despite this tension, the U.S./U.S.S.R. Church Relations Committee of the NCCC decided to go ahead with its most extensive study and exchange program in its almost 30-year history, as evidence that in both nations, there was also a yearning for significant contacts with people who shared a deep desire for peace.

In May of 1984 a total of nineteen Soviet religious leaders visited rural areas as well as cities in the United States — eighteen Christian and one Jewish Rabbi. The June 1984 seminars were the latest in a growing number of contacts between the two Christian communities (only one of five specific exchanges during 1984–85). The seminars were designed to give 266 local church people from the United States a first-hand experience of Soviet church life.

After three days of briefing at Riverside Church in New York City, this largest group of Christians to visit the U.S.S.R. embarked on their experience. Among the 266 were Roman Catholic nuns, a Syrian Orthodox Archbishop, denominational executives, the moderator and vice-moderator of a major Protestant denomination, canons and deacons of Episcopal cathedrals, and university and seminary presidents. The delegation also included Hispanics, blacks, and Asian-Americans, and it was evenly divided between men and women.

Once in the Soviet Union, the entire group stayed together in Moscow, Zagorsk, and Leningrad; then they divided into 10 smaller groups of about

26 each to travel different regions and visit two cities in each from Tallin to Tashkent. Itineraries included factories, schools, farms, pioneer camps for children, national memorials, cultural events, museums, and extensive contacts among a great variety of churches. Baptist, Lutheran, and Roman Catholic churches were given priority, but interaction was also provided with Russian, Armenian, and Orthodox churches.

Visitors found that war experiences (especially World War II) had left most Soviet people with a passion for peace woefully lacking among too many people in the United States. However, their mutual concern for peace with justice was so central to the hopes and prayers of both Soviet and United States participants in this 1984 study and exchange program that they did not hesitate to address hard and difficult questions about national policies wherever they met, especially in forums held in Moscow and Washington, D.C.

An article in the report by Claire Randall called attention to three major reasons which motivated the two groups to continue their relationships:

• The Church is the body of Christ, which transcends national boundaries and political and ideological differences.

• Christians are called to respect God's creation, "both human and earthly." Thus, they must reach out to other peoples/nations (especially to nations sharing the power to destroy humanity and the earth); and in accordance with Christ's greatest commandment of love.

• Participants want to strengthen the churches of the U.S.S.R.

In Dr. Randall's closing paragraph, she stated:

The National Council of Churches has come to a new and exciting stage in its building of relationships with the churches in the Soviet Union. We have now begun to make it possible for hundreds of American Christians to experience Christianity in the U.S.S.R. so that they might bear a witness for peace in the world.

In another article in the report, V. Bruce Rigdon stressed their attempt to convince people inside and outside the church that it is possible for us in the U.S. and U.S.S.R. to live together, acknowledging our differences and resolving our conflicts without destroying one another. "That, simply stated, is why we and our Soviet fellow believers have worked so hard and risked so much." He pointed out that Americans are sometimes shocked to discover that among people who are supposed to be their enemies, there are many who are, in fact, their "brothers and sisters in Christ." He continues to remind us that the Gospel transcends ideologies and that Christians throughout the centuries have lived in all kinds of societies. In each situation they shared the common calling to care for justice, mercy, and peace.

At the close of the report, the Committee lists the following accomplishments of its 1984 program:

• Expansion of ecumenical contacts to include large numbers of persons in both countries.

• Involvement of local and regional councils of churches as well as United States denominations.

• Initiation of a significant national dialogue on U.S.–Soviet relations with a Christian perspective.

• Encouragement and strengthening of the life and witness of churches in the U.S.S.R.

• Enrichment and spiritual renewal of many American Christians and congregations.

• Preparation of printed and audiovisual materials on the people and churches of the U.S.S.R.

• Creation of a network in the United States of informed persons, committed to continuing this dialogue.

Since the initial survey, the NCCC has shared additional materials, including:

• Its Fall/Winter 1987 issue of *MIRror,* its U.S.S.R. Travel Seminar newsletter. (The name *MIRror* incorporates the Russian word for peace, "mir.")

• A brochure about plans for 1987–88 Travel/Study Seminars in the U.S.S.R. in observance of the one thousandth anniversary of the Russian Orthodox Church.

• A brochure entitled *Peoples and Churches of the U.S.S.R.* available from Friendship Press.

## Peace Corps

At his inaugural on January 20, 1961, President John F. Kennedy laid down his challenge: "Ask not what your country can do for you; ask what you can do for your country." Since President Kennedy formally established the Peace Corps by an executive order on March 1, 1961, over 100,000 Peace Corps volunteers have responded to his call.

The essential purposes of the Peace Corps were defined by the United States Congress in 1961 as follows:

It is the policy of the United States ... to promote world peace and friendship through a Peace Corps, which shall make (volunteers) available to interested countries and areas....

It then set forth three goals for volunteers:

• to help people of developing countries meet their needs for trained personnel;
• to help promote a better understanding of the American people on the part of the people served; and

• to promote a better understanding of other peoples on the part of Americans.

These three goals are met through the constant efforts of the Peace Corps volunteers—American citizens of all ages and backgrounds who willingly serve two years or more in a developing nation, sharing skills and knowledge in an effort to better the lives of Third World peoples.

Extensions beyond the initial two years of service have been common in many areas. Worldwide, the extension rate has been about 14 percent.

President Kennedy appointed his brother-in-law, Sargent Shriver, as the first director of the new independent agency. Shriver and his staff laid the foundation for the selection, training, project selection, and administration of volunteer services; and by September 1961, the first volunteers began work in their assigned countries.

As it began to function, the Peace Corps enjoyed favorable responses from the United States government, the public, the volunteers themselves and their host nations, whose requests for volunteers far outstripped the supply. (In 1966, the Peace Corps fielded more volunteers and trainees—a total of 15,556—than in any other year. By 1974, in its 24 years of existence, the Peace Corp had sent more than 100,000 Americans to over 90 developing nations.)

Throughout its history, the fundamental operation of the Peace Corps has not changed. Interested individuals, age eighteen and older, apply for volunteer service and are selected on the basis of their experience and qualifications. They are matched with requests from foreign governments to work side by side with host country nationals on projects in agriculture, rural and urban community development, health and nutrition, forestry, fisheries, small enterprise development, architecture, engineering, water sanitation, animal husbandry, and education (including teacher training, English, math, science, vocational education and special education). Volunteers are not only selected for their skills, but for their commitment to helping less privileged people to make the most of their resources.

After eight to sixteen weeks of training (usually in the country of assignment), these volunteers give 24 months of service in improving the lives of thousands of people in developing countries. They use technology that is affordable and ecologically sound, benefitting the community while preserving local culture and values. Peace Corps's accomplishments endure because the mission is not to do things for people, but to act as catalysts to help people do things for themselves; and volunteers aim to "work themselves out of a job."

Volunteers are trained in language, culture, and skills before assuming their assignments. They may be based in a large city or a remote village; they may live in comfortable or austere surroundings. They receive a subsistence allowance for living expenses at the level of their host counterparts; and they work as equals, not as supervisors. They immerse themselves in their communities, and become part of the local life by sharing language and culture.

Above all, volunteers work for peace and friendship. They are unique in their status as *individuals* overseas; the Peace Corps is not and never has been included as a segment of United States short-term foreign policy. The public diplomacy role of volunteers, and thus their overall effectiveness, would be undermined if the agency were perceived as a political instrument of United States foreign policy. This policy of Peace Corps autonomy has allowed the United States to demonstrate its continued humanitarian interest in countries during periods of strain and even during periods when agencies of the diplomatic mission have been withdrawn.

It is difficult to document the exact nature of Peace Corps's effects on the developing nations of the world due to the nature of the Peace Corps mission. Its successes cannot easily be measured by concrete criteria such as miles of roads paved, numbers of schools built or wells dug or children vaccinated, because the accomplishments of Peace Corps are, more importantly, the accomplishments of the host country's people. Volunteers gauge their effectiveness by how responsive their counterparts are to upgrading their own living conditions, because it is the role of the volunteer to teach and encourage self-sufficiency, not to do the work while villagers stand by. A 1978 Peace Corps survey found that volunteers had a direct impact on the lives of nearly one million people in a month.

In many ways, the Peace Corps's most valuable contribution has been to give hundreds of thousands of Third World children the chance to go to school. Not only have volunteers provided classroom instruction and teacher training in math, science, English as a foreign language, and other subjects, they have broadened available educational opportunities to include libraries, audiovisual methods, sports clubs and other extracurricular activities. Perhaps most importantly, Peace Corps teachers have encouraged their students to think independently from the structured outlines of their textbooks, to challenge the status quo, and to question the causes and effects of outside forces on their lives and their country.

The contribution of Peace Corps volunteers to world peace and friendship is furthered by the cross-cultural exchange which occurs in the country of assignment and in the United States when volunteers return.

Volunteers are living examples of the United States desire to promote peaceful relations among peoples. Each volunteer acts by example as an ambassador of American goodwill, and the cumulative effect of Peace Corps involvement in a country over many years is often significant.

Returned volunteers make significant contributions to the education of Americans in international development, global interdependence and, ultimately, achieving peace between the nations of the world. They hold positions in the United States Agency for International Development (AID), the State Department, Foreign Service, United States Congress, private voluntary organizations including International Voluntary Services, Cooperative for American Relief Everywhere (CARE), and Volunteers in

Technical Assistance; and in the private sector, as bankers, businessmen, educators, and journalists. Their first-hand knowledge of the realities of the Third World and their perceptions of the struggles for international cooperation give volunteers and Americans in general an edge in shaping United States policies for the future.

In 1963 Sargent Shriver wrote, "Peace is the fundamental goal of our times," and he "believed the Peace Corps could contribute to its attainment, for while armaments can deter war, only men can create peace."

The mission of the Peace Corps is still thriving under Director Loret Miller Ruppe, who has headed the agency since 1981. She oversees the activities of more than 5,000 volunteers in 59 countries spanning Latin America, Africa, the Near East, Asia, and the Pacific.

In the early years, the Peace Corps was criticized for expanding too fast and sending too many liberal arts graduates with insufficient technical training. However, in recent years, because of shrinking budgets, the Peace Corps has become leaner with better-trained volunteers.

In some areas, the Peace Corps was charged with espionage, but spying has never been proven against any Peace Corps volunteer. Such charges led to the Peace Corps regaining its status as an independent and separate agency in 1981.

The American Ambassador to Kenya, William C. Harrop, reported to the State Department, "There is no – repeat no – U.S. overseas program that yields as much return for the taxpayers' dollar as the Peace Corps." In fiscal 1983, the Peace Corps cost $110 million (about equal to the cost of a half-dozen Air Force fighter planes) out of a total foreign aid expenditure of $7.7 billion. (By contrast, the Defense Department spent $210.5 billion.)

Senator Paul Tsongas (Mass.), a former Peace Corps volunteer in Ethiopia in the 1960s and a staunch supporter of the Peace Corps, pointed out, "The United States benefits from the volunteers coming home. It produces a steady stream of people who understand the Third World."

Important dates in Peace Corps history include:

**Sept. 22, 1961.** Congress passed an act creating the Peace Corps.

**June 8-9, 1981.** Twentieth Anniversary Peace Corps Conference at Howard University, Washington, D.C., with over 1,600 participants.

**Dec. 29, 1981.** President Reagan signed legislation designating the Peace Corps as an independent agency.

**Feb. 24, 1982.** Self-help role of nearly 1,000 volunteers was emphasized by President Reagan's inclusion of the Peace Corps in his announcement of the Caribbean Basin Initiative.

**April 18, 1982.** Older Americans' roles as volunteers highlighted by President in first Rose Garden ceremony honoring the Peace Corps since the 1960s.

(See section in this chapter on the National Council of Returned Peace Corps Volunteers.)

# World Conference on Religion and Peace

Preparations for the first Assembly of the World Conference on Religion and Peace began with a 1968 symposium in New Delhi, India. Its first world assembly was held in Kyoto, Japan, in 1970; and since then, it has met in Louvain, Belgium, in 1974; in Princeton, New Jersey, U.S.A., in 1979; and in Nairobi, Kenya, in 1984. Some of the highlights of its last two assemblies are given in this report.

In WCRP III, held in Princeton in 1979, there were 358 participants including Buddhists, Christians, Confucianists, Hindus, Jains, Jews, Muslims, Shintoists, Sikhs, Zoroastrians, and representatives from several miscellaneous religions from 47 countries. Participants pledged themselves to continue to grow in mutual understanding and their work for peace, justice, and human dignity. They chose as their conference theme: "Religion in the Struggle for World Community."

Participants were convinced that "peace is possible," and that "world community, built on love, freedom, justice, and truth, is another name for *peace.*" In the Princeton Declaration, they stated:

> We believe that, as religious people, we have a special responsibility for building a peaceful world community, and a special contribution to make. . . . We are all commanded by our faiths to seek justice in the world in a community of free and equal persons. In this search, conscience is given to every person as a moral guide to the ways of truth among us all. . . . We believe that peace in world community is not only possible, but is the way of life for human beings on earth, as we learn it in our prayers or meditations and by our faith.

The mobilization for peace of WCRP III was organized around the following concerns: (1) a just international economic order; (2) nuclear and conventional disarmament; (3) human rights; (4) environment and energy crises; and education for peace.

Nearly 600 from 60 countries attended the Fourth World Assembly in Nairobi in 1984, again with representatives from most of the world's religious traditions and from the traditional cultures of Asia, Africa, Europe, North America, South America and others. From this diversity, they met to address a theme of common concern: "Religion and Human Dignity," and to address their common goals of "human dignity and world peace." They were encouraged by the participation of over 100 youth delegates and the contributions of over 150 women. (Participation is open to all, not just clergy.) Over half of the participants were from Asia, Africa, and Latin America.

This Fourth Assembly enabled participants to build trust and to discover once again that differences of cultures and religions should be viewed as treasures rather than threats to one another, to view this multiplicity as a source of strength. They were united in their common pursuit of peace. Those present were convinced that a new priority of the WCRP must be to address regional tensions and conflicts in South Africa, the Middle East, South and Southeast Asia, Central America, and Europe. They committed themselves, as religious men and women, to undertaking the work of reconciliation and peacemaking.

Another outcome of the Fourth Assembly was its reaffirmation to work for disarmament. To all of them, from various traditions of faith, nuclear weapons and all weapons of mass and indiscriminate destruction are immoral and criminal; and the stockpiling of such weapons with intent or threat to use them erodes the foundations of moral civilization. Members of WCRP join with scientists, physicians, educators, and students who have taken an active role in opposing the arms race. This commitment to disarmament includes conventional weapons and halting the spread of militarization and the commercial exploitation of developing countries by trade in arms, leading to military and political dependency.

The commitment to peace of WCRP is based upon the interrelationship between disarmament and development. It seeks liberation from perpetual fear and insecurity, from hunger and poverty, from injustice and oppression.

Human rights, along with disarmament and development, are an important part of WCRP's commitment to peace. It believes the UN's Universal Declaration of Human Rights can be the foundation of a just and humane society. These rights must never be postponed or suspended in the name of "national security." (See Appendix D for the text of that declaration.) The WCRP states, "Wherever and in whatever way, human rights violations occur, it is our concern internationally and interreligiously."

This same report on WCRP IV states:

> Essential to peace education is learning about and coming to understand those of different religions, ideologies, and cultures with whom we share our community, our nation, and our world ... and ... educational efforts must be made that fear may begin to give way to trust.

Among its actions, WCRP IV endorsed a brief statement on the Middle East, prepared jointly by a Lebanese Muslim, an Israeli Jew, and a Palestinian Christian, which covered eight common affirmations for bringing peace to the area.

In a January 1985, open letter, Dr. John Taylor, the WCRP's new Secretary-General, writes:

> One way in which WCRP/International hopes to strengthen its commitment to the U.N. is to ensure that a multireligious staff team is available both in our New York and Geneva offices. Not only shall we try to revive our presence in New York with other NGOs, especially in concerns of disarmament, but we shall pursue possibilities of bringing the discussion of inter-religious cooperation into some of the specialized agencies' work; for example in the field of refugees, of disaster relief, of education for peace, of promoting human rights, etc.

He also states:

Young people are sometimes leading the way in showing their commitment to build and to pray for peace with justice. One of the priorities for WCRP/International must be to encourage such dedication. A series of youth camps is being planned for the international Year of Youth. It is to be hoped that in places as far apart as Thailand and England, North India and South India, Kenya and Senegal, there may be co-operative ventures of young people of various religious traditions who come together to tackle some concrete issue of humanitarian need or communal reconciliation.

In his closing remarks, Dr. Taylor points out:

The tasks of rooting out the causes of conflicts, let alone the tasks of responding to their symptoms, are so vast that none of our religious or ideological traditions is capable of solving the problem alone. The international work of the U.N. supported by non-governmental agencies like WCRP/International, needs all our support.

The WCRP's newsletter on interreligious dialogue and action for peace is called *Religion for Peace.*

## Pax World Foundation

Pax World Foundation was organized in 1970 to promote international understanding, reconciliation, and development by providing financial support for selected programs and projects. Its two primary objectives are peace and Third World development.

To meet the Foundation's objective of peace, it funds projects that further peaceful relations among peoples. Priority is given to projects that:

• Encourage understanding and reconciliation between peoples across national boundaries.

• Offer effective action for immediate threats to peace; the greater the urgency, the higher the consideration given to it.

• Contribute to long-range, as well as short-range, needs for building effective peacemaking constituencies.

• Affect substantial numbers of people and have some prospect of making a difference.

• Focus upon building bridges to peoples of adversary nations, regardless of official governmental positions.

To meet its second objective, Third World activities emphasize basic human needs through small-scale community-based initiatives. Priority is given to Third World projects that:

• Directly involve beneficiary groups in the planning, implementation, direction and evaluation.

• Reflect long-range planning.

• Are small-scale, easily replicated once successfully demonstrated, and compatible with local customs, available materials, and cultural values.

• Support proposed technologies that are inexpensive, appropriate and simple to maintain.

• Show significant financial or in-kind commitment by the local group.

• Are sponsored by nonprofit or voluntary organizations engaged in meeting pressing human needs at the local level.

• Integrate health, agriculture, education and forestation, and stress the role of women.

The Pax World Foundation, along with the World Council of Churches, is convinced that science and technology for the Third World should be *"just, participatory, and sustainable."*

To be *just,* Third World development has to reach out to the poor families in the villages of a given country rather than simply assist urban dwellers or members of the wealthy class. Effective economic assistance cannot be measured adequately by a developing nation's gross national product (GNP) — which may be spread very unevenly among the population. Instead, its effectiveness is better gauged by the extent to which the poorest people within a country enjoy better nutrition, lower infant mortality, improved health, and useful education.

Community development must be *participatory.* Innovations which are imposed upon people of developing countries will not result in true technology transfer. Local people must be involved at the decision-making level and must conclude that they want the services and technology offered. It is preferable to use indigenous materials for any technological improvements.

*Sustainable* technology means that equipment has to be readily reparable and maintained without waiting for months for costly parts from overseas. It also means the community must be organized in such a way that it can undertake the maintenance of the project set in place.

While the Pax World Foundation believes technology is a part of any Third World project, its primary concern is for human development.

Examples of *peace projects* getting financial support from the Pax World Foundation include:

*U.S.-U.S.S.R. Citizens Dialogue.* The Foundation continues to support the U.S.-U.S.S.R. Citizens Dialogue and recently participated in the cultural exchange of 23 Soviet citizens in the U.S. for several weeks. These community leaders from the U.S.S.R. visited in San Antonio, Des Moines, and Oakland. U.S. citizens from these and several other cities made a memorable trip to the Soviet Union in the spring of 1983. It is hoped that through this project, mutual confidence building will occur and a modest contribution will be made toward improving the climate for disarmament and peace.

*Peace and Reconciliation in Central America.* The Foundation provides modest financial support for groups on reconciling missions to Central America, particularly in Nicaragua, El Salvador, and Honduras.

***Bishops' Pastoral Letter on Peace and War.*** When the Catholic Bishops published their statement on peace and war, Pax World realized how important it was to get the information widely distributed. Subsequently, the Foundation sent out 12,000 paperback editions free of charge to nearly 200 theological seminaries of every major denomination for use in ethics classes.

In his May 1987 progress report to "Foundation Friends," J. Elliott Corbett, President of Pax World Foundation, enthusiastically began:

> What's new? Quite a bit. We have completed a successful Friendship Tour to Central America. We have found a new use to our Buffalo Gourd plant — burning the dried roots as fuel. Our Water Purification Device is being publicized by a number of organizations for employment in the Third World.

In more detail he reported that 21 people had participated in the Friendship Tour to Honduras, Nicaragua, and Costa Rica in February of 1987; and that another Friendship Tour of the Middle East was being organized for the first two weeks of June.

He explained that researchers at Washington University in St. Louis, Mo., had discovered the buffalo gourd's roots could be a good source of efficient fuel in the Third World. (They had already found the plant to have a high yield in vegetable oil and its seed to be a source of flour when ground.) Pax World is continuing to provide seeds of the Giant Leucaena, a fast-growing tree especially useful as fuel wood.

In Third World countries without mountain springs or other clean water sources, news of Chris Ahren's water purification device has been most welcome.

Funding is obtained through voluntary contributions from the general public as well as from shareholders of the Pax World Fund. The Foundation keeps expenses to a minimum and depends upon substantial voluntary efforts from its board members, project directors, and the public. No compensation is paid to its officers or directors or executives operating the Foundation.

## Ulster Project Delaware

The Ulster Project Delaware began in 1976 as a joint experiment in reconciliation involving youth from Ulster, Northern Ireland and a number of families in Wilmington, Del., U.S.A. The Wilmington families shared a deep concern about the effects of the conflict in Northern Ireland on that country's young people. Encouraged by an earlier experience in Manchester, Conn., members of Wilmington's interfaith organization, *Pacem in Terris,* made arrangements to bring a group of Catholic and Protestant teenagers from Northern Ireland to Delaware for a three-week experience of peace and reconciliation. The first experience was so well received that Catholic and Protestant youth between ages fourteen and sixteen from the Ulster area have been spending the month of July visiting host families with teenagers of the same age in Delaware for the past twelve years, getting to know one another apart from the fear and mistrust in their native land.

Through social, service, and ecumenical activities in a strife-free environment, the Northern Irish teens have built bridges of trust leading to mutual understanding. Through experiences such as area sightseeing, recreation (such as canoeing the Brandywine), athletic and cultural events, special workshops on prejudice, and joint worship, the Northern Ireland youth discard many of their stereotypes of each other, and the American teens grow in their international understanding and experience peacemaking firsthand.

Participants are selected each year by their churches in Northern Ireland for their leadership potential; and they are evenly divided between Catholic and Protestant youth and between male and female.

At first the Irish youth came from the town of Portadown near Belfast. They now come from nearby Bambridge. The project serves both Northern Ireland and Delaware by fostering tolerance, understanding, and friendship among future leaders.

An open letter from Delaware about the project stated:

> Over the years more than 200 local families and over 300 teenagers have been involved in the project. For many of them the summer experience has grown into lifelong friendships that have prompted more than 50% of our teens to visit their Ulster brother or sister. Many of our teens take part-time jobs after school for a year or more to earn money for their air-fare. Such industry and dedication on both sides of the Atlantic speak well for our young people and our project. In addition, local teens also raise funds for the project by holding carwashes.

The Ulster-Delaware relationship has been rewarding on both sides of the ocean, and it has spread to communities in other states such as Illinois, Maryland, Minnesota, Ohio, Tennessee, Texas, and Utah.

While it will take years to fully assess the ultimate impact of these projects on Northern Ireland, there have been signs of hope. Private correspondence, visits, and follow-up programs of volunteers in Northern Ireland have shown that the projects have had and continue to have a profound, positive impact in the lives of the hundreds of young people who have participated. In the words of one Catholic participant: "We'll be able to say to our children, 'I have Protestant friends and you can too! We are the parents of the future.'"

## Friendship Force International

The Friendship Force was founded in 1977 by the *Reverend Wayne Smith,* a Presbyterian Minister in Atlanta, Georgia, with encouragement from *Rosalyn* and *Jimmy Carter*. Having served as a missionary in Brazil, Reverend Smith accompanied Governor and Mrs. Carter from Georgia on a goodwill visit to Brazil in 1972. This led to a series of exchanges between the citizens of Georgia and the state of Pernambuca, Brazil. In the summer of 1976, Reverend Smith approached the Carters with a proposal to expand into a global exchange program.

On March 1, 1977, less than two months after taking office, President Carter announced the formation of the Friendship Force at a dinner in the White House for state governors and their first ladies. He said, "This is the kind of involvement that each of us can do that is a little above and beyond government." President Ronald Reagan echoed that enthusiasm in 1982 when he wrote, "Your organization helps to create an international environment for mutual respect and understanding between nations." In all Friendship Force countries, including the U.S.A., there are no formal ties with any government or any political party.

The Friendship Force is a private, nonprofit, citizens' exchange program which brings people of all ages and backgrounds together in friendship across the barriers that divide them — barriers of distance, culture, language, or politics.

The stated purpose of the Friendship Force is "to create an environment in which seeds of friendship can be sown across the barriers that separate people." The Friendship Force seeks to provide a means by which people can cross international boundaries to meet other people and share their lifestyles. This is accomplished largely through volunteer efforts. Participants in the program share the conviction that the knowledge, understanding, and friendships developed through these personal contacts will promote the cause of world peace. Out of shared lifestyles, common concerns about the present and mutual dreams for the future, come lifelong friendships. They believe that a world of friends can become a world of peace.

Participants in the Exchange Program serve both as visiting ambassadors and hosts. As ambassadors of goodwill, they have a sense of adventure and a concern for world understanding, and are willing to travel anywhere on earth to promote it. As host families, they are dedicated to international friendships and are glad to share their lifestyles with people from another culture. Participants discover that the peoples of the world are more alike than they are different.

The "pledge" of a Friendship Force ambassador reads:

As a member of the Friendship Force, I recognize that I can make a difference. I recognize that I have a mission. That mission is to be a friend to the people in the world. As I embark upon this adventure, I know that others will be watching me. I know that through my example to my own fellow citizens and the people of other nations, the cause of friendship, love, and peace can be furthered. *I can make a difference.*

Friendship Force offers two programs: the *Exchange Program* and *Friendship Missions*. In the former, participants serve as hosts and are welcomed as guests in each other's homes. In the latter, where hosting is not practical, participants stay in hotels but have contacts with citizens through a series of formal and informal meetings and activities. Both programs seek the same goal: bringing people from two nations together in friendship and understanding.

The basic Friendship Force experience includes a homestay (or mission) of one or two weeks. A wider look at the host country during the second week of the visit is also possible through independent travel.

Each traveling ambassador pays an induction fee, which covers transportation costs to and from the host city and administrative costs of the volunteer committees in both cities. Participants may make their own arrangements for independent travel after the first week, but must return to the gateway city at the end of two weeks (or three weeks) for the return home.

A small professional staff coordinates the efforts of a worldwide network of volunteer leaders. Exchanges or missions are implemented locally by small committees under the supervision of a volunteer. The committee coordinates the matching of ambassadors and hosts by their shared occupations and interests, and prepares participants for their experience. Preparation includes workshops and correspondence between ambassadors and hosts-to-be whenever time permits.

In its first six years, the Friendship Force formula fostered over 200,000 personal friendships. Close to 60,000 ambassadors traveled to offer warm handshakes to over 150,000 host families. In the U.S.A., Friendship Force Clubs sponsored the program in 43 states. Worldwide, 38 countries have been involved, and more are joining each year.

From its beginning, the Friendship Force has emphasized the belief that people are more important than places, that making friends is more vital than touring, and that *you,* as an individual, *can* make a difference!

## Buddhist Peace Fellowship

The following are direct quotations from a brochure published by the Buddhist Peace Fellowship.

Buddhists of many traditions are joining together in the Buddhist Peace Fellowship to explore the possibilities of direct response to the suffering in the world caused by political, social and ecological ignorance. Drawing on the power of wisdom and compassion, recognizing the essential unity of all beings, its members work to awaken peace where there is conflict, to bring insight into the institutionalized ignorance of political systems, and to help wherever help is needed. This is done in the spirit of harmony and loving kindness.

The Buddhist Peace Fellowship (BPF) was founded in 1978. It seemed time to bring a Buddhist perspective to the peace movement, and the peace movement to the Buddhist Community. As a network of individuals and local chapters, the Fellowship serves to promote communication and cooperation in the Sangha's work of nourishing all beings as it, at the same time, resists the forces of exploitation and war. BPF has already taken on several national and international projects and is helping to bring about an international alliance of concerned Buddhists.

Purposes listed are:

- To make clear public witness to the Buddhist way as a way of peace and protection of all beings.
- To raise peace and ecology concerns among American Buddhists and to promote projects through which the Sangha may respond to these concerns.
- To encourage the delineation in English of the Buddhist way of nonviolence, building from the rich resources of traditional Buddhist teachings a foundation for new action.
- To offer avenues to realize the kinship among groups and members of the American and world Sangha.
- To serve as liaison to, and enlist support for, existing national and international Buddhist peace and ecology programs.
- To provide a focus for concerns over the persecution of Buddhists, as a particular expression of our intent to protect all beings.
- To bring the Buddhist perspective to contemporary peace and ecology movements.

At present, BPF publishes a quarterly newsletter, provides articles and reprints, and offers assistance to local groups in developing their projects. Members and local chapters have been involved in disarmament, ecological, and human rights activities, including campaigns opposing political oppression of Buddhists in such places as Bangladesh and Tibet.

Local chapters carry on many of BPF projects and programs. While operating within the broad guidelines of the purposes of BPF, chapters retain their autonomy.

The Buddhist Peace Fellowship is one of sixteen religious peace fellowships that have affiliated with the Fellowship of Reconciliation. The BPF was warmly welcomed by the FOR as its first affiliate outside the Judeo-Christian tradition; and the association has proven mutually beneficial. (See section on FOR in this chapter for more information.)

## Center on Law and Pacifism

The Center on Law and Pacifism was founded in Philadelphia in 1978 and has grown into a national service organization providing legal and theological counseling for people in conflict with the law or legal institutions because of their religious conscience. The Center was first founded

because of religious and conscientious war tax resistance and civil disobedience, and it responds to the needs of both individuals and groups who
become engaged in civil disobedience or war tax resistance because of
religious or moral conscience.

The Center believes that peace is a means as well as an end, and that
there is a distinctly peaceful approach to issues such as militarism, war
taxes, the death penalty, criminal punishment, poverty, abortion, environmental abuse, and overconsumption. As a service and educational
organization, the Center functions as a witness to this pacifist approach.

The three primary purposes of the Center on Law and Pacifism
are:

• To provide legal research and opinion, legal counsel, and court
representation.

• To educate, including the above, and helping prepare individuals
and groups to write their own briefs and represent themselves in court and
before government agencies; also to provide workshops and classes in law,
theology, and criminal justice.

• To serve as a channel for support, encouragement, motivation, and
organization for individuals and groups in the community who are involved
in the risk and isolation of religious pacifist activities.

The Center on Law and Pacifism supports other peace groups for disarmament, an end to institutional violence, and the right of people to survive in a nuclear age. It also supports legislation and other measures to provide conscientious objector status for military tax refusers. The Center is
also concerned with a balanced environment based on creative, nonex-
ploitive relationships among all forms of life.

## World Peacemakers

Since 1972, members of the Church of the Saviour, an ecumenical
church in Washington, D.C., have included the following statement in their
membership commitment:

> Realizing that Jesus taught and exemplified a life of love, I will seek to
> be loving in all relations with other individuals, groups, classes, races,
> and nations, and will seek to be a reconciler, living in a manner which
> will end all war, personal and public.

Early in 1978, *Gordon Cosby, Richard Barnet, Bill Branner,* and *Bill
Price,* all of whom were associated with the Church of the Saviour, called
World Peacemakers into being as a response to the serious crisis they saw
in the buildup of armaments in the United States and the world. They
agreed that to meet this crisis responsibly, Americans needed to work and
to pray for world peace, especially in their church communities.

They started World Peacemakers with a wide distribution of a 1978

World Peace Paper, "A Time to Stop," by Richard J. Barnet, which called upon the churches of the United States to urge their government to negotiate a bilateral freeze on the testing, manufacture, and deployment of nuclear weapons. This first World Peace Paper was followed by eight additional World Peace Papers entitled:

- "Moving Toward True Security"
- "No Room in the Lifeboat"
- "The Arms Race: Is Paranoia Necessary for Security?"
- "Our Choice Is Life"
- "Hope in the American Crisis"
- "A Vision of Peace: Redeeming the American Dream"
- "Peace in the Reagan Era"
- "Christ of the Americas: Dying, Rising, and Coming Again"

World Peacemakers, Inc., seeks to help churches take faithful action in light of the current crises in foreign and military affairs by building on its church's emphasis on a spiritual formation, a disciplined inner life, mission groups with a balanced inward/outward approach, a membership commitment to work for peace, and broad ecumenical network of relationships with churches throughout the world.

World Peacemakers, Inc., calls individuals to:

- Confess Jesus Christ as Lord and to live out Christ's call to peacemaking in both the personal and public domain.
- Start by reaching out to others, expressing concern; and by praying for world peace and for guidance.
- Contact their denominations about their particular program for peacemaking.
- Reach a decision to combine reflection with action, action with reflection.
- Invite others to join them in forming a group with an "inward and outward" approach to peacemaking.
- Claim the power of Biblical faith to undergird their peacemaking efforts to move the world toward peace.

World Peacemakers offers to:

- Provide resources for small groups with a balanced inward and outward approach.
- Lead workshops for training local leadership in the search for real security by combining Christian Faith and citizenship.
- Provide retreat experiences for leaders of peacemaking groups.
- Help local leaders design special events encompassing a spirituality of peacemaking and peace action.
- Provide consultations in developing small groups.

In November 1986, World Peacemakers published a summary paper entitled, "World Peacemakers' Journey Pursuing Peace with Justice." The following skeleton outline of that paper provides an overview of their progress:

A. Milestones to the Present
   1. The Church of the Saviour/World Peacemakers' Heritage.
   2. World Peacemakers Founded in the Church of the Saviour. (World Peacemakers founded by C of S members in 1978.)
   3. World Peacemakers Quickly Became a National Peace Organization Serving the Religious Community. (By 1982, a series of eight World Peace Papers had been published and distributed throughout the United States.)
   4. Small Groups as Leaven in Local Communities. (In 1979, World Peacemakers published its *Handbook for World Peacemaker Groups* by Gordon Cosby and Bill Price.)
   5. World Peacemakers as a Support/Catalyst for Denominational Peace Initiatives. (From its inception, World Peacemakers has worked directly with the denominational staffs of both "mainline" and "historic peace" churches.)
   6. Promoting Real Security.
   7. Pioneering in the Religious Communities' Resistance to United States Central American Policy.
   8. Pioneering in Merging Religious Faith and Responsible Citizenship to Pursue Peace with Justice.
B. The Continuing Program of World Peacemaking
   1. Looking More Deeply into the Church's Unique Role.
     a. Focus on the Church of the Saviour as a "peace church."
     b. Growing as "makers of history."
     c. Supporting a church-centered debate on the United States national security policy.
     d. The Church's ministry to our nation.
   2. Sharing What We Are Learning.
     a. Quarterly newsletters.
     b. Handbooks/study guides.
     c. Personalized communication.
     d. Serving as resource for denominational and other national peace organizations.

In response to the worldwide crisis of growing military arsenals, especially the escalation of the nuclear weapons buildup, the churches of the United States, almost with one voice, have declared in resolutions, pastoral letters, and newly initiated peacemaking programs their concern for peace. The composite of these actions by all the major denominations is a significant theological declaration of the churches to the nation.

## National Council of Returned Peace Corps Volunteers

The National Council of Returned Peace Corps Volunteers (NCRPCV) was organized in 1979 out of a grass-roots desire on the part of a group of individual returned volunteers to, in some organized fashion, bring their Peace Corps experience back home. These individuals are united by the belief that their respective experiences abroad have given them a perspective of the world that is worth sharing, and by their willingness to share their experiences through a national organization. Thus, members of NCRPCV continue to work for the third goal of the Peace Corps; namely, "to promote a better understanding of other peoples among Americans."

The following are the more specific goals of the National Council:

• To create an awareness among the American public, Congress, leaders and other organizations and sectors concerning the Third World.

• To teach, to organize and to otherwise facilitate the education, and affect the actions of Americans regarding developing nations, Third World peoples, and development issues in an attempt to "Bring the World Home."

• To promote support for the beneficial functions which Peace Corps performs.

• To foster a strong organizational network on a national basis among returned Peace Corps volunteers, their affiliated local organizations, supporters, and other parties to facilitate achievement of all these NCRPCV goals.

• To provide a voice for input by its members into political, commercial and policy matters relating to development, foreign aid, foreign relations, and similar issues.

• To contribute to Peace Corps' policy-making processes in an effort to assist Peace Corps in being fully responsive to the needs of Third World peoples, of volunteers in service, and of returned Peace Corps volunteers.

• To provide returned Peace Corps volunteers with informational, educational, social, employment, and career services and advice.

• To extend Peace Corps ideals and volunteerism in the form of involvement with local communities, local organizations, and social programs.

• To assist refugees, immigrants, foreign visitors, foreign students, and otherwise be generous hosts, in the same spirit with which Peace Corps volunteers were and are being received as guests in foreign lands.

Since 1961, more than 130,000 Peace Corps volunteers, including approximately 5,000 who currently serve, have made a difference in the lives of people in over 90 countries. The success of the Peace Corps lies also in what America has received in return. The friendships and experiences, the technical and language skills, and the first-hand knowledge of other people and cultures form resources and rewards for America.

The National Council of RPCV's is attempting to help use these resources back home. It is a national, voluntarily operated, nonprofit organization of individual RPCV's, local RPCV groups, and affiliated private voluntary organizations.

The National Council believes its returned Peace Corps volunteers have a special sensitivity toward international development and global understanding which should be shared and translated into action in the United States.

The National Council is independent of the Peace Corps and serves as a focal point for a growing network of former volunteers, volunteer groups, and friends.

## Council for International Understanding

The Cathedral of Peace Institute, a center for the study of religion and international affairs, was founded in 1981 by *Moorhead Kennedy,* a former 20-year veteran of United States government foreign service and the third-ranking foreign service officer among the hostages held by Iran for 444 days. In 1983, its name was changed to the Council for International Understanding (CIU) and it became a part of the Myrin Institute for Adult Education.

In a recent brochure, the purpose of the CIU was described as follows:

> The Myrin Institute's Council for International Understanding (CIU) mounts educational programs designed to help Americans overcome psychological and cultural barriers to the understanding of foreign affairs. Such barriers include a lack of sensitivity to viewpoints different from ours, assumptions of moral and cultural superiority, and the delusion that American solutions to problems are necessarily of universal validity. These diminish our nation's capacity for leadership, which ultimately depends not on power alone but on our ability to listen, to articulate, and to exemplify the deepest aspirations of those with whom we hope to be effective partners.
>
> When we fail to listen, terrorist groups have found ways to make us aware of long-standing grievances. Over the short term, we must defend ourselves through improved security measures, military and covert action, and diplomatic initiatives. But these by themselves provide no lasting remedy unless we also address terrorists' root causes. In order to deal effectively with the terrorists, just as with other serious challenges from abroad, we need first to sharpen our own perceptions of other cultures and our moral criteria, through innovative educational programs. CIU makes use of topical issues, such as terrorism, in order to stimulate awareness of the need for shifts in long-established popular attitudes on foreign affairs.

The Council serves as a resource, assisting Americans individually and collectively to develop workable criteria of moral judgment, and correct those popular American attitudes that present obstacles to an effective foreign policy. These include the delusion that the perspectives of other nations and cultures do not differ from our own; the win/lose syndrome, in contrast to the necessity for compromise that we accept in our personal and institutional relationships; and attitudes toward and difficulty in understanding unfamiliar forces, such as the link between terrorism and religion. The Center also helps Americans to identify, articulate and introduce fresh insights into public opinion, through personal contact, public affairs forums, churches, academic institutions and the media, and to make their views politically effective.

The Council for International Understanding cooperates with local media, religious organizations, fraternal and patriotic organizations, and academic institutions.

In one of his open letters as executive director of the Council, Moorhead Kennedy emphasized:

> We are not another single issue group, advocating what are often unrealistically simple solutions to complex problems. Nor are we among those institutions which merely impart information. Rather, our purpose is to encourage the development of a constituency of intelligent Americans who are able to influence our political leadership toward sounder foreign policy formulation and execution.

In his book *The Ayatollah in the Cathedral: Reflections of a Hostage* (sponsored by the Myrin Institute and published by Hill and Wang, New York, 1983), Moorhead Kennedy explores the mistakes the United States made during the Iranian hostage crisis and continues to make in its foreign policy. His book makes specific recommendations to help correct faulty American attitudes about foreign affairs and how they "trip us up" again and again as we try to relate to foreigners, to international issues, and as we try to develop a more realistic understanding of other cultures.

## Volunteers for Peace (International Workcamps)

Volunteers for Peace, Inc., operates a program of international workcamps. It is a Vermont nonprofit, nondenominational membership corporation that has, since 1981, been coordinating international workcamps in the U.S.A. and abroad. The field volunteers of VFP provide consultation and placement services for workcamp volunteers and hosts.

They call themselves Volunteers for Peace because their membership is composed of people who volunteer their time, energy, and resources toward promoting world peace through travel and community service. They promote no doctrine and believe in caring, sharing, and celebrating the love of people for people everywhere. Their work is in coordination with 35 other organizations doing similar work in 36 countries.

The stated purpose of Volunteers for Peace is

> to promote international goodwill and peaceful relations among nations through coordinating international workcamps: environments where people can learn to live and work together for the benefit of humanity.

An article in its 1987 issue of *The International Workcamper,* the annual newsletter of VFP International Workcamps, entitled "What Are International Workcamps," tells their story so well, it is reprinted below:

> International Workcamps are an inexpensive and personal way that you can travel, live and work in a foreign country. Sometimes described as a fully internationalized short-term "peace corps," workcamps are a time-tested avenue of "people-to-people" exchange. These projects receive universal support from countries of all political persuasions and are sanctioned by the United Nations.
>
> Workcamps are sponsored by an organization in a host country, but coordinated by people in a local community. We're talking about really getting to know people by working with them to improve their lives in some tangible way.
>
> You will learn a lot about one another, yourself, and about some of the social, cultural, and political conditions that exist in other countries. This is a meaningful way to travel and demonstrate your concern for the well-being of other people. They are a fun-filled adventure in international education.
>
> Workcamps can vary greatly in living conditions. Generally, 10–20 people from four or more countries arrive on a given day in a host community. You may be housed in a school, church, private home or community center. Living arrangements are generally cooperative, like a family, with workcampers coordinating and sharing the day-to-day activities such as food preparation and entertainment.
>
> The work involved is casual. Construction, restoration, environmental, social, agricultural and maintenance workcamps are common.
>
> Formal and informal discussions of issues of common concern are an integral part of every workcamp. A great deal of communication and sharing takes place at workcamps. Free-time activities and excursions to local points of interest are usually arranged by community hosts.

The article closes with information about its *International Workcamp Directory* listing over 800 workcamp opportunities. The directory becomes available each April and can be obtained by contacting the VFP headquarters. (See Appendix B for address.)

In this same 1987 issue, they provide the following summary of Workcamp Facts:

| | |
|---|---|
| For Whom? | Anyone age 18 and up (also limited opportunities for ages 13–18). Average age is 22. |
| Why? | Promotion of international goodwill through people-to-people exchange and community service. |
| When? | Year round. 90% of workcamps are in July through September. |
| Where? | 36 countries in East and West Europe, North and West Africa, Central and North America including Canada and the U.S.A. |
| How? | Through UN sanctioned cooperating organizations. |
| Cost? | $75 per workcamp with $15 refund when submitting brief |

report to VFP by Oct. 1. $90 in Eastern Europe with $15 re-
fund. U.S.A. Workcamp $75.

Duration?     Two–three weeks. (Volunteers often apply for multiple
              workcamps in the same or different countries.)
Insurance?    Coverage is usually for accident only, depending on spon-
              soring organization.
Language?     No foreign language proficiency required.

Another article in a previous newsletter called attention to ways in
which their volunteers promote international goodwill:

- By promoting dialogue and understanding.
- By providing an indelible personal experience in international coop-
  erative living.
- By being a cost-effective medium of community development.
- By engineering public consciousness to think globally while acting
  locally.
- By being the least expensive avenue of international travel.
- By being the only sizable avenue of exchange encouraged by govern-
  ments in Western and Eastern Europe.

Workcamps are a program of dialogue *and* deeds!

## The All Children Together Movement (Lagan College)

Lagan College in Belfast, Northern Ireland, is not what the name im-
plies to those who think of colleges as four-year post-secondary institutions. Lagan College is an integrated, all-ability, post-primary school for
boys and girls (ages 11–17) which was founded by the All Children Together
Movement in 1981. Established in response to pleas from parents for integrated education, it is operated in accordance with the philosophy of the
All Children Together Movement (founded in 1974), in particular:

- Its belief in educating Protestant and Catholic children together
equally.
- Its belief that an integrated school should be Christian rather than
secular in character.
- Its emphasis on the involvement of parents in the life and work of
an integrated school, and
- Its desire for co-operation with the churches.

Quoting from Sister Anna's portion of the 1981–83 Report of Lagan
College:

A large element in the troubles in Northern Ireland is the gross ignorance of one section of the population for the other, upon which fear
and violence feed. This is based on polarized housing and social habits,
and a segregated education system. . . . Part of the problem in N. Ireland
arises from the Catholic and Protestant religious traditions and the Irish

and British cultural traditions being viewed as antagonistic, rather than mutually enriching and complementary. Fourteen years of agony has left over 3,300 people killed and some 30,000 mutilated....

The All Children Together Movement was founded in 1974 to seek the establishment of shared Christian schools where parents wished, so bringing together the two main Christian traditions and the two cultures in their fullness, in close cooperation with the churches. It is thought that where children grow up together in mutual respect they will no longer fear and even hate each other, for in truth, Christ does not divide; he is our solid ground of unity. Members desire to awaken in the children a faith and love of God and man that is unitive, ecumenical, exciting, unfettered.

The trustees and governors also believe that educating Catholic and Protestant children together will contribute positively to peace and reconciliation in Northern Ireland. The motto of Lagan College is, "Ut sint unum" ("That they be one").

Catholics and Protestants are equally represented amongst pupils, parents, staff, and governors. The school attempts to be Christian in ethos, and has the services of six chaplains who look after the pupils of their own denominations and advise on the teaching of religious education within the curriculum.

As well as being co-educational, the college admits pupils of all abilities, attempting to balance its intake to reflect society generally. No pupil has ever been refused admission because of inability to pay.

The school opened with 30 children, age 11, its first year. The second year there were 90 children, ages 11 and 12; and the third year, there was an enrollment of 163, ages 11, 12, and 13. The school has continued to grow in like manner, adding a grade level each year. In the 1985–86 academic year, there were 457 pupils.

An important stage in the school's development was reached when Lagan College was recognized and accepted by the Department of Education of Northern Ireland as a "voluntary grant-aided" school as of April 1, 1984. This new status made the school eligible for partial government support for the first time.

Another milestone was reached in 1986 when Lagan College graduated its first class of "fifth formers." After taking their public exams and completing their terms at Lagan College, 57 confident young people took their next steps into a challenging and uncertain world.

In my correspondence with Sister Anna of Lagan College, she shared the following verses written by two first-year pupils there:

*Our School*

Monday morning, at the stroke of nine,
we're off to school and feeling fine.
Protestant, Catholic, it does not matter,
through the gates we all do clatter.

Boys and girls from all around
   in this place are to be found.
After prayers the lessons start:
   math and English, biology and art.
Because it's new and very clear,
   the eyes of the world are on us here.
Togetherness is what we're after,
   combining this with peace and laughter.
A first step in this troubled land
   to help us to walk hand in hand.
Patricia McIlwraith—1981

*Peace*

Peace is a candle that has to be lit.
A spark is beginning to show,
   but its light is so small
   it's not yet seen by all.
But our school is making it grow.
Kiera O'Neill—1982

## Children as the Peacemakers Foundation

The Children as the Peacemakers Foundation has evolved from the *Round Table Foundation* to the *Children as Teachers of Peace Foundation* to its current name. It was established in 1982 in San Francisco by *Patricia Montandon* . . . to promote world peace by creating an opportunity for children and adults to interact constructively on a wide range of peace-related activities, all inspired by the clear, straightforward views of children. It is now expanding to include children, teenagers, and adults as "the Peacemakers."

In line with its stated purpose, the Foundation sponsors two major programs: (1) its World Peace Missions, and (2) its Annual International Children's Peace Prize. The former enables children to meet with heads of state and youth organizations to discuss their wishes and concerns for a peaceful world. In the January 3, 1986, fact sheet sent in response to this survey, the Foundation reported having had five missions to 20 countries, including talks with world leaders such as Chairman Vitaly Petrovich Ruben of the Soviet Union, Premier Zhao Ziyang of China, Chancellor Helmut Kohl of West Germany, and Pope Paul II. Approximately 60 children have traveled on these missions.

One of its most publicized sponsorships enabled the eleven-year-old Soviet schoolgirl Katerina Lycheva to visit the United States in 1986 (prompted by the 1983 Soviet tour by Samantha Smith of the U.S.A.).

The Foundation's Annual International Children's Peace Prize program is open to all children, and its stated purpose is to "honor children, ages six through eleven, for their efforts on behalf of the critical issue of our times—PEACE. The prize and ceremonies focus world attention on peace and bring together nations around the globe in constructive sharing of ideas to further world understanding." Since its inception in 1983, over 15,000 children have participated by submitting original works of art, music, dance, poetry, essays, statements, and sculpture designed to further the cause of peace. Children have also been nominated for their outstanding acts of peace.

The Children's Peace Prize has been presented to 55 children from 32 countries since 1983. Judges have included panels of children in the organization, and presentors have included Ms. June Lockhart of the U.S.A., Madame Jehan Sadat of Egypt, Dr. Linus Pauling of the U.S.A., and the Rev. Kiyoshi Tanimoto of Japan.

The third and largest group of presentations was made in San Francisco in 1985, with award recipients from Australia, Belgium, Bulgaria, Canada, China, Costa Rica, Czechoslovakia, Egypt, Ethiopia, France, German Democratic Republic, Greece, Hungary, India, Italy, Israel, Japan, Kenya, Korea, Malta, Mexico, New Zealand, Northern Ireland, Norway, Philippines, Poland, Turkey, U.S.A., U.S.S.R., West Germany, and Yugoslavia.

Each recipient receives a beautiful Children as the Peacemakers glass sculpture, which presents three generations of hands reaching for the dove of peace (inspired by the Foundation's logo). The glass represents the honest, clear vision of children; the hands reaching toward heaven symbolize hope for wisdom and peace.

## The John T. Conner Center for U.S./U.S.S.R. Reconciliation

The John T. Conner Center for U.S./U.S.S.R. Reconciliation was organized in September of 1983. Begun as a regional effort in Illinois and Indiana, it developed into a national network of people concerned about a reconciliation between the religious communities of the United States and the Union of Soviet Socialist Republics. It is an ecumenical center working toward reconciliation from a religious base; and it works with the National Council of Churches and its Committee on U.S.–Soviet Church Relations.

In June 1984, the National Council of the Churches of Christ in the U.S.A. sponsored a two-week trip to the Soviet Union. Ninety clergy and 180 lay persons participated, and the Conner Center provided a co-leader for the tour. The purpose of the trip was to build bridges between American and Soviet religious communities. They shared in worship, met church and government leaders, and toured Russian Orthodox, Evangelical Baptist, Roman Catholic, and Lutheran churches. Some groups also visited synagogues and spoke with Moslem officials.

This visit was one in a series of NCC-sponsored exchanges that have taken place since 1956. In October 1984, a group of American church leaders traveled to the Soviet Union; and a group of Soviet church leaders and seminary students visited the United States in 1985.

The Conner Center prepares study materials for use in local churches and religious groups who wish to know more about religious life in the Soviet Union. It is also becoming involved in the translation and interpretation, from Russian to English and vice versa, of emerging materials to keep both communities current with regard to materials that can assist in studies leading to reconciliation.

The Conner Center publishes a monthly newsletter called *Rapproachment,* which focuses on center activities, upcoming conferences and broadcasts, book reviews, and occasional papers from guest writers.

For example, the January 1987 issue alerted readers to the upcoming mini-series "Amerika," to be aired by ABC the following month. Its April issue announced the Second Annual Conference on U.S.–Soviet Relations — "Citizen Action to Bridge the Gap" — to be held at International House, University of Chicago on May 9, 1987. The May 1987 issue of *Rapproachment* announced the Third Annual Summer School of the Conner Center on the "Study of Religion in the Soviet Union," to be held on the campus of Purdue University, in cooperation with Purdue's Religious Studies Program, June 29–July 4.

Other publications of the Center include:

• *The First Reader on U.S.-U.S.S.R. Reconciliation* (A 150-page handbook including 22 articles on religion in the Soviet Union and the script of "The Church of the Russians," a two-part documentary broadcast by NBC.)

• Occasional papers.

• Study materials used by participants in the trip to the Soviet Union.

## Center for Innovative Diplomacy

The Center for Innovative Diplomacy (CID) was founded in 1983 in Palo Alto, California, by three Stanford University graduates: *Hal Harvey,* a civil engineer; *Eric Horvitz,* a physician; and *Michael Shuman,* a lawyer. They were determined to use their skills to reduce the risk of nuclear war.

The Center now has about 4,500 members. Roughly half of these members joined CID directly. The other half were members of Local Elected Officials of America (LEO/USA) and Local Elected Officials for Social Responsibility (LEO/SR), both of which merged with CID in 1986 to become part of CID's LEO Project. With this merger, nearly 1,000 mayors, city council members, and county supervisors came under CID's umbrella.

Publications from CID include the books *Citizen Diplomats: Pathfinders in Soviet-American Relations; Local Elected Officials Handbook;* and *Having International Affairs Your Way.* They also publish two periodicals: *Bulletin of Municipal Foreign Policy* (4/yr.), and *The CID Report* (2/yr.). Examples of lead story headlines in *the CID Report* follow:

- "International Institution Building: the Missing Link for Peace."
- "CID Policy Statement Captures National Attention."
- "Municipal State Departments: The Wave of the Future?"
- "CID Helps Organize First U.S. Workshop on Municipal Foreign Policy."
- "The World's Mayors Meet in Hiroshima."
- "CID Visits the Evil Empire."
- "CID's Fifth Year."

The Winter 1986–87 issue of *The CID Report* gave an excellent overview of its operations, including explanations of CID's LEO (Local Elected Officials) Project and its 3-2-1 Proposal, Municipal Foreign Policies, Citizen Diplomacy Project, PeaceNet, and Alternative Security Project. The following are selected quotations from these sections of the report.

Under *CID's LEO Project:*

> ... America's local officials have come to understand that the nuclear arms race is, indeed, a local issue. For those of us who hold local office, it is painfully evident that even if the massive arsenals of nuclear weapons are never used, the relentless production of armaments is inflicting tragic economic and social damage upon our communities and our people.

*The 3-2-1 Proposal* concluded with:

> Now, therefore, be it resolved that the President and members of Congress be urged to cut military spending by at least $60 billion and re-direct these funds on a "3-2-1" basis to achieve deficit reduction ($30 billion), the re-enactment and enlargement of General Revenue Sharing ($20 billion), and the re-allocation of remaining funds to other public purposes as determined by the Congress and the President ($10 billion).

Final suggestions given in this section were:

> Get your county supervisors, mayor, city council members, and school board members to join the LEO Project network and sign on to the "3-2-1 Proposal." If they refuse, recruit their opponents to join and make a campaign issue out of the adverse local impacts of military spending.

On *CID's Municipal Foreign Policy:*

> More than 1,000 state and local governments of all political stripes are participating in foreign affairs, and their numbers are expanding daily.
>
> The trend of "thinking globally and acting locally" may both weaken national governments' traditional autonomy over foreign affairs and open new conduits for citizens to shape global politics directly, through the governments to which they are closest.
>
> America's politicians may be starting to view municipal foreign policies as an inevitable, indeed laudable, step in the maturation of democracy.

As a beginning, cities should agree to suspend any further investment of public funds in firms that directly or indirectly benefit from the production of weapons of mass destruction.

Let the Nuclear Armistice free our most talented citizens to help invent the ways and means for actually achieving the conversion from preparation for war to preparation for peace.

## Under its *Citizen Diplomacy Project:*

In *Having International Affairs Your Way,* CID authors Michael Shuman and Jayne Williams lay out the five essentials of citizen diplomacy:
- preparing yourself with the appropriate intellectual, communication, and psychological skills.
- developing your agenda.
- picking the right action network.
- choosing the right tools of persuasion, pressure, and agreement.
- mapping out a strategy of fund raising and publicity.

The main effort of CID here has been its book entitled *Citizen Diplomats: Pathfinders in Soviet-American Relations.*

## Under its *PeaceNet* (a global computer network):

Through PeaceNet, peace activists in 70 countries are no farther than a local telephone call away from one another.

PeaceNet is bringing America's fragmented peace movement together and giving it a new coherence, vision, and power. What's more, by providing affordable overseas communication, it is helping Americans collaborate and coordinate with activists in Canada, Costa Rica, Great Britain, the Soviet Union, Australia, and Japan.

With PeaceNet's electronic mail service, national peace groups such as Beyond War and the Nuclear Freeze are sending action alerts to their regional offices and grassroots membership. By being able to send a hundred copies of a letter with a single electronic command, they are reducing the need for costly and burdensome printing, folding, stuffing, and stamping. They are also helping users get messages more quickly, organize them more easily, and respond in a more timely fashion.

## Under its *Alternative Security Project:*

The cornerstone of their approach is that the United States should try to increase the security of all nations, especially its adversaries. Historic efforts to decrease the security of adversaries such as the Soviet Union, the study argues, are entirely counterproductive.

An alternative security agenda would direct U.S. foreign policy to deal with conflicts at three different levels:
- eliminating their roots.
- resolving them without force.
- where necessary, employing the minimum levels of nonprovocative defense to halt the conflicts.

... an alternate security agenda also foresees an increasing role for citizens, organizations, and cities.

... an alternate security agenda envisions nations retaining purely defensive forces to repel any attacker. Forces that are unambiguously defensive....

... an alternative security would have the United States phase out first strike weapons from its arsenal and try to convince other nuclear nations to do likewise.

In *Summary* (from a recent CID information sheet):

Dedicated to reducing the risks of nuclear and conventional war by encouraging greater citizen participation in foreign affairs, CID works toward this agenda by: promoting municipal foreign policies, organizing local elected officials against the arms race; analyzing Soviet-American citizen diplomacy; and helping to build an international computer network for the peace movement (PeaceNet).

# 3. Instructional Approaches

*Examples of Organizations Promoting Peace Primarily
Through Knowledge and Action in Research,
Publishing and Education*

The majority of responding organizations are promoting peace primarily through research, publishing, and educational efforts. All of these groups are deeply concerned over public apathy and feelings of frustration and inadequacy about war and peace issues. Most of these organizations are trying to convince the public, political leaders, and foreign relations and military personnel that peace efforts are not only essential to the survival of humanity, but that they will pay big dividends economically and socially. Their composite message is, "War is the road to global suicide. Peace with justice is the way to freedom from fear and want. Peace can bring prosperity and make food, clothing, health, and happiness a possibility for all."

As in Chapter 2, reports of these responding organizations will be presented in order of founding.

## World Peace Foundation

The World Peace Foundation was created in 1910 by *Edwin Ginn,* of Ginn and Company, an educational book publisher based in Boston. The Foundation seeks to advance the cause of peace through studies of current international issues and the dissemination of its findings to the public through conferences and publications. As stated in its by-laws, the purposes of the World Peace Foundation include: "educating the people of all nations to a full knowledge of the waste and destruction of wars, and, generally, by every practical means to promote peace and good will among all mankind."

The Foundation is a privately operating foundation that organizes its own projects and funds them from the income of its endowment and outside grants.

The early work of the Foundation was on the development of international law and the League of Nations, and later on the United Nations. In more recent years, the Foundation has shifted its attention to regional issues that require international cooperation. For example, the Foundation has conducted regional studies concerning U.S.–Canadian relations, the conflicts in southern Africa, and collective security in the Western Hemisphere.

Its studies are currently focused on Latin America and Africa. Representative studies include:

* United States foreign policy toward Portuguese-speaking southern Africa — Angola and Mozambique — and South Africa.
* United States policies toward Africa in the 1990s.
* The Inter-American Collective Security System, its decline, and the possibility of resuscitating or replacing it.
* How to promote sustainable economic development in Latin America in spite of the debt crisis, a project that engages younger economic policymakers from the region.
* A study of the successes and failures of United States attempts in the last century to promote the development of democracy in the Western Hemisphere and the lessons of that experience that are relevant to the future.

Aside from conferences, the World Peace Foundation sponsors monthly luncheons on different themes of United States foreign policy. Most recently, the luncheons have dealt with the Central American conflict. The Foundation also publishes a quarterly journal, *International Organization*. The Foundation's archives are included in the Swarthmore College Peace Collection, Swarthmore, Pennsylvania.

## Women's International League for Peace and Freedom

The Women's International League for Peace and Freedom (WILPF) grew out of an International Congress of Women presided over by *Jane Addams* and held at the Hague in 1915 during World War I with 1,136 women from 12 nations in attendance. The Congress sent delegates to the heads of both neutral and warring nations, urging constant negotiations until peace was established.

At a Second Women's Peace Conference in 1919, women from 16 countries voted to continue their organization permanently as the Women's International League for Peace and Freedom. The WILPF was headed by Jane Addams from its beginnings until her death in 1935.

Throughout its history, WILPF's slogan has been "Listen to the Women for a Change." It is a well-organized, worldwide community of activists working on international issues, with a strong network of grass-roots branches in the United States. Its programs for peace and social justice have held the loyal commitment of supporters through more than 70 years of world achievement.

Recent actions and coalition work of WILPF have included:

* Feed the Cities not the Pentagon Campaign (1976).
* Nuclear Weapons Freeze Campaign (1979).

- Conference on Racism (1979).
- Stop the Arms Race Campaign (STAR) (1980).
- March for Jobs, Peace and Freedom (to commemorate the twentieth anniversary of historic civil rights march (1983).
- Women's Peace Encampment (1983).
- Listen to Women for a CHANGE (including the Women's Poll Project and work with the Women's Vote Project) (1983).
- Women's Speaking Tour on Central America (1984).
- Campaign for Comprehensive Test Ban (1984).
- International Cruise Missile Alert (1985).
- The Women's Budget and "Take Back the Budget" Campaign (1986–87).

Also, in 1987, the Wisconsin branch of WILPF engaged in an active pilot legislative campaign for WILPF, a Campaign to Stop "Star Wars."

In a recent WILPF brochure entitled *70 Years as Pioneers,* the following statement is set aside in a box:

The Women's International League for Peace and Freedom has been working since 1915 to unite women in all countries who oppose war, exploitation and oppression. Through sections in 26 countries and 130 activist branches across the U.S., WILPF enables women to find their voice, and increase their power. We know that one person can work effectively for social change when connected to a larger network. We know the strength of cooperation and of direct non-violent action in the name of peace and freedom.

During this study, I first became aware of WILPF through its excellent curriculum materials for peace education in elementary and junior high schools. (See description of the Jane Addams Peace Association, the education affiliate of WILPF, included in this chapter.)

# The League of Women Voters

On February 14, 1920, six months before the Nineteenth Amendment to the United States Constitution was ratified, delegates from the National American Woman Suffrage Association met for a victory celebration in Chicago. With the realization of votes for women, they founded the League of Women Voters.

From its beginnings, it was apparent that the legislative goals of the LWV would not be exclusively related to women's issues. Instead, the primary role of the League of Women Voters was to become one of providing citizen education aimed at the entire electorate. In its 68 years of service, the League has helped millions of men and women become informed participants in government.

Throughout its history, the LWV has taken a stand on a wide variety of issues, including international relations. In its 1923 convention, it disagreed with the prevailing attitude of isolationism as "neither wise nor possible for this nation." When the League of Nations could not stop the Japanese invasion of Manchuria in 1931, the LWV pointed out that the League of Nations would have been stronger if the United States had been a member. In the following year, 1932, the LWV took a firm position in support of United States membership in the League of Nations.

The League of Women Voters continued its efforts in international affairs by working for United States membership in the World Court, and in 1932, it presented a trunkful of petitions to the Disarmament Conference in Geneva. It also worked for implementation of the *Kellogg-Briand Pact,* which renounced war as an instrument of national policy. In 1939, the League began its consistent support for trade expansion rather than trade-restrictive legislation. The League opposed the principle embodied in the Neutrality Acts in the 1930s that the United States should treat all belligerent nations the same.

As the 1944–45 Dumbarton Oaks proposals for a United Nations were developed, the League of Women Voters launched a vigorous citizen education effort. Ever since, the LWV has been a strong supporter of the United Nations, free world trade, and a United States foreign aid policy that improves the quality of life for the people in the developing nations.

Since World War II, the League has given equal emphasis to domestic and international affairs. The League of Women Voters Education Fund (LWVEF) was founded in 1957 as a citizen education and research organization. At the national level, the LWVEF received much-deserved recognition for sponsoring presidential debates in 1976, 1980, and 1984.

The Education Fund also publishes special reports such as a recent paper entitled "Promoting Peace: Agenda for Change," by staff specialists Laureen Andrews and Alice L. Hughey.

In the 1960s, the League did a two-year evaluation of United States relations with the People's Republic of China, and in 1969, it announced its position, calling for normalization of relations with the Chinese and an end of United States opposition to representation from the People's Republic of China in the United Nations.

The LWV has been in the forefront on all major issues, including equal rights and environmental issues. Its advocacy agenda for 1987 included promoting a safer world and creating a positive climate for nuclear arms control through policy and spending decisions on national weapons programs; and promoting humane and equitable United States relations with developing countries in Central America by opposing United States military aid to the Nicaraguan "contras."

Membership was broadened in 1974 to include men, and within six years, more than 3,000 men had joined the League.

The basic goals of the League of Women Voters remain the same as they were stated back in 1919. They are included in the following 1919 quotation:

The organization has three purposes:
* to foster education in citizenship,
* to promote forums and public discussion, and
* to support needed legislation.

## War Resisters League

The War Resisters League was organized in 1923 to enroll men and women opposed to war and to support conscientious objectors who did not feel at home in the religious pacifist movement. The national office of WRL is located in New York City and it has three regional offices, in Durham, North Carolina; Norwich, Connecticut; and San Francisco, California. Since its founding, it has evolved and grown to include over 17,000 members. The League's early support of imprisoned World War II C.O.'s led to a radicalization of WRL as these resisters left prison and joined the League. Its membership now includes "anarchists, feminists, socialists, Democrats, agnostics, Jews, Protestants, atheists—even a few Republicans" according to WRL literature.

The War Resisters League is the United States section of War Resisters International (WRI), which has sections in more than eighteen countries around the world. WRI has official status with the United Nations.

The War Resisters League believes war is a crime against humanity and advocates Gandhian nonviolence to create a democratic society free of war, racism, sexism, and human exploitation. Quoting from a recent WRL brochure:

> The radical pacifism of the League is an effort to use education and nonviolent actions to deal with the complex political, social, economic, and psychological causes of war. . . .
> The War Resisters League views nonviolence as an experiment, which, because it is different, seems radical and yet is necessary for survival. Our job is developing ways of social change which bring justice without the injustice and tragedy of violence. Pacifists are not looking for power—but for ways of changing society so it is a better place for all. . . .

The program of the WRL centers on education and action. Of special importance are its Annual Peace Calendar, its WRL Organization Manual, and various action packets, posters, slide shows, etc. Although its program focuses on militarism and disarmament, WRL is also committed to eliminating the causes of war as well as war itself, and various task forces have been established to develop action programs to address these causes.

During the 1950s, the WRL stressed support for civil rights and opposition to nuclear weapons testing. In the 1960s, the League's membership grew dramatically, and it organized marches, rallies, draft card burnings, war tax resistance, and civil disobedience at induction centers. It also worked in coalitions to oppose the Vietnam War. Since the end of the

Vietnam War, the League initiated the Continental Walk for Disarmament and Social Justice in 1976 and helped start the Mobilization for Survival organized in 1977. It has continued to work on numerous anti-nuclear actions up to the present. For example, to demonstrate the futility of defense when there exist in the world enough nuclear weapons to destroy us all several times over, the League has developed a national educational campaign against the government's civil defense program.

Both WRL/New England and WRL/Southeast played leading roles in the anti-Trident campaign; and all three regional offices have contributed creatively to the anti-apartheid movement. The WRL/NE is also a national clearinghouse for the international *Stop War Toys* campaign. The WRL/SE helped initiate the campaign against Star Wars contracts.

The WRL is one of the few United States organizations specifically supporting nonviolent resistance in Central America.

In 1986, WRL produced "Daring to Change: Perspectives on Feminism and Nonviolence," a complete packet of materials which included useful feminist and pacifist analyses of militarism and its effects on women everywhere.

In March 1987, a call was mailed to all WRL members urging them to participate in a "Mobilization for Justice and Peace in Central America and Southern Africa." This "Appeal to the People of the U.S." was a call for a mass mobilization and a civil disobedience action on April 25–27, 1987, in Washington, D.C., to protest United States foreign policy in these two regions. Initiated by labor and religious leaders, this Spring Mobilization for Peace and Justice in Central America and South Africa was sponsored by WRL and a broad coalition of religious, labor, anti-apartheid, peace, and social justice organizations.

With this same mailing was enclosed a brochure about WRL's 1987 Ten Day Training Program for Organizers to be held at Woolman Hill, a Quaker Center in the Berkshire Mountains of Massachusetts, July 24 through August 2. Every year, participants in this program learn new skills and develop their approaches to local organizing.

A brief notice was also given of WRL's National Conference to be held in Raleigh, North Carolina, August 13–16, 1987.

The magazine of the War Resisters League, *The Nonviolent Activist,* is published eight times a year and includes current political news as well as news of WRL activities.

## Jane Addams Peace Association

The Jane Addams Peace Association was incorporated in 1948 and has its headquarters in New York City. It sponsors and finances the educational programs of the Women's International League for Peace and Freedom (WILPF). (See separate report on WILPF earlier in this chapter.) These programs include the following listed in order of founding:

**1953.** The *Jane Addams Children's Book Award* is presented to the children's book of the previous year that most effectively promoted the cause of peace, social justice, world community, and the equality of the sexes and all races. Honor books are also given recognition.

**1961.** The *International Seminars* program arranges meetings both in the United States and abroad to provide opportunities for women from various countries to discuss mutual concerns related to world peace.

**1967.** The *Living Memorial Fund* receives memorials and other gifts to be used to publish and distribute materials on peace and freedom to schools, libraries, and religious institutions. Through this fund, thousands of books and pamphlets, as well as peace curricula for younger ages, have been made widely available to the public.

**1976.** The *Committee on Education* develops curricula for peace and justice studies, and implements them, preschool–college, through community, parent, and teacher publications and programs. It also conducts an ongoing review of peace education materials.

**1980.** Its *Racism Task Force* writes articles and provides workshops on racism. A nationwide network of monitors reports on incidents of racism in their respective regions.

**1981.** The *International Disarmament Fund* publishes materials on disarmament negotiations and meetings, and provides assistance to national and international workshops on disarmament.

Each January, Ruth Chalmers, Executive Director of the Jane Addams Peace Association, sends to friends of JAPA a brief report of the previous year's activities along with her note of appreciation for past support and encouragement of continuing support. Actions reported in recent years have included:

• Support of WILPF Conference in Lisbon, May 3–6, 1984, on Nicaragua and Peace in Central America.

• Help with the cost of the 1984 Women's Poll, a project of WILPF in which 18,000 women (mostly non–WILPF) in 49 communities and 23 states were asked six key political questions (re: the nuclear freeze, reducing military spending, decreased military involvement in Central America, increased support for child care, the Equal Rights Amendment, and the right to choose an abortion).

• Received money to finance the Peace Tent at the final conference of the Decade for Women on the campus of the University of Nairobi the summer of 1985.

• Helped to finance a WILPF Latin American Conference, March 17–22, 1985, in San Jose, Costa Rica, attended by women from sixteen countries in Central and South America.

• Published the *Women's Budget,* a booklet which envisioned cutting the military budget and redistributing the money to social programs that benefit women and their families.

• Sponsored the Ninth Conference of Soviet and U.S. Women in Estes Park, Colorado, in June 1986.

- Accepted an invitation from the All China Women's Federation to have a delegation of three WILPF leaders visit China, September 29 to October 17, 1986.
- Bought a small building in Washington, D.C., to house the Washington office of WILPF in 1987.

Not everyone is aware that Jane Addams, in addition to her social work career at Hull House, Chicago, was the first American woman to win the Nobel Peace Prize (awarded in 1931). This award came to her because of her work for world peace through the Women's International League for Peace and Freedom (WILPF). From her experience with people of different national backgrounds working and living together, Jane Addams was convinced that disagreements among nations could be settled around a conference table without resort to war. She also believed the highest form of patriotism lay in building a world free from hunger and oppression.

Besides establishing Hull House, one of the first social settlements in the United States, Jane Addams helped to found the National Association for the Advancement of Colored People and the WILPF. The latter grew out of an International Congress of Women held at the Hague in 1915, over which Jane Addams presided. The WILPF was headed by Jane Addams until her death in 1935.

After her death, the WILPF continued to grow, nationally and internationally. By the mid–1940s, it was deemed necessary to establish a separate organization to carry on some of the WILPF educational programs. This new organization, appropriately named the Jane Addams Peace Association, was founded on December 23, 1948. Its stated purpose is to promote understanding among the peoples of all nations and races so that war and strife may be avoided and a lasting peace enjoyed.

## The National Committee for an Effective Congress

The National Committee for an Effective Congress (NCEC) was founded in 1948 by Eleanor Roosevelt and other distinguished Americans to confront the powerful vested interests dominating politics, e.g. big oil, big steel, big utilities, and Wall Street.

The founding of NCEC created a powerful new political concept: public concern for congressional races on a national basis.

In 1954, NCEC confronted Senator Joseph McCarthy and coined the term "the radical right" to describe him and his supporters.

In the early 1960s, a coalition of Old Guard Republicans and Democratic "Dixiecrats" was still able to block civil rights legislation, but NCEC led the fight to break the conservative hold on the House Rules Committee and to defeat the obstructionists at the polls by 1965.

The NCEC was one of the first national organizations starting to oppose the Vietnam War in 1966. By 1972, NCEC led the attack on entrenched House conservatives supporting the war and the huge military/industrial complex.

In 1974, after leading the fight for the first campaign fund reform law, NCEC helped to send a new breed of men and women to Washington. They led the campaign to abolish the seniority system, establish ethical standards in Congress, and open up the legislative process to public scrutiny.

The above examples suffice to define the NCEC as a group interested in helping to elect liberals to Congress to counteract the "radical right." In the *National Journal,* Nell Gregory stated:

> The National Committee for an Effective Congress ... might better be labeled "an effective committee for a national Congress"—effective because the candidates it endorses and helps finance usually get elected and national because its aims are directed toward foreign policy and other issues usually removed from parochial interests of a Congressional district.

The NCEC supports candidates committed to *reversing* the following policies in national government:

• Escalating the arms race and increasing world tension by resorting to military rather than diplomatic intervention.

• Causing record budget deficits which mortgage the lives of our children and cripple our ability to compete in world markets.

• Despoiling the environment.

• Demanding trillion-dollar increases in defense spending.

• Dismantling Medicare, Social Security, pension programs and other commitments to senior citizens.

• Coddling the big corporations by cutting their taxes and curbing regulatory agencies.

• Pushing through constitutional amendments prohibiting abortion and requiring school prayer.

In its 38 years of service, the NCEC has come to be recognized as one of the most effective political forces in the country. It provides candidates with expert assistance in planning, organizing, and managing campaigns, and provides the best in professional polling, targeting, media, and fund-raising.

## World Policy Institute

The World Policy Institute (formerly the Institute for World Order) was founded in 1948. Its agenda emphasizes the development and promotion of policies in three major areas: (1) the peaceful resolution of global conflicts, (2) the building of an equitable and sustainable world economy, and (3) the protection of human rights and the global ecology. The Institute sponsors research in these areas performed by its staff and by specialists from throughout the world.

Key projects of the World Policy Institute (WPI) are its *World Policy Journal* and its *Security Project.*

The Institute's quarterly journal, *World Policy Journal,* provides a forum for the assessment of United States and world economic and security policies and is open to new writers and analysts from around the world. It has a circulation of 10,000, and copies of each issue are sent to Congress, journalists, and organizational leaders. Article reprints are available for classrooms and the general public. The Journal provides progressive internationalist perspectives, bold policy proposals, fresh new "voices" in its debates, book reviews, essays, special reports from crisis spots, and in-depth interviews with national and international leaders. The *World Policy Journal* is for educators and scholars, public officials and policy-makers, opinion-makers, political activists, and concerned citizens.

The Institute initiated its *Security Project* in 1983 to develop an integrated set of United States economic, political, and military policies. This set of policies has been shared with presidential and congressional candidates and incumbents, and with the media, national organizations, universities, and civic groups. The Institute illustrates ways in which the Security Project's proposed policies could benefit American security, and how the policies might be applicable to changing areas throughout the world. Some 48 studies were commissioned in 1983 on issues most central to United States security in the 1980s.

The first report of the Security Project, released in June 1984, outlined comprehensive proposals for the 1980s and beyond and was presented in a series of briefings for members of Congress, House and Senate aides, and for leaders of 30 activist groups and research organizations. *Post–Reagan America,* published in 1987, contains studies representing the culmination of the research phase of the Security Project.

As a not-for-profit educational organization, WPI is involved in the publishing and distribution of books and curriculum guides. Institute fellows and staff also prepare articles for newspapers and magazines, and give numerous speeches and briefings before public, congressional, and university audiences.

The WPI's 1987 *Publications Catalog* included a listing of available *World Policy Journal* reprints; a listing of reports on the Security Project; an annotated bibliography of recent books; and a backlist of available books, journals, World Policy Papers, and working papers. Recent books listed were:

• *International Law: A Contemporary Perspective* (Volume II: Studies on a Just World Order Series), by Richard Falk, Friedrich V. Kratochwil, Saul H. Mendlovitz, eds. Boulder CO: Westview, 1985.

• *Making Europe Unconquerable: The Potential of Civilian-based Deterrence and Defense,* by Gene Sharp. Cambridge MA: Ballinger, 1986.

• *Peace and World Order Studies: A Curriculum Guide* (4th edition), by Barbara J. Wien, ed. New York: World Policy Institute, 1984.

• *Proposals for Third World Development: Out from Under,* by James H. Mittelman. London: Macmillan, 1987.

- *The Quest for a Just World Order,* by Samuel S. Kim. Boulder CO: Westview, 1983.
- *Sexism and the War System,* by Betty Reardon. New York: Teachers College Press, 1985.
- *Toward Nuclear Disarmament and Global Security: Search for Alternatives* (Volume IV: Studies on a Just World Order Series), by Burns Weston, ed. Boulder CO: Westview, 1984.
- *World Military and Social Expenditures,* by Ruth Leger Sivard. Washington, D.C.: World Priorities, 1986.

A transnational activity of the World Policy Institute is the co-publishing of a quarterly journal, *Alternatives,* with the Centre for the Study of Developing Societies in New Delhi. *Alternatives* provides analyses of major views, processes, and strategies for confronting problems such as militarism, underdevelopment, dependency, exploitation, and ecological destruction.

## Promoting Enduring Peace

*Promoting Enduring Peace* was organized in 1952 by Dr. James Davis. He was a Quaker and a staunch believer in nonviolence; and he recognized a need for a grass-roots citizens' peace organization that would seek out truth and make it available to "ordinary" persons. He began collecting "liberal" articles and sending copies to people free of charge.

During the Vietnam War, millions of articles opposing United States involvement were distributed for classes, workshops, leafletting, and other purposes. This practice has continued and remains a vital part of the program of *Promoting Enduring Peace* (PEP).

Free peace materials are mailed by PEP on a quarterly basis. Anyone can get on its mailing list by request. (See address of PEP in Appendix B.) There are no dues, but most send in a tax-exempt contribution once a year to help cover costs.

Quarterly mailings usually include five, six, or more selected articles/materials accompanied by an order form listing over 40 items available free of charge except for postage. In April 1987, for example, the mailing included:

- "The Arms Race: How to Stop It and What Stands in the Way," by Prof. George Wald. 1/12/87.
- "Making Peace Here and Now," by Michael T. Klare and Andrea Ayvazian. *Fellowship.* 1 & 2/87.
- "Worldwide, Military Priorities Leave Social Programs in the Dust," by Peter Grier. *Christian Science Monitor.* 12/4/86.
- "Preaching Peace While Testing Weapons," by Senator Paul Simon. 3/16–22/86 (weekly column).
- "Respect, Please, for Nicaraguans' Rights," by Keven M. Cahill. *The New York Times.* 2/14/87.

- Plus a descriptive announcement about a new documentary film entitled, *Faces of the Enemy,* to be aired by PBS starting May 27.

With each mailing, Alice and Howard Frazier, co-directors, of PEP, send their own enthusiastic summary report of peace happenings since the last mailing. For example, the opening sentence of their April 17, 1987, cover letter read, "The People's Appeal for Peace Campaign is going strong!" and their first paragraph ended with, "Thus the effects of the campaign will continue long after the petitions are presented to President Reagan, General Secretary Gorbachev, and to the Secretary-General of the United Nations on August 6."

Their summary also covered the highlights of the successful Mississippi River Peace Cruise PEP sponsored the previous summer (with twelve co-sponsors), and announced that the Volga Peace Cruise for July 21–August 9 was already fully booked.

Once a year, PEP awards its *Gandhi Peace Award* to a person who has made a significant contribution to world peace and international understanding. Included in its list of recipients have been Eleanor Roosevelt, Linus Pauling, A.J. Musti, Norman Thomas, Dorothy Day, and Helen Caldicott.

In addition, PEP has conducted international *peace seminars* in various countries, including tours to the U.S.S.R. and the People's Republic of China, Cuba, and Mongolia. Tours in the Soviet Union for high school students have been taken for several years during the spring recess.

Promoting Enduring Peace is a member of the Mobilization for Survival coalition and incorporates the activities and goals of that organization into its own program. (See report on MfS in this chapter.) It also works closely with the American Friends Services Committee and the Women's International League for Peace and Freedom, and other peace organizations. (See report on AFSC in Chapter 2 and report on WILPF in this chapter.)

In August 1987, Promoting Enduring Peace was one of 25 co-sponsors of an International Bicentennial Symposium on Strengthening the United Nations held in Philadelphia, Pennsylvania. (For more information on the symposium, see the section for WFA in Chapter 4.)


## SANE/FREEZE

National SANE, a Committee for a Sane Nuclear Policy, was formed in 1957 at a time of public concern about the testing of nuclear weapons on the desert flats of Nevada. These tests were polluting the atmosphere and spreading deadly, cancer-causing radioactivity throughout the nation and the world. SANE was on the forefront of the public demand for a bilateral agreement with the Soviet Union to end all above-ground nuclear explosions.

The successful outcome of their efforts was the Limited Test Ban Treaty of 1967, an agreement that has been honored by both sides.

In the 1960s, SANE was one of the first national organizations to oppose the Vietnam War. In 1969–70, SANE took the lead in another successful citizens' effort, the campaign to prevent both sides from building an ABM (anti-ballistic-missile), which would have increased the risk of nuclear war at that time.

More recently, SANE played a leading role in blocking mobile basing of the MX missile in Utah and Nevada. Currently, SANE is continuing to oppose its being based in other areas of the West and is attempting to stop all new MX basing schemes.

With over 120,000 members, SANE is one of the largest citizens' organizations in the United States focusing on reversing the arms race. Drawing on its experience of many years of working for peace, SANE has become a respected source of knowledge and creative thinking on how to reduce the nuclear threat and plan for economic alternatives.

In a recent open letter, David Cortright, Executive Director of SANE, stated:

> We don't just hope and plead for peace — we work for it!
> We disseminate facts about nuclear war and military spending to decision-makers in Washington.
> We have established our own political action committee, SANE PAC, to assist political candidates who support arms reduction.
> We provide newspapers, magazines and radio and television stations with data to counter Pentagon propaganda.
> We distribute filmstrips and research materials to schools, civic groups and others.
> We are building a Rapid Response Network which quickly activates thousands of citizens throughout the country when public pressure is needed to influence policy decisions in Washington.
> We have our own half-hour radio program presenting rational alternatives to the nuclear arms race on more than 150 stations every week.
> We established the first national door-to-door canvass for peace, speaking personally to hundreds of thousands of people.

In another letter, following the reelection of President Ronald Reagan, Mr. Cortright called for an organized drive to support candidates in the 1986 United States Senate race who are against the buildup of nuclear arms. Members of SANE worked for peace candidates by talking at town meetings, canvassing door to door, meeting with the press, appearing on television, and printing and distributing campaign letters.

Mr. Cortright invited all groups and individuals working for peace to unite and become "a part of the biggest, strongest drive for peace ever mounted in this country."

National SANE's formidable peace and arms control lobby in Washington is powerfully confronting the arms constituency with its network of activists throughout the country. It points out:

> Our nation can be made stronger, not weaker by the nuclear weapons freeze and other disarmament measures. These measures would enable the

U.S. to focus its energies on its most precious commodity: its people.

Instead of channeling trillions into "star wars" weapons, let's give our children a better education. Instead of overkill nuclear weapons, let's provide job training to the millions of underprivileged and displaced workers who need it. Instead of continuing to stuff an overweight Pentagon, let's develop better health care programs.

Again, quoting from SANE's Executive Director, David Cortright:

Together, this SANE team — lobbyists, activists and members — has taken on the military Goliath that dominates our nation's future. And not just our military, but the future of our health care programs, our education programs, our jobs programs . . . our lives.

In urging individuals to get involved in working for peace, Mr. Cortright quoted from Jonathan Schell's *The Fate of the Earth:*

Because everything we do and everything we are is in jeopardy, and because the peril is immediate and unremitting, every person is the right person to act and every moment is the right moment to begin, starting with the present moment.

The members of SANE are kept informed of important developments through its monthly newsletter, *SANE WORLD.*

*Addendum*: The foregoing has been a summary of SANE's initial response to this survey of positive efforts to promote peace. Since then, SANE has merged with the Nuclear Weapons Freeze Campaign. This merger brought together SANE's 150,000 members with the FREEZE's 1,800 state and local chapters, creating the largest active peace organization in United States history. Since SANE and FREEZE have worked together over the years on various legislative campaigns, this merger was a natural culmination of their collaborative efforts. The Reverend William Sloan Coffin, Jr., became the first president of the merged SANE/FREEZE organization on a part-time basis in the fall of 1987 and full-time in January 1988. The name of its quarterly publication was changed from *SANE WORLD* to *SANE World/FREEZE Focus.*

## World Without War Council

Although the *World Without War Council* was not founded until 1967, it grew out of *Acts for Peace* (1958–61), and *Turn Toward Peace* (1961–66). The first was active primarily in Northern California, and the second spread up and down the West Coast (California, Oregon, and Washington) and had offices in Chicago and New York. Now, the World Without War Council has offices in Berkeley, Chicago, New York, Seattle, and Washington, D.C., and it has meetings and events throughout the United States. The wwwc also operates a bookstore in Chicago.

The basic goal of all three organizations has been the same: to develop international legal and political institutions capable of resolving inevitable conflicts between nations; i.e., institutions that are not likely to come into being without significant leadership provided by the United States. However, the strategies for reaching that goal have changed with each name change.

The current World Without War Council seeks to develop the structures, ideas, leadership training, and processes to enable the United States to provide that needed leadership in developing the above institutions.

Information sheets on wwwc sent in response to this survey brought out that the World Without War Council is not a membership organization. It sees itself as a management/consultant agency with America as its client and thus, in its work, touches almost every sector of our society. The wwwc is a research, publication, training, initiating, coordinating, and organizing center that challenges many of the guiding ideas of the present peace movement even as it works to develop alternatives to the Pentagon's. It is hard to locate on the present political spectrum because it deliberately brings people from widely varying positions on that spectrum into its work.

The wwwc conducts some of the best overview and coordinating efforts in the American and world affairs field, but it also works as a catalyst and trainer with individual institutions and organizations, setting in motion projects, structures and events which aid in making America a leader in progress toward a world that resolves international conflict without war. More specifically, wwwc's current tasks include:

• Linking in a common work process key leaders of the major non-governmental structures in the country interested in America's role in world affairs.

• Improving relations between leaders of independent sector organizations and those in the Department of State, the International Communication Agency and other governmental centers, in ways which maximize the chances for agreement on a common sense of purpose and direction in our country.

• Enlarging the base of funding for the field and helping develop more sophisticated leadership in the philanthropic community.

• Recruiting and training leadership capable of sustained and effective work in the range of non-governmental organization.

• Adding to those organizations whose central purpose is work on foreign policy and world affairs problems other agencies not previously active in the field.

• Sustaining a commitment to sound and creative local work.

• Work on current issues.

• Idea development and publications programs.

• "Other" undertakings which aid in progress toward a world without war.

In his "Reflections on the Freeze and a Peace Effort Worthy of the Name," Robert Pickus, President of wwwc, states:

> But an effective peace strategy would not focus on weapons alone. It would recognize the central problem: the absence of legal and political alternatives to weapons in the resolution of conflict, and it would propose ways to secure Soviet cooperation in bringing them into being.

Thus, special note should be made of wwwc's *American Initiative Project,* which is aimed at securing Soviet agreement on progress toward nonviolent resolution of international conflicts.

Mr. Pickus closed his paper with:

> At the center of any genuine peace effort is a spiritual resistance to the idea that millions of human beings should be treated as our enemies and that we should prepare to destroy them. That affirmation of human community moves in the Freeze. It is an essential requisite for any genuine peace effort. But in the present peace movement it is submerged in waves of fear and the hatred that emerges from that fear. Those emotions can dissolve our own political community. They cannot build the wider one we so desperately need.

## Physicians for Social Responsibility

*Physicians for Social Responsibility* (psr) was formed in 1961 by a group of United States physicians who were deeply troubled by the health implications of nuclear weapons testing in the atmosphere and by the lack of data on the medical consequences of nuclear war. Since its founding, psr has become a strong national, nonprofit, nonpartisan organization of over 30,000 members, including physicians, osteopaths, dentists, and medical students dedicated to professional and public education on the medical hazards of nuclear weapons and nuclear war. It works through its 160 chapters "to halt and reverse the arms race, beginning with a bilateral freeze, and to create a citizenry so well informed about the dangers of nuclear weapons that, in time, we will eradicate the threat of nuclear war itself."

A major role was played by psr in developing public understanding of the devastating capabilities of thermonuclear weapons and contributed to the signing of the Limited Test Ban Treaty of 1963. Although it was hoped the Treaty would be a major step to control the nuclear arms race, the threat has steadily intensified.

From its beginning, psr recognized that a nuclear war would be the "final epidemic." It has worked to reach fellow physicians and, through them, the American people with that message. Through its efforts, Americans have begun to question the sanity of the arms race. Eighty-nine percent of all Americans now believe there can be no winners in a nuclear war.

Physicians for Social Responsibility sees ending the nuclear arms race as its most urgent task. It advocates a verifiable bilateral freeze on the testing, production, and deployment of nuclear arms by both the United States and the Soviet Union.

In just a few years, PSR has demonstrated the tremendous impact physicians can have when they address the health issue of nuclear technology. In 1981, the American Medical Association passed a resolution calling on its member organizations to educate physicians and the public on the medical consequences of nuclear weapons and nuclear war.

Because of the United States administration's commitment to the biggest arms buildup in history, Physicians for Social Responsibility was compelled to issue the following warning, based on medical and scientific analysis:

- Nuclear war, even a "limited" one, would result in death, injury, and disease on a scale that has no precedent in the history of human existence.
- Medical "disaster planning" for nuclear war is *meaningless. . . . There is no possible effective medical response.* Most hospitals would be destroyed, most medical personnel dead or injured, most supplies unavailable. The vast majority of the "survivors" would die.
- *There is no effective civil defense against nuclear war.* The blast, thermal and radiation effects would kill even those in shelters, and the fallout would reach those who had been evacuated.
- *Recovery from nuclear war would be impossible.* The economic, environmental and social fabric on which human life depends would be destroyed in the U.S., the U.S.S.R., and much of the rest of the world.
- *There can be no winners in a nuclear war.* Worldwide fallout would contaminate much of the globe for generations and atmospheric effects would severely damage all living things, as well as food and water supplies.
- *In sum, there is no cure for nuclear war, only prevention.*

Dr. Helen Caldicott once explained:

Having taken the Hippocratic oath, this is our issue: the life and wellbeing of all people on the planet are in our hands. This cause, it seems to me, is the ultimate form of preventive medicine.

According to *Time* magazine, March 29, 1982, "PSR may be the most effective group in the anti-nuclear movement." It helps its members by providing the PSR quarterly newsletter, an up-to-date digest of facts and analysis; Washington reports and briefing papers; research on the nuclear issue; and regional meetings, national conferences, and medical symposia.

Members of PSR are working with physicians around the globe, including Soviet physicians, through the International Physicians for the

Prevention of Nuclear War, a federation of physicians' groups, including PSR of the United States. (See report on IPPNW in this chapter.)

## Council for a Livable World

In response to this survey, I received three brochures from the *Council for a Livable World:*

*To Combat the Menace of Nuclear War* (a general brochure about the CLW).

*What We Don't Know About the Nuclear Arms Race Could Destroy Us All* (a brochure about the Council for a Livable World Education Fund).

*Council for a Livable World Education Fund Speakers' Bureau* (a brochure on how to obtain speakers).

The first brochure provided historical information about the Council and brief descriptions of its Washington Program and its political action committee.

The Council for a Livable World (CLW) was founded in 1962 by the eminent nuclear physicist *Leo Szilard* and other scientists who were pioneers in the development of atomic weapons. The goal of these men and women who knew first-hand the nature of nuclear weapons was to warn the public and Congress of the threat of nuclear war and to lead the way to rational arms control.

The Council's *Washington Program* monitors and influences arms control legislation in the United States Senate. (The Council's affiliate, Peace PAC, supports candidates for the United States House of Representatives; see report on Peace PAC in this chapter.) Council board members and other knowledgeable authorities outside of government provide valuable technical, scientific and strategic information to senators and their staffs at regular Council seminars. These off-the-record sessions, often attended by as many as one-third of the Senate, give plain–English explanations of the nature and dangers of present weapons systems such as the MX missile and of future technologies such as "charged particle beams," an anti-missile device still under research.

The Council also helps initiate and draft legislation, monitors appropriate committees (from the initial hearing to final markup), produces expert witnesses for important hearings, and keeps accurate headcounts before crucial arms control votes are taken.

In Congress, the Council is working *for* mutual and verifiable nuclear weapons reductions, a comprehensive nuclear test ban treaty, and strategic arms negotiations; and *against* "Star Wars," space weapons and chemical weapons.

The Council widely distributes a printed record of votes by members of Congress on key nuclear arms issues.

Six thousand Council supporters in all 50 states have formed a grass-roots network and have volunteered to respond when their personal lobbying of Congress is needed on critical arms control votes.

The CLW maintains a nuclear arms control hotline which explains what is happening in Congress on arms control and what action is needed to influence senators and representatives.

The Council also serves as a resource for local peace groups and activists, distributing fact sheets, reprints and articles free of charge to every state in the country.

The Council has enjoyed considerable success. It was instrumental in the passage of the 1963 Limited Nuclear Test Ban Treaty, halting ABMS, banning biological weapons, defeating the proposed 4,600 shelter MX deployment, advancing the SALT process under four presidents, and slowing nuclear proliferation.

The success of the Council in helping elect 75 United States senators in 24 years has been due to the sophisticated and unique methods of its political action committee. Of the 5,000 PACs in the United States, the Council provides more campaign contributions to nuclear arms opponents than any other political action committee. This proves to candidates the existence of a large constituency that cares deeply about nuclear arms control. Unlike any other candidate assistance group, the Council lets its supporters decide which of its endorsed candidates they prefer to support. Thus Council supporters make contributions to candidates of their choice, but through the CLW.

The Council's political action program begins with exhaustive political intelligence gathered months, even years, before the elections take place.

While the Council for a Livable World is continuing to educate "Washington," it established its Education Fund in 1980 to educate the rest of the country. The Council for a Livable World Education Fund (CLWEF) was formed to educate the public about nuclear weapons, the nuclear arms race, and nuclear arms control by promoting discussion, publishing books and pamphlets, and arranging intensive coverage in the print, radio and television media. The CLWEF has joined with Physicians for Social Responsibility in organizing a series of nationwide symposia on "The Medical Consequences of Nuclear Weapons and Nuclear War." (See report on PSR in this chapter.)

Although it refers to the consequences of nuclear war as "unthinkable," the CLWEF sees its mission as one of making people think about this "unthinkable," so they will start thinking about ways to avoid it. It is using knowledge as a weapon against this "unthinkable." One of its strongest efforts is to promote a no-first-use policy on nuclear weapons. The CLWEF has sponsored No-First-Use conferences in major cities such as New York, Chicago, San Francisco, and Cleveland, which have had intense media coverage.

To meet a growing demand for information, the CLWEF formed a Speakers Bureau. Distinguished physicists, chemists, physicians, arms control specialists and political scientists have agreed to participate within the limits of their schedules. Their Speakers Bureau brochure lists available speakers and tells how to obtain them.

## United World Colleges

The *United World Colleges* currently consist of six schools devoted to fostering international understanding through education "suited to the needs of our times." They are, in order of founding:
- The UWC of the Atlantic at St. Donat's Castle in Wales, founded in 1962.
- Waterford KaMhlaha UWC of Southern Africa in Mbabane, Swaziland, founded in 1963.
- Lester B. Pearson UWC of the Pacific in Victoria, British Columbia, Canada, founded in 1974.
- The UWC of South East Asia in Singapore, founded in 1975.
- The UWC of the Adriatic in Duino Aurisina (Trieste), Italy, founded in 1982.
- Armand Hammer UWC of the American West in Montezuma, New Mexico, United States, founded in 1982.

These six United World Colleges offer young people from all over the world, ages 16 to 19, a unique and challenging educational experience. They provide excellent programs in preparation for entry into the finest colleges and universities (usually with advanced standing), and an international living situation that deepens their understanding of themselves in relation to the world in which they live.

At these UWC campuses, students gather from around the globe in order to share a two-year program of living, working, and studying together. They enjoy a variety of formal and informal activities designed to help them mature intellectually and physically, and at the same time develop first-hand knowledge and appreciations for many of the world's cultures and societies.

The curriculum in the UWCs is the International Baccalaureate, roughly equivalent to the last year of high school and the first year of college in the United States. In addition to the International Baccalaureate and multi-cultural living environment, the schools offer challenging community service programs which are an integral part of the UWC educational philosophy.

Admission to UWCs is based on merit, and scholarship assistance is provided for those demonstrating need.

While each UWC is distinct, all are committed to promoting international understanding through education, and to the proposition that a step toward international understanding is a step toward world peace.

Students of UWC enjoy a wide variety of activities. In addition to their required community service and traditional recreational programs in sports, art, and music, they may choose to learn a local craft, help produce a special event such as an International Day, or join one of many informal discussion groups on world issues. Different geographical locations allow for different training; e.g., the proximity to the ocean has led some to concentrate on sea rescue; the Pecos Wilderness area of the American West provides opportunities for training in wilderness search and rescue. (One of the founders of uwcs, Dr. Kurt Hahn, was also the founder of the Outward Bound Movement.)

Each United World College has its own board of directors or trustees that operates under the guidelines of the International Board. The International Board is advised by an International Council of distinguished individuals, and the first President of the Council was Lord Mountbatten, who worked diligently to expand the uwc movement. In 1978, His Royal Highness the Prince of Wales became its president. He, too, has been working for international growth of the uwcs. Plans are being made for an agricultural college in Venezuela, and another uwc on the Asian subcontinent is under consideration.

***The Armand Hammer United World College of the American West.*** Lord Mountbatten had hoped to establish a United World College in the United States; and when Prince Charles assumed the uwc presidency, he energetically pursued Mountbatten's dream. In 1980, he approached Dr. Armand Hammer, noted citizen diplomat, philanthropist, humanitarian, and Chairman of Occidental Petroleum Corporation.

In August of 1981, Dr. Hammer purchased a beautiful 110-acre site in the mountains of New Mexico, approximately 70 miles northeast of Santa Fe and 120 miles from Albuquerque. The property, 6,500 feet in elevation, still had several buildings from a former health resort and still had natural hot mineral springs flowing on it.

Renovation of five buildings and landscaping of the property were sufficiently completed in time for opening in September of 1982. The school opened with 102 students, 53 young men and 49 young women, from 46 countries. It now operates with a capacity of 200 students, ages 16 to 19, representing more than 60 nations.

The *Academic Program* requires each student to complete six subjects drawn from each of the following groups:

**1. Language A.** (Most fluent language.) Including world literature.

**2. Language B.** A second language.

**3. Study of Man.** Anthropology, economics, history, and psychology.

**4. Science.** Biology, chemistry, applied chemistry, and physics.

**5. Mathematics.** A range of courses appropriate to different levels of ability and interest. Computer studies are available.

**6. Options.** Art, music, or second course from groups 2, 3, or 4.

The *Service Program* at the uwc of the American West, Montezuma, New Mexico, requires all students to participate in both social and wilderness service. As well as providing benefits to the community, these services provide students with opportunities for group responsibility, teamwork, leadership, and the furthering of friendship and understanding.

Examples of community service might include working with visually handicapped, hearing impaired, or developmentally disabled people; or assisting
professionals in the state psychiatric hospital. The wilderness component
offers training in search and rescue, rock climbing, and environmental
studies; and assisting the New Mexico State Police or United States Park
Service on rescue missions or in improving local trails or maintaining
mountain facilities.

## Conference on Peace Research in History

The Conference on Peace Research in History was formed in 1964 to
encourage, support, and coordinate peace research among historians and
social scientists.

In its brochure, the CPRH points out that "viewing war and its causes
as among the most serious problems confronting humanity, members of
CPRH seek to apply intellectual resources to the quest for a peaceful world.
They include diplomatic historians, writers on transnational institutions,
analysts of military policy, chroniclers of movements for peace and social
justice, and those interested in their work. Many members teach related
courses in colleges, universities, or secondary schools; others are students,
peace activists, or members of the general public."

Members are drawn increasingly from around the world as well as
from the United States. They are concerned with making peace research
relevant to the scholarly disciplines, to policy-makers, and to their respective societies.

The CPRH grew out of a 1963 ad hoc committee of the American Historical Association (AHA). At that time, they realized that little effort had
been made in their field to study the "causes of peace." Subsequently, the
CPRH has become an affiliate of the AHA, and it has joined the Consortium
on Peace Research Education and Development for the Promotion of History. It has also acquired non-governmental organization (NGO) status at
the United Nations.

The CPRH has sponsored major conferences including meetings on
Peace and Sovereignty, Wars and Society, Peace Research and Its Impact on the Curriculum, and the Multinational Corporation as a Historical Phenomenon. As it has conducted its meetings on war and peace
research, it has gathered papers which it distributes to members and interested libraries, and it has compiled lists of relevant research in progress.

In addition to its own meetings, CPRH has been responsible for putting
peace research on the agendas of the AHA and numerous other professional
organizations.

Since 1972, the Conference on Peace Research in History has published its own quarterly journal, *Peace and Change,* which features scholarly articles, book reviews, poetry, and reports on peace research and peace

movements around the world. It also includes news of CPRH and the Consortium on Peace Research, Education and Development.

In addition to its quarterly journal, CPRH has a quarterly newsletter covering news of interest to members such as relevant sessions at various conferences, new publications, research announcements and queries, and peace research programs at colleges and universities.

## International Peace Research Association

The International Peace Research Association (IPRA) was founded in 1964. Its current headquarters is in Rio de Janeiro, Brazil. Past headquarters have been in Groningen, Netherlands; Oslo, Norway; Tampere, Finland; Tokyo, Japan; and Columbus, Ohio, U.S.A.

The IPRA is the sole worldwide association of peace researchers. Its stated purpose is:

> To advance interdisciplinary research into the conditions of peace and the causes of war and other forms of violence. To this end, IPRA shall encourage world-wide cooperation designed to assist the advancement of peace research and in particular:
> (1) To promote national and international studies and teaching related to the pursuit of world peace,
> (2) To facilitate contacts and cooperation between scholars and educators throughout the world,
> (3) To encourage the world-wide dissemination of results of peace research.

There are three classes of membership in IPRA: individual scholars, scientific institutions, and scientific associations. IPRA also has contributing members.

The IPRA *Council* members are from Australia, Austria, Denmark, Egypt, Federal Republic of Germany, Hungary, India, Malaysia, Mexico, Netherlands, Nigeria, Norway, Peru, Puerto Rico, Senegal, U.S.A., U.S.S.R., and Zimbabwe. Its *Peace Education Commission* includes members from Argentina, Australia, Canada, Costa Rica, Federal Republic of Germany, Hungary, India, Italy, Netherlands, New Zealand, Nigeria, Norway, Pakistan, Philippines, U.K., U.S.A., and U.S.S.R.

The IPRA holds consultative status B with UNESCO (UN Educational, Scientific and Cultural Organization) and is financially supported by it through the ISSC (International Social Science Council). It also holds NGO status with UNCTAD (UN Conference on Trade and Development).

The IPRA publishes an annual *Activities Report;* and in its 1986 report, it announced plans to move IPRA headquarters to Rio de Janeiro, Brazil, in April of 1987 to share facilities with Development Alternatives for Women for a New Era (DAWN). The same report told of the Association's Eleventh

General Conference held at the University of Sussex, England, April 13–18, 1986, with approximately 328 participating from 52 countries.

The years and locations of previous IPRA biennial conferences have been:

**1965.** Groningen, Netherlands.
**1967.** Tallberg, Sweden.
**1969.** Karlovy Vary, Czechoslovakia.
**1971.** Bled, Yugoslavia.
**1973.** Varanasi, India.
**1975.** Turku, Finland.
**1977.** Oaxtepec, Mexico.
**1979.** Konigstein, Federal Republic of Germany.
**1981.** Orillia, Canada.
**1983.** Gyor, Hungary.

The IPRA maintains study groups on communications, food policy, human rights, weapons technology and disarmament, nonviolence, peace movements, and women, militarization and disarmament.

In addition to their own conferences, IPRA members participate in other international conferences and symposia throughout the world, encouraging peace research and offering their services. The group collaborates with the Latin American Council for Peace Research, the Asian Peace Research Association, and the Consortium on Peace Research Education and Development. It also works with and through member institutions such as the Austrian Institute for Peace Research, the Hungarian Academy of Science's Center for Peace Research Coordination, the Geneva International Peace Research Institute, the International Peace Research Institute of Oslo, the Institute for Alternative Development Research (also in Oslo), the Centre Interdisciplinaire de Recherches sur la Paiz et d'Etudes Strategiques of Paris, the Italian Peace Research Institute, and the United Nations University headquartered in Tokyo. Plans are being developed for two new peace research institutes in Canada and Australia.

The *International Peace Research Newsletter* provides a quarterly forum for peace researchers and educators. The editorial office of the newsletter is now located at the Brazil IPRA headquarters.

As stated in the conclusion of a recent IPRA report:

> There is no doubt that, in the light of global militarization on the one hand, and the counteracting popular movement that is emerging transnationally, on the other, IPRA will continue to assume a great responsibility as the nucleus of the worldwide community of peace researchers and educators.

## Clergy and Laity Concerned

Clergy and Laity Concerned (CALC) was first founded in 1965 to mobilize opposition to United States involvement in Southeast Asia. Over the past 20 years, it has grown into an interfaith, interracial network with over 28,000 supporters and 53 chapters throughout the United States. The men and women of CALC come from all religious groups — Protestants, Catholics, Jews, Muslims, Buddhists — from big cities and small towns in every state of the Union. They are united in a common concern about those who are denied justice or enough food or their basic human rights; and they are working to right these wrongs.

Clergy and Laity Concerned has

• Opposed the growth in the nuclear arms race, and supported a nuclear freeze.

• Co-sponsored tours of European and Asian peace leaders, including Pacific nationals whose islands were threatened by nuclear testing.

• Supported Italian peace fighters working to keep cruise missiles out of their country.

• Kept up a constant struggle against the production of nuclear weapons.

• Faced armed opposition in its tactics of civil disobedience.

The organization is concerned about:

• The quality of human life in this country and throughout the world.

• Arms buildups that are created primarily to give more power to the military and more hefty profits to arms manufacturers.

• The plight of poverty-stricken women who are being denied basic, fundamental needs by our government while it spends trillions on the arms race.

• Political injustice.

• Human rights and hunger, both here and abroad.

Clergy and Laity Concerned believes it would be un–American *not* to criticize its country when it does wrong. It believes that hunger and poverty are the fruits of social injustice. While America puts trillions of dollars into a senseless arms buildup, its own poor are getting poorer, its own hungry are getting hungrier.

To help get at the source of hunger and poverty, CALC has established an education-action program to help concerned Americans challenge United States foreign policy and corporations that contribute to the problems of hunger and poverty. It has also sponsored a broad-based coalitional effort to increase public awareness of food and hunger problems and to build grass-roots support for solutions to these problems.

In its human rights program, CALC has helped unite people in their efforts to oppose repressive governments in South America, Central America, South Africa, and Asia; and it has called upon the religious community to give sanctuary to political refugees who are in danger of death if they return to their homelands.

Also, CALC has helped to bring about the withdrawal of state and municipal funds previously invested in South Africa, due to its system of apartheid.

Clergy and Laity Concerned has expanded its Peace Sabbath into a Peace with Justice Week. This gives churches and synagogues a powerful and effective means of exploring how to achieve not only peace — but peace with justice.

## Center for War/Peace Studies

The Center for War/Peace Studies in New York was established in 1966, and its stated purpose reads:

> An explosion of technology has made our world so small and dangerous that the only hope of humanity for a reasonably happy survival lies in vastly greater cooperation among the nations and peoples than the world has yet witnessed. We need new ideas, new social inventions. The Center for War/Peace Studies seeks to develop such new ideas under its motto: "Applied Research Toward a World of Peace with Justice...."

One of the criteria used by CW/PS in selecting issues to study is to ask, "Is the issue critical to progress toward a world of peace with justice?" Four areas of interest have been singled out for current CW/PS efforts:
- The Law of the Sea and the provision of global sharing of ocean resources, including oil and gas beyond the twelve-mile limit.
- Disarmament, and most urgently, the reversal of the out-of-control arms race.
- The development of a comprehensive and even-handed proposal for peace in the Middle East.
- International decision-making processes, including proposals to change the one-nation, one-vote system in the UN General Assembly and the veto system in the Security Council, as well as proposals for alternative voting systems on the Law of the Sea Treaty.

In line with the above fourth area of study, the Center for War/Peace Studies, under the leadership of Richard Hudson, has developed a recommendation called "The Binding Triad System of Global Decision-making" for the United Nations.

On the cover of its brochure on the *Binding Triad,* CW/PS states, "The world needs a way to make up its mind — to prevent World War III." In order to provide a peace system in place of the war system of international relations, it would be necessary to make two amendments to the articles of the UN Charter.

The first amendment, to Article 18, would change the voting system in the UN General Assembly. Important decisions in the Assembly would still be adopted with a single vote, *but with three simultaneous majorities* within that vote. Approval of a resolution would require that the majority vote include 2/3 of the combined population of nations whose representatives are present and voting, and nations representing 2/3 of the contributions to the regular UN budget of those present and voting. (Abstentions would not count.) Thus, in order for a resolution to be adopted it would have to be supported strongly by most of the countries of the world, most of the population of the world, and most of the political/economic/military strength of the world.

The second amendment, to Article 13, would increase the powers of the General Assembly in most cases, making its decisions binding instead of recommendations as at present. However, the Assembly would not be permitted "to intervene in matters which are essentially within the jurisdiction of any state," as the Charter already provides. Whenever jurisdiction is in doubt, the issue can be referred to the World Court, and if the court rules the question is essentially domestic, the Assembly could not act. Furthermore, the Assembly would be prohibited from employing military force to carry out its resolutions; this would remain the prerogative of the Security Council, as at present. However, the Assembly could provide peacekeeping forces to carry out a mandate. The Binding Triad system would be applicable not only to peace and security questions, but also to economic and social problems.

Thus, the three legs of the Binding Triad would be: (1) *one nation, one vote,* based on the sovereign equality of states; (2) *population,* based on the population of states — the democracy leg; and (3) *contributions* to the regular UN budget, based on assessments on members for contributions to the organization's regular budget — the realpolitik leg.

An obvious problem with the third leg is that the current level of contributions calls for 16 percent from the Soviet bloc, and 25 percent from the United States. The cw/ps's suggested solution would require the U.S. to reduce its contribution to 22 percent and permit the Soviet bloc to increase its contribution to 22 percent. (This 22 percent figure represents 2/3 of a veto.)

The cw/ps newsletter, *Global Report,* on progress toward a World of Peace with Justice is published four to six times each year, depending upon events and the production of cw/ps Special Studies and other materials.

The 1984 Nov./Dec. issue of *Global Report* was an open letter to the President of the UN General Assembly and the UN Secretary-General from Richard Hudson, Executive Director of cw/ps and author of the Binding Triad system. In his letter, Hudson stated:

> The major thrust of the United Nations at this stage of history, in my opinion, should be to develop itself into an organization that can confront all our multifarious global problems and produce fair, imaginative, specific solutions to them.

## Common Heritage Institute

Common Heritage Institute of Villanova University is a "think tank" that studies international problems and suggests solutions to them. Since its founding in 1967, the Institute, under the leadership of John Logue, has been concerned with many policy problems, but it has placed special emphasis on four closely related problems: (1) how to make the best use of the enormous wealth of the world's oceans; (2) how to improve and strengthen the United Nations; (3) how to bridge the widening gap between rich and poor nations; and (4) how to reverse the arms race.

Quoting from one of CHI's brochures:

> The phrase "common heritage" suggests the Institute's belief that each generation of the human family has an obligation to use our planet's physical and other resources wisely and justly and while doing so, to consider the needs of future generations.

The Institute tries to focus public and scholarly attention on the need for a more just, peaceful and humane world order. It makes and evaluates policy proposals which may help bring that kind of world order into being. The Institute is associated with the United Nations as a non-governmental organization.

The "ocean program" of CHI reflects its belief that the recent advances in ocean technology have brought mankind great opportunities as well as great problems. One of these opportunities is to implement in an appropriate way the view of some thinkers that the oceans are, in some sense, "the common heritage of mankind."

In the nine-year, 160-nation UN Conference on the Law of the Seas, the Common Heritage Institute worked with key diplomats and non-governmental organizations interested in building more effective ocean institutions and ensuring that some of the immense wealth of the oceans be used to assist developing nations and to fight marine pollution. The theme of CHI's 1971 conference was "The Fate of the Oceans," which resulted in publishing a book by the same name in 1972. "Peace, Justice, and the Law of the Sea" was the theme of its 1977 conference.

The Institute is also concerned about the future of the United Nations. It believes the world needs stronger and more effective international institutions if human life and freedom are to be preserved and peace and justice strengthened.

The first CHI conference held in 1969 was "On the Future of the United Nations." In 1978, the Institute hosted a conference to examine President Carter's modest proposals to reform and restructure the UN. In 1980, CHI published a book entitled "United Nations Reform and Restructuring."

"Youth and World Order; Pathway to Action" was the theme for the Institute's 1981 conference.

At its 1983 Conference on Peace, Justice, and International Institutions (jointly sponsored by 27 organizations), participants again examined proposals for UN reform, including bold proposals for developing the UN into a world federation with power and authority to enforce world law and to provide economic and social justice.

Another major concern of the Institute is the relationship between "developed" and "developing" nations. The Institute points out that the success of efforts to strengthen the United Nations may well depend on the reconciliation of "North" and "South" through ongoing global negotiations on economic issues.

The CHI has sponsored a number of educational events focusing on the nature and implications of the arms buildup and alternative proposals for ending the buildup. It sees the continuing buildup of nuclear weapons as the most immediate threat to peace—to human life itself. Again quoting from Institute materials:

> A just and peaceful world order, for which the Institute has worked since its founding can never be achieved until a way has been found to stop the rush for bigger and more destructive nuclear weapons.

This was also one of the themes of the 1983 conference.

The CHI has used several methods to help carry out its mission. It has published scholarly studies, the books previously mentioned, a variety of educational materials, several monographs, its newsletter, *Common Heritage,* typically published four times a year, and an extensive bibliography on arms control and nuclear arms. Other means have included seminars, public lectures, working lunches for UN diplomats, and large conferences, some of which have already been mentioned.

Participants in CHI's programs have included scholars, students, media representatives, government officials, members of the UN Secretariat, non-governmental organizations associated with the United Nations, and diplomats from more than 60 countries.

Common Heritage Institute was one of three initiating sponsors of an International Bicentennial Symposium on Strengthening the United Nations held in Philadelphia, Pennsylvania, August 6–9, 1987, along with the World Federalist Association (U.S.A.) and the World Association of World Federalists. (See section on WFA in Chapter 4 for more information on the symposium.)

# Fund for Peace

The *Fund for Peace* is a multi-project institution dedicated to a single purpose: the survival of human life on earth under conditions which make life worth living. It was established in 1967, in the shadow of the Vietnam War, by a group of concerned citizens from the private, academic, and nonprofit sectors. It promotes greater knowledge and understanding of global problems that threaten human survival.

Through its research, publications, radio and television broadcasts, the Fund has focused the attention of Congress and the general public on:

- The growing threat of nuclear war.
- The continuing increases in military spending by both developed and developing nations.
- The systematic abuse of basic human rights by governments throughout the world.
- The disparity in economic and social welfare between industrialized and developing nations.
- Violations of civil liberties in the name of "national security."

The Fund for Peace works in Washington and New York through a national office and specific projects, each of which plays a critical role in promoting Fund objectives. Acting as a catalyst and godparent, the Fund has helped launch the following projects:

*The Center for Defense Information.* Directed by admiral Gene R. La Rocque, the Center is a nonpartisan research organization that provides objective analyses of United States military programs for members of Congress and other top decision-makers, the news media, key opinion leaders, and private individuals throughout the United States. The Center supports a strong defense, but opposes excesses and waste in military spending and programs that increase the danger of nuclear war. (See separate report on CDI in this chapter.)

*The Center for International Policy.* Directed by William Goodfellow, this Center analyzes the impact of United States foreign policies, particularly economic and military assistance, on human rights and social and economic needs in the Third World. CIP monitors the World Bank and other international financial institutions and insists on respect for economic, political and civil human rights. Its Indochina Project seeks to improve relations between the United States and the countries of Indochina.

*The Center for National Security Studies.* Directed by Morton H. Halperin, this Center monitors the practices of intelligence agencies (including the CIA and FBI) and alerts Congress and the public to violations of civil liberties in the name of "national security" and in efforts at covert intervention. In collaboration with the ACLU, the Center works with the executive branch, Congress, and public interest groups to develop a consensus on ways to meet government responsibilities without undermining individual freedom.

*The Institute for the Study of World Politics.* Directed by Dr. Kenneth W. Thompson, the Institute awards fellowships in an annual national competition. The program assists scholars working to develop new knowledge and understanding without which complex global issues cannot be resolved. Since 1971 it has enabled more than 200 young men and women from universities throughout the United States to examine current problems of nuclear arms control, regional conflicts and the worldwide crises of population, food, poverty, and energy.

Currently, the Fund's national office has several activities underway:

*Joel Brooke Memorial.* Publishing FIRST STEPS TO PEACE, an annotated resource guide. Its aim is to increase the effective cooperation between national peace groups and concerned citizens at the local level.

*Alternative Defense Project.* Encouraging public and official discussion about alternatives to "star wars." A series of briefing papers will examine six alternative world security systems, analyzing their economic costs and benefits.

*Regional Conferences.* Focusing on the historic relationship between arms control negotiations and international economic and financial policies, these conferences explore why free trade is the policy most conducive to a peaceful world.

*Citizens Dialogue Program.* To improve U.S.-U.S.S.R. relations by expanding citizen dialogue and contact. The Fund for Peace and the Soviet Peace Fund have initiated an annual exchange of delegations to discuss issues of concern to each peace fund.

*International Conference on Accidental Nuclear War.* To be co-sponsored with the Center for Defense Information and to be held in Washington, D.C. This conference will examine how a nuclear war could start, and how the risks of an accidental nuclear war could be reduced.

*Entertainment Summit.* Jointly sponsored by the Fund and Mediators Productions, Inc., of California. This experimental program will seek to improve the climate of Soviet-American relations by critically examining the image through which each society portrays the other in popular film and TV shows.

The national office of the Fund provides back-up funding, administrative support and coordination for all of the Fund's operational units and special projects.

Thus, the Fund for Peace combines the functions of research, training, and public education on urgent issues of the day, as well as on the long-range prospects for survival and achievement of a just and decent world.

The Fund is open to new, creative, and productive proposals for achieving its aims of eliminating war as a means of settling international disputes and the attainment of a just, free, and peaceful world.

## International Association of Educators for World Peace

The International Association of Educators for World Peace (IAEWP) was officially established in 1969, although it dates its origin back to 1967. It now has over 15,000 members with 50 chapters in countries around the globe. It was founded and operates on the premise that

through education and organized activity we can enlarge areas of cooperation between peoples of different nations, eliminate fear and mistrust, articulate humanity's desire for peace, and promote practical, international oriented projects. We are providing models that are trustworthy, and then asking nations to trust.

The IAEWP's international officers and their countries as of March 1987 were as follows: *President,* Professor Norman Marcus, South Wales, U.K.; *Executive Vice-President (and Founder),* Dr. Charles Mercieca, Alabama, U.S.A.; *Vice Pres. for Financial Affairs,* Helen G. Deer, Illinois, U.S.A.; *Vice Pres. for African Affairs,* Dr. George J. Amurun, Nigeria; *Vice Pres. for the Arab States,* Dr. Walid Kamhawi, Jordan; *Vice Pres. for Asian Affairs,* Dr. Saroj Srivastava, India; *Vice Pres. for European Affairs,* Jorgen Laursen Vig, Denmark; *Vice Pres. for Latin American Affairs,* Dr. Rodrigo Carazo Odio, Costa Rica; *Vice Pres. for North American Affairs,* Dr. John R. Petry, Tennessee, U.S.A.; *Secretary-General,* Dr. George Valdeanu, Romania; *Deputy Secretary-General,* Dr. Surya Nath Prasad, India; *United Nations Ambassador,* Dr. Prachoomsuk Achava Amrung, Thailand; and *Plenipotentiary Envoy,* Dr. Seo Kyung-Bo, Korea. In addition to these international officers, each of the 50 chapters has a National Chancellor.

At the beginning of each of its annual *Peace Progress* journals can be found a listing of officers and the following statement:

> IAEWP is a member of NGO (International Non-Governmental Organization) groups of the Economic and Social Council of the United Nations (Category II), and UNESCO Category B. Its objectives are:
> 1. Promoting the kind of education which will stress the release of full potential of the individual in terms of his or her development in the family, the local community, his or her country and whole family of nations.
> 2. Encouraging the development of Colleges and Universities for peace research, including support of UN efforts in this regard.
> 3. Using fully ways of communications and clarifying controversial views and issues in order to achieve maximum understanding.
> 4. Developing the kind of education which will contribute to the formation of characters capable of delaying aggression so that conflict situations may be solved in a positive manner.
> 5. Helping put into practice the Universal Declaration of Human Rights. [See Appendix D.]

Articles and papers published in *Peace Progress* are from writers throughout the world. The 1985 journal, for example, had within its section on "World Peace Ideas" an article by the UN Secretary-General, Javier Perez de Cuellar, and five other authors from Czechoslovakia, France, India, Ireland, and Poland. Other sections of the journal are headed "World Peace Studies," "World Peace Activities," and "Book Reviews." Each section has several articles or papers from various parts of the world. Of particular interest in each issue are "Brief World Records" containing: (1) a summary of world events toward world peace during the past year, (2) a listing of peace group meetings during the past year, and (3) a listing of upcoming peace events and meetings for the next year.

In addition to the annual journal, IAEWP publishes its *World Newsletter,* which keeps members informed of happenings and planned events. The newsletter's summary of IAEWP's 1980–84 Quadrennial Report listed the following as its leading international conferences:

**1980.** Third Asian Convention, Ankara, Turkey, on the Promotion and Prevention of Peace.

**1981.** First Latin American Convention, Bogata, Colombia, on International Understanding and Cooperation.

**1982.** Third World Congress, Washington, D.C., U.S.A., on Education and Survival.

**1983.** Third European Convention, Odense, Denmark, on Varieties of Peace Education.

**1984.** Second National Convention, Trivandrum, India, on People's Education for World Peace.

The summary continued:

> During this period, 1980–84, the Association's documents and brochures were printed in a number of languages including English, Spanish, Italian, Japanese, Thai, and Hindi. In addition, the Association sends regular representatives to participate in major United Nations and UNESCO sessions. Besides, most of the officers travelled extensively around the world to participate in a large number of conferences which dealt with social and educational concerns.

To enlarge on one example, IAEWP's Third European Convention was held at Hesbjerg Peace Research College in Denmark in August of 1983. Although its general theme was "Peace Education," this was divided into: Religion and General Values, and Peace Education (first day); School Education and National Endeavors, and Peace Education (second day); and Politics and Law, and Peace Educaton (third day). The presentation of papers on these subjects and critical discussions were the major activities of the convention.

Since the Quadrennial Report, the IAEWP had its Fourth World Congress in Austria in November 1986, with the theme of "Peace Education in Teacher Training Programs."

A Fifth World Congress is being planned for November 1990, to be held in the People's Republic of China.

## Union of Concerned Scientists

The Union of Concerned Scientists (UCS) was founded by a group of scientists and students at MIT (Massachusetts Institute of Technology) in 1969 to encourage more humane use of scientific and technical knowledge. Over the years it has become a national organization of scientists and citizens concerned about the impact of advanced technology on society. Its early years coincided with America's national awakening to its deteriorating environment. Since, two *primary* goals have emerged: (1) a safe, sensible course for America's energy program, and (2) a world free from the threat of nuclear war.

The UCS is an action-oriented organization. The following are examples of the diversity of its work (taken from the Spring 1984 15th Anniversary issue of its news magazine, *Nucleus):*

**1969.** The UCS sponsored teach-ins at 69 universities, nationwide, focusing on the dangers of the proposed anti-ballistic system (ABM). This helped build public support for the 1972 U.S.-U.S.S.R. ABM Treaty. Also, the UCS released a report calling for the United States to do everything possible to prevent the legitimization, proliferation, and use of chemical and biological weapons.

**1970.** The UCS report called attention to New England's most serious environmental dilemma—air pollution caused by emissions from the region's fossil-fueled power plants—and the hazard related to storage and transportation of liquefied natural gas.

**1971–72.** The UCS was the principal group responsible for bringing about Atomic Energy Commission (AEC) hearings and exposing major weaknesses in the design of emergency cooling systems, the principal protection against serious reactor accidents. This helped initiate public discussion on the subject. Also, the UCS's analysis of the first major accident at a nuclear power plant, the fire at Brown's Ferry, Alabama, forced the AEC to improve regulations governing reactor fire protection.

**1974.** A UCS report to a Senate committee charged that the AEC's structure allowed political and economic considerations to outweigh safety considerations. As a result, the AEC, with its dual role of regulating and promoting nuclear power, was split in 1975 into two federal agencies, the Nuclear Regulatory Commission (NRC) and the Energy Research and Development Administration.

**1975.** The UCS's critique of the Reactor Safety Study, started by AEC and completed by NRC in 1975, sparked the reevaluation that culminated in NRC's eventual disavowal of the report's central findings on major accident probability.

**1977.** The UCS's Declaration on the Nuclear Arms Race, calling for United States initiatives to halt the production of nuclear arms, and UCS's petition supporting ratification of the SALT II Treaty were both signed by thousands of scientists, engineers, and other professionals. Also, continuing UCS litigation concerning the Indian Point and the Three Mile Island reactors helped call public attention to similar problems with the safety of nuclear generation plants.

**1979.** The UCS opposed the MX Missile as an unwarranted weapon that would endanger arms control agreements and destabilize the nuclear arms race.

**1981.** The UCS began convocations and teach-ins on nuclear war which have been attended by hundreds of thousands of citizens at public education events on college campuses in all 50 states. These have stimulated a growing public awareness of the threat of nuclear war.

**1982.** Convocations expanded to more than 500 programs with the focus on "Solutions to End the Arms Race." Also, the UCS's film on "No-First-Use" had its national premier on over 300 campuses. The UCS has continued to be a leading advocate of an American no-first-use policy regarding nuclear weapons. Also in 1982, the USC released its "Framework for a New National Security Policy" to update its 1977 "Scientists' Declaration on the Nuclear Arms Race." Forty-six Nobel Laureates in science and medicine and more than 500 members of the National Academy of Sciences endorsed this new UCS framework. It called for the United States and its allies to pledge not to be the first to use nuclear weapons, and it called for a bilateral freeze on strategic weapons and delivery systems, a comprehensive nuclear test ban, negotiated deep cuts in nuclear arsenals, and the development of a program to curtail nuclear weapon proliferation.

**1983.** Convocations expanded to a full week of programs co-sponsored with five other arms control organizations, on the theme, "The New Arms Race or New Ways of Thinking? A Week of Education." These activities took place during the first week of November in more than 1,000 locations nationwide.

Since its fifteenth anniversary, along with continuing efforts in the above areas, UCS has been very active in opposing militarization of space as proposed by the Reagan Administration's Strategic Defense Initiative (SDI) or "Star Wars." They published an "Appeal by American Scientists to Ban Space Weapons," which read as follows:

> The development of antisatellite weapons and space-based missile defenses would increase the risk of nuclear war and stimulate a dangerous competition in offensive nuclear arms. An arms race in space poses a great threat to the national security of the United States.
>
> Outer space must remain free of any weapons. It should be preserved as an arena for non-threatening uses: peaceful cooperation, exploration, and scientific discovery among all nations.
>
> We call upon the United States and the Soviet Union to negotiate a total ban on the testing and deployment of weapons in space. To create a constructive environment for the negotiations, both nations should join in a moratorium on further tests of antisatellite weapons. The Soviet Union should bring the Krasnoyarsk radar into conformity with the ABM Treaty, or dismantle it.
>
> We ask the United States and the Soviet Union to reaffirm their commitment to the 1972 ABM Treaty, which prohibits the development, testing, and deployment of space-based ABM systems. We support the continuance of a program of research on ABM technologies in strict conformity with the provisions of the 1972 ABM Treaty.

In addition to its domestic work, the Union of Concerned Scientists has been active in international efforts to promote safety in nuclear energy programs of Great Britain, the Netherlands, the Philippines, and Sweden, as examples.

The UCS is also actively involved with the problem of radioactive waste produced from reactors. The UCS and other environmental groups have led a fight to ensure a safety-first approach to a permanent disposal program. Taking a positive approach, UCS has also been active in researching solar energy and other renewable sources of energy.

The following are excerpts from UCS's open letter dated May 1987. Regarding the UCS Legislative Program:

> Over eight thousand members of the scientific community participate in our Scientists Action Network, sharing their technological expertise with the public in national as well as local forums. Eminent scientists testify before Congress under UCS sponsorship, while others are helping to educate citizens on the threat of nuclear war and alternatives to the arms race.
>
> These efforts by the scientific community are made even more effective by letters and phone calls to members of Congress from the nearly twenty thousand UCS sponsors who have joined our Legislative Alert Network.

Regarding the education of the American Public:

> The real foundation for any constructive change must come from an aware and educated public. That is why so much of the work of UCS focuses on helping Americans understand the issues of Star Wars, nuclear weapons, and arms control. This effort includes many television appearances, books, articles, and brochures, as well as our pioneering use of advanced video technology.
>
> UCS held a highly successful educational conference in February [1987]. Titled "Scientists, Educators, and the Strategic Defense Initiative," the program drew some 250 scientists and educators from 40 states. Participants attended a series of workshops on the technical aspects of SDI, and training sessions on improving media relations and public speaking.
>
> We have produced many documentary films and video tapes, which have been widely distributed for use in colleges and high school courses and for viewing by local civic and arms control groups.
>
> Finally, UCS has created many advertisements that have been printed in newspapers and broadcast on television. Last summer [1986] we ran a series of "editorial" ads in the *New York Times* and hope to carry out similar campaigns in the future.

Regarding their Satellite Summit:

> Last November [1986], UCS sponsored the "Satellite Summit," a video conference featuring a live link between the International Scientists' Peace Congress in Hamburg, a UCS conference of scientists in Washington, D.C., and gatherings of citizens in hundreds of communities across the U.S. The program was co-produced in West Germany by one of its leading television stations and cable networks.

# National Impact Network

The *National Impact Network* (Impact) was organized in 1969 and is headquartered in Washington, D.C. While the National Impact focuses on the United States Congress, state Impact affiliates address state issues.

Impact is an interfaith network which provides information on legislation and on opportunities for citizen action. It is composed of contact persons in local churches, synagogues, and parishes. The cover of its promotional brochure reads:

> Your Voice is Needed! Impact provides information about Congress and state legislatures — and Impact offers the opportunity to make an impact on your elected representatives — For Peace! And for Social Justice! Join Impact today!

Impact addresses a broad spectrum of issues pertaining to international peace and social justice. The Impact agenda focuses on three main priorities: (1) halting the arms race, (2) protecting human rights, and (3) securing economic justice. These reflect the deeply felt concerns of sponsoring Protestant, Roman Catholic and Jewish groups.

As Impact defines these terms, *halting the arms race* means

> supporting arms control initiatives. This addresses such issues as the nuclear freeze, the comprehensive test ban treaty, non-proliferation measures, and the opposition to escalations in the arms race.

*Protecting human rights* means

> promoting domestic and foreign policies which will advance the cause of human rights throughout the world. Some of the areas of concern addressed under this priority include civil and religious liberties, immigration and refugee policies, human rights and foreign policies and Native American concerns.

*Securing economic justice* means

> working towards equitable domestic needs programs, international and domestic economic policies and domestic and international development. This priority item addresses issues such as jobs, welfare, agricultural policies, security and development assistance, women's issues, and the balance between environmental protection and economic concerns.

Impact keeps its members informed through:

• Study reports in *Prepare* which examine pressing issues and project options for future legislative action.

• Legislative alerts in *Action* which provide information on bills before Congress along with Impact recommendations for constituent action. Alerts go to Impact members whose senators or representatives are crucial to the outcome of a vote.

• A monthly newsletter, *Update,* which keeps members informed about developments in Congress in all of Impact's issue areas. The *Update* features a "Priority Action Call" focusing on a critical legislative issue. This gives all network members the chance to communicate with their elected representatives every month.

• A supplementary publication, *Hunger,* which addresses such issues as global hunger and poverty, international development assistance, agricultural policy and food stamps.

• State affiliate *Prepares, Actions,* and *Updates* on state issues.

The National Impact Network is sponsored by the following national religious bodies (or their program agencies):

American Baptist Churches.
American Lutheran Church.
Catholic Committee on Urban Ministry.
Christian Church (Disciples).
Church of the Brethren.
Church Women United.
Episcopal Church.
Episcopal Urban Caucus.
Friends Committee on National Legislation.
Jesuit Conference.
Lutheran Church in America.
National Council of Churches.
Presbyterian Church, U.S.A.
Reformed Church in America.
Union of American Hebrew Congregations.
Unitarian Universalist Association.
United Church of Christ.
United Methodist Church.

## Institute for Peace and Justice

The Institute for Peace and Justice began as a center for peace studies at Saint Louis University, St. Louis, Mo., in 1970. Under the leadership of Kathy and Jim McGinnis, this independent, ecumenical, not-for-profit institute is committed to the challenge: "If you want peace, work for justice." Also, the following is quoted from its mission statement:

> . . . the institute is engaging in creating resources and providing learning experiences in peace education and social justice for schools, religious institutions, families and family life leaders. . . .

In line with its mission, IPJ assists individuals, families, educators, and religious leaders in their active quest for peace, addressing issues such as:

• Global economic justice, including hunger, United States and Central America, global interdependence, and a new international economic order.

• Peacemaking, including the nuclear arms race, nonviolent conflict resolution, peacemaking for congregations, Gandhian nonviolence, and militarism in schools.

• Racism and sexism, including countering stereotypes, challenging institutional racism and sexism, and multiculturalizing education.

Faith and justice, including spirituality of peace and justice, Biblical basis and church teachings, and lifestyle responses.

The IPJ's *Action Program* includes both its *Direct Service* (works of mercy; i.e. helping the victims of injustice meet immediate needs) and its *Work for Social Change* (works of justice; i.e. action aimed at correcting conditions that victimize and oppress people). Services listed by IPJ include:

• Resource development: audio-visual and printed materials. (IPJ's catalog describes a wealth of available educational and parenting resources including books, booklets, puppets, filmstrips, and videotapes.)

• Advisory services, through action initiatives, community forces, letter-writing to legislators, and responses to other groups.

• Newsletters, including the *IPJ Newsletter* and the *PPJN Newsletter.*

• Teaching and leadership training, including workshops, faculty in-service training, summer institutes, seminary courses, and family camps.

Along with in-service training, elementary and secondary teachers in public and parochial schools are assisted with curriculum and resource development, and consultative assistance is provided school administrators concerning school policy. Assistance is also given at the college level and in seminaries. Some of IPJ's most creative work has been in the area of multicultural education.

People and institutions assisted are:

• Schools, including public and parochial school educators, college faculties, seminaries, and campus hunger ministries.

• Religious bodies, including parishes or congregations, religious communities' denominational leaders, religious publications, ecumenical action groups, NCC and USCC family life commissions.

• Individuals and families, including the United States and Canadian Parenting for Peace and Justice Network (PPJN), families, family life leaders, and IPJ shareholders—those people who support the Institute.

• Justice and peace networks (national and international), including advocacy groups on disarmament, hunger, and human rights, Latin American/North American Linking groups, national boards, COPRED, and Pax Christi.

• St. Louis Area peace and justice groups.

Many of the Institute's resources have an explicit Christian dimension. However, other resources have been developed for use in public schools and for families who come from a Jewish tradition.

The Institute's Parenting for Peace and Justice Network (PPJN), coordinated by Kathy and Jim McGinnis, has local coordinators in more than 150 cities in the United States and Canada, and has groups in Australia, Brazil, the Philippines, and South Africa. This Network received national recognition on the Phil Donahue Show in 1983 when three PPJ families interacted with a lively audience on topics such as children and television, multicultural living, consumerism, the arms race, family meetings, nutrition, and the Nestle boycott. An available video tape of this show includes an overview of PPJ.

## The International Peace Academy

The International Peace Academy (IPA) of New York City was founded in 1970. It is a professional training institute devoted to the development and refinement of practical skills in mediation and negotiation for dispute settlements, conflict management and resolution, and peacekeeping.

The Academy is wholly transnational in its board of directors, administration, program staff, and publications, and it is funded by grants and contributions from foundations, corporations, and individuals. Host facilities and participant tuition fees from governments also help support IPA programs.

Civilian and military participants in training programs have come from 125 nations and include academicians, theorists, and practitioners; diplomats, military officers, and policy-makers; from East and West, North and South.

The Academy focuses its work in three areas: (1) conducting training seminars in peacekeeping and multilateral regulations; (2) initiating research in conflict studies and third-party roles in the peaceful resolution of conflicts; and (3) publishing and collecting materials and information relating to its basic training seminars.

Its first Peacekeeping Seminar was held in Vienna in 1970 and it has since become an annual event. These seminars are hosted by the Austrian government and have approximately 40 participants from 30 countries at each. They deal with various aspects of international and regional peacekeeping. The Academy's peacekeeping model has been widely adopted, for example in the Nordic countries and national military academies. A growing number of countries and organizations, including Finland, Japan, Jordan, Nigeria, Peru, Venezuela, and the Organization of American States, have invited the Academy to conduct modified forms of its basic model for them.

The Academy's first annual Seminar for UN Diplomats was held in 1980; and in 1981, the Academy began conducting regular off-the-record round table meetings of military and diplomatic representatives of the UN missions and members of the UN Secretariat to discuss current issues related to peacemaking and peacekeeping.

The IPA established its first Task Force on Technology in 1979. It included representatives from industry, international and regional organizations, diplomats, and military officers; and they held conferences on the use of various devices that could help with peacekeeping efforts, such as ground sensors, remote control television, radar, and other improved equipment. Their analysis led to the conclusion that technology could strengthen peacekeeping capabilities, reduce costs, improve communications, and enhance security.

The IPA produces books, reports, simulation exercises, case studies, newsletters and research and teaching materials of immediate, practical use by professionals in government and institutes of higher education. Since 1970, more than 35 titles have been published and distributed worldwide.

*The Peacekeeper's Handbook* of IPA has become a textbook for the training of peacekeepers by the international community, and it is available in English and French editions. The IPA lists several other publications and reports, many of which were produced for or by its various seminars and studies. Its *Coping with Conflict* gives a yearly review of the work and progress of the International Peace Academy, Inc.

The International Peace Academy Program for 1987, as an example, included off-the-record workshops and discussions in:

• Kingston, Jamaica, for diplomats, business people, and military officials on Peace, Development and Security in the Caribbean Basin.

• Dar es Salaam, Tanzania, on Peace and Security in Southern Africa.

• Jakarta, Indonesia, for government officials, business and military professionals on regional security, Kampuchea, and the role of ASEAN, cosponsored by the International Institute of Strategic Studies, London.

• New York City, for UN and New York diplomatic community on topics of current interest, four or five times during the year.

1987 Training Seminars were provided by IPA in:

• Philadelphia, Pennsylvania, for mid-level career diplomats on multilateral negotiations, mediation and third-party roles.

• Vienna, Austria, for senior-level professionals in the military and diplomatic fields on the political and military practice of international peacekeeping and negotiation, hosted by the Austrian government.

• Bridgeport, Connecticut, for junior diplomats on the formal and informal operating procedures of the United Nations.

• Lima, Peru, for senior-level diplomats, government and military officials on regional cooperation for development and the peaceful settlement of disputes in Latin America.

• Dar es Salaam, Tanzania, for senior officials, co-sponsored by the Center for Foreign Relations.

• University Training Seminars for graduate students are regularly conducted at institutions such as Columbia University in New York and York University in Canada.

In one of its brochures, IPA includes the following statement from Javier Perez de Cuellar, Secretary-General of the United Nations:

> Since its establishment in 1970, the International Peace Academy has made an increasingly significant contribution to the study of peacekeeping and peacemaking, and in particular to the development of skills and techniques for the greater efficiency of peacekeeping operations. The seminars held by the Academy have demonstrated how new ideas can be generated by blending the firsthand experience of veteran peacekeepers, civilian and military, with the conceptual contribution of scholars and diplomats. It is this fortunate combination of theory and practice which has made the Academy such a unique and exceptionally fruitful institution.

## Center for Defense Information

The Center for Defense Information (CDI) was founded in 1972 by former military personnel, educators, and public officials as a project of the *Fund for Peace* (see report on Fund for Peace) to make independent, informed analyses of United States defense policies available to the general public, government officials, journalists, and interested scholars. It is a respected research organization and its military experts monitor the military buildup in every country in the world and project future United States military requirements. The CDI staff includes retired admirals, generals, and other military officers, along with civilians with extensive training and experience in military analysis. They believe in an effective defense but also believe there will be no winners in a nuclear war.

The CDI's reputation as an authoritative and impartial monitor of the military has grown steadily over the past 15 years. The Center works on behalf of all citizens to support an effective but not excessive military program, eliminate waste in military spending, reduce military influence on United States domestic and foreign policy, and avert nuclear war.

In addition to informing the public through the media, the Center provides assistance to the federal government upon request from Pentagon and State Department officials and Congressional committees such as the House and Senate armed services committees, and the House Foreign Affairs Committee. However, it should be noted that CDI is supported entirely by the public and accepts no military contracts or remuneration for its services from the government or military industries.

The most influential publication of the Center is its *Defense Monitor,* published ten times a year. Materials from the Monitor are regularly reprinted in the Congressional Record and often quoted in news features and editorials across the country. Other publications include a Nuclear War Prevention Kit and three films: "War Without Winners, Parts I and II," and "A Step Away from War," all featuring Paul Newman. CDI also maintains a speakers bureau, offers internships, and sponsors conferences, seminars, and meetings to share its findings. CDI speakers are featured in many programs in the United States and abroad.

A recent CDI brochure quotes the following statement from its director, Admiral Gene R. La Rocque:

> There's nothing mystical about stopping the arms race, and we don't have to change our whole society to do it. Its simply a question of adjusting our national priorities. . . . Today military spending is driving the arms race, rather than the arms race driving military spending.

The Admiral urges Congress to "take the profit motive out of preparing for war. . . ."

In recognition of the important role of women in determining national policies, the *Women's Agenda of CDI* was organized in 1985 to provide a medium for the expression of women's views on nuclear and other military policies and on other aspects of national security.

## Global Education Associates

Global Education Associates (GEA) of East Orange, New Jersey, was founded in 1973. The Association conducts educational and research programs, publishes educational materials, and aims to generate a transnational, multi-issue movement for a world order based on the values of social and economic justice, peace, ecological balance, and participation in decision-making. Toward the attainment of that goal, the Association has conducted over 1500 workshops, institutes, and leadership seminars in Africa, Asia, Europe, North America and South America.

There are actually five affiliated organizations coordinating their efforts: (1) the Global Education Associates headquartered in New Jersey; (2) the Genesis Farm, a reflection center and organically farmed acreage near Blairstown, New Jersey; (3) the Global Education Associates of the Upper Midwest; (4) a Ministry of Concern for Public Health, especially concerned with levels of radiation; and (5) the Philippine Council for Global Education. They are all working on some aspects of world order within certain contexts. Much of their work is through seminars and leadership institutes.

After publishing one of its Whole Earth papers entitled "Star Wars and the State of Our Souls," GEA sent a copy to each United States representative and senator.

The Association continues its efforts to educate the general public and its legislators on issues imperative to creating a more human world order. Examples of such educational efforts include distribution of its quarterly publication, *Breakthrough,* with articles such as:

• "Star Wars, ASATS, and Pershing IIs," by Dr. Robert M. Bowman.

- "Why I Oppose Space Weapons," by Senator Dave Durenberger.
- "How the U.S. Administration Is Preparing for 'Star Wars,'" by Carol Rosin.
- "A Space Policy for Humanity," by Howard Kurtz.
- "Cooperation in Space: An Alternative to 'Star Wars,'" by Carol Rosin.

In the same (Winter 1985) issue carrying the above article on cooperation in space was a short item about a cooperative operation already in place. COSPAS/SARAT are the acronyms for the Satellite Search and Rescue programs of the Soviet Union and the United States. This cooperative use of satellites to locate victims of marine, air, or other disasters has resulted in the rescue of approximately 300 persons to date.

## Global Learning, Inc.

Since its beginnings in 1973, Global Learning, Inc., has worked on a threefold approach toward its goal of promoting a global perspective in elementary and secondary education.

The first approach has been to gain *legitimization* for the concept of global education. The second aspect has been to provide *training for teachers* in the conceptual framework of global education and practical classroom resource materials and learning activities with a global perspective. The third factor has been to build *community support.*

The legitimization component has entailed working with the State Department of Education, county superintendents, and professional education associations. The teacher education component has been implemented through scores of workshops, conferences, teacher in-service days, consultation services, and graduate level courses in universities.

To develop community support, Global Learning has conducted several one-day and weekend workshops for church-related educators and other community organizations. It has also provided numerous workshops and displays at church and community group meetings; and it has worked closely with church-related hunger task forces.

Other accomplishments of Global Learning, Inc., include:

- Forming a statewide Consortium for Global Education, consisting of more than 30 organizational members, i.e., key professional associations and educational institutions, as well as interested individuals.
- Publishing a newsletter, *Gleanings,* about and for consortium members and others with a mailing list of 2,000.
- Developing and implementing a Global Learning School Improvement Program to aid in the infusion of a global perspective within the ongoing curricula.
- Publishing three manuals to share experience with others: *Global Learning Teacher Education Manual, Coalition Building for Global Perspective, and Global Studies Teacher Manual* (high school level).

• Co-editing a compendium of global education evaluation instruments.

• Organizing a Hunger Program which helped teachers focus on problems of world hunger.

Global Learning has also developed a project entitled "New Jersey in the World." This project is funded by the New Jersey Department of Higher Education, International Education Grant Program, and includes ten college learning modules. Global Learning has completed its first year of this project on the undergraduate level and has applied for second-year funding of the project, involving eleven colleges and universities.

Global Learning has begun to work with several groups in providing resources for social studies teachers who will be required to teach a new high school class in 1988 on "World History/Cultures."

One of the most exciting endeavors of Global Learning was its development and marketing of the software for four cooperative computer games. These games offered players opportunities to compete against a challenge rather than against each other, develop problem-solving skills, and learn to work collaboratively. (Global Learning, Inc., is working to expand the number of computer systems on which the games can be played.)

## United Nations University — Tokyo

In 1969, the UN's Secretary-General, U Thant, asked the General Assembly of the United Nations to consider the establishment of a United Nations University that would be truly international and devoted to the UN Charter's objectives of peace and progress. In 1972, the Japanese government pledged $100 million (in United States dollars) for an endowment fund and offered a site in Tokyo for the university.

The General Assembly voted to accept Japan's offer and approved the charter for a United Nations University in December 1973. Although the University is sponsored by the United Nations and UNESCO, its charter specifies that it shall enjoy autonomy within the framework of the UN and that it shall have the academic freedom required for the achievement of its objectives, with particular reference to the choice of subjects and methods of research and training, and the selection of persons and institutions to carry out its tasks.

According to its Charter, the United Nations University (UNU) is to be "an international community of scholars, engaged in research, postgraduate training and dissemination of knowledge in furtherance of the purposes and principles of the Charter of the United Nations." It is enjoined to "devote its work to research into the pressing global problems of human survival, development, and welfare that are the concern of the United Nations and its agencies." This work is carried out, as the Charter instructs, through a network of research and postgraduate training centers in both the developed and developing countries, with planning and coordination provided by the central headquarters in Tokyo.

Also, UNU's charter stipulates, along with its guarantee of academic freedom and complete autonomy to manage its own affairs, that it is not to be financed by annually assessed contributions to the UN from governments. Instead, it is financed by project funds and by voluntary contributions to the endowment fund and annual operating funds.

The UNU is governed by a 28-member Council made up of distinguished educators and leading citizens, each from a different country, and serving as individuals rather than as governmental representatives. Twenty-four members are appointed by the Secretary-General of the United Nations and the Director-General of UNESCO (UN Educational, Scientific, and Cultural Organization) and serve six-year terms. The Rector, who is appointed by the UN's Secretary-General with the concurrence of the Director-General of UNESCO to serve as the designated Chief Executive Officer of the University, is also a member of the Council. There are three ex-officio members on the Council: the Secretary-General of the UN, the Director-General of UNESCO, and the Executive Director of UNITAR (the UN Institute for Training and Research).

As the UNU Council convened to put the Charter into effect, it selected three priorities for immediate attention: (1) world hunger, (2) human and social development, and (3) the use and management of natural resources. Recognizing that other agencies were already working on these problems, the Council reasoned that the UNU could help "fill gaps in knowledge."

The UNU has only a small academic and administrative staff at its headquarters in Tokyo. Its research and training activities are carried out in more than 60 countries at 37 associated institutions, by research units, by individual scholars organized into networks and by fellows appointed for advanced training.

Actually, the UNU did not come into being until the academic year of 1975-76. It has no students, no tenured professors, no campus, no athletic teams, and it does not grant degrees. Instead of a traditional student body and faculty, the Council decided to institute a fellowship program. UNU also established an "associate status" for existing institutions/organizations, linking them to UNU.

The first associate agreement was with the Institute of Nutrition of Central America and Panama when the first fellow began working there in 1976. Since, the University has dispatched more than 775 fellows to trouble spots around the world.

Fellows are selected from governments, universities, and the private sector, and they include both experienced specialists and qualified students seeking training and experience in the field of development. The UNU pays living and travel expenses of fellows while on assignment, after which they are expected to return to their home countries to apply what they have learned.

In addition, UNU is beginning to establish research and training centers of its own, in accordance with the provisions of its charter. The first of these are the UNU World Institute for Development Economics Research, which was established in Helsinki, Finland, in 1984, and more recently, a natural resources institute for Africa.

As listed in a recent brochure, the main aims of UNU are:

• To foster intellectual cooperation among scholars and scientists of the world to help understand and solve urgent problems beyond the capabilities of single nations or regions.

• To increase the practical impact of research and advanced training by organizing networks of collaborating individuals and institutions.

• To increase the ability of developing countries to solve their own problems by cooperation in the strengthening of their research and advanced training capabilities.

• To improve the outreach of institutions all over the world by involving them in international cooperative efforts to deal with global problems of concern to all nations.

At present, the University is working in the areas of five priorities: (1) peace, security, conflict resolution, and global transformation; (2) global economy; (3) hunger, poverty, resources and the environment; (4) human and social development and co-existence of peoples, cultures, and social systems; (5) science and technology and their social and ethical implications.

The UNU's newsletter "provides a sampling from publications, reports, working papers, and other sources of the United Nations University and highlights recent University news." The following article headings from its November 1984 issue will illustrate the scope of topics covered:

• "Diverting Science to the Cause of Peace."
• "Using Space Technology to Prevent Wars," by B. Jasani.
• "Communications Serving the Cause of Peace," by F. Chong-cheng.
• "Conflict Management in International Relations," by R. Vayrynen.
• "Monitoring for Peace."
• "Competing with the Motivations to 'Go Nuclear,'" by S. Paribatra.
• "The Long-term Cure: Dissolution of Military R & D," by T. Toyoda.
• "Military Budget-cutting to Close the Technology Gap," by J.M. Perczynski.
• "Asian Countries Trade Traditional Technology to Provide Better Nutrition," by H.A.B. Parpia.
• "Oneness and Multiplicity Woven Together: A Symposium on the Management of Complexity," by C. Descamps.

The UNU's Newsletter is published in English, French, Spanish, and Japanese.

# Global Perspectives in Education, Inc.

Global Perspectives in Education, Inc., (GPE) is but one example of the many good publishers of materials now available for global and international education as well as peace education. The GPE has been publishing quality curriculum materials at affordable prices since 1977. It works with a broad range of institutions, organizations, and individuals to help prepare young Americans for the challenge of citizenship in a global age. As a nonprofit, nonpartisan educational organization, GPE receives support from private foundations, corporations, government agencies, and individuals.

The GPE curriculum materials promote the critical thinking skills students will need for the challenge of the culturally diverse and interdependent world they will face as adults. These materials feature complete lessons and activities, thought-provoking readings, and exciting ideas for teaching. Most materials are easily integrated with ongoing curriculum plans, and most of GPE's publications can be easily duplicated for classroom use.

The GPE publications catalogue lists its materials under the following headings:
- Introducing a Global Perspective.
- For the Elementary and Middle Grades.
- United States History.
- Humanities and Language Arts.
- Culture and Area Studies.
- Global Issues and Trends.
- Environmental Studies.

Among its services, GPE offers a subscription to its *Access* magazine, which has eight issues per year. It is filled with current and exciting ideas and materials on global and international issues, and information on important global conferences and events. Another option is a package including *Access* plus five of GPE's curriculum publications at considerable savings.

Another GPE magazine, *Travel and Learning ABROAD,* is offered on a subscription basis. This bimonthly provides timely news and activities on international exchange, study abroad, special interest travel, internship or volunteer opportunities, scholarships and grants, and meetings and conferences. News about international activities and programs that can be enjoyed in local schools and communities is also included.

# National Mobilization for Survival

Mobilization for Survival (MFS) was organized in 1977 as a project of Survival Education Fund, Inc. It is a national coalition of local and national disarmament, anti-intervention, safe energy, religious, and community organizations working for the goals of zero nuclear weapons, a ban on nuclear power, reversing the arms race, and meeting human needs.

As a multi-issue coalition, MFS highlights the connection between nuclear weapons, military spending, and the lack of commitment to social and economic justice.

As stated in one of its brochures:

> MFS believes that the necessary changes in national priorities require a national movement based in communities throughout the nation and reflecting a cross-section of the country. MFS's primary focus is to nurture this grassroots movement by reaching out to community based organizations, providing resources and assistance to carry forward their work. MFS promotes a wide range of protest and educational activities, from demonstrations and non-violent civil disobedience to referenda and lobbying.

Thus, Mobilization for Survival provides opportunities for diverse, local organizations to join together with similar groups around the country to develop a common, multi-issue program. The MFS acts as both a network for local groups and as an initiator of national activities. For example, it:

- Assists local groups in organizing local components of national campaigns.
- Assists local groups in developing organizational and other technical skills.
- Provides a forum in which local organizations can participate concerning national issues and activities.
- Initiates and promotes national activities and campaigns to further its goals.
- Brings together activists working on similar issues around the country.

Communication among affiliates is the most important service of MFS. The national office keeps in touch with affiliates and other local groups through regular mailings, phone calls, occasional visits, and its quarterly publication, *The Mobilizer*. MFS keeps its affiliates advised of pressing national and international developments, and helps coordinate simultaneous local events around the country, particularly when circumstances require immediate action. Two examples of MFS's recent mailings were signed by Dr. Benjamin Spock and L.T. Matthesen, Bishop of Amarillo. One asked for help in keeping nuclear disarmament a key issue in 1985, and the other was on the folly of "Star Wars," the Reagan Administration's Strategic Defense Initiative.

Resource materials available from MFS include leaflets, research reports, educational pamphlets and publications, and organizing guides. In addition, MFS compiles lists of speakers and resource materials on topics such as nuclear weapons, nuclear power, the social and economic impact of military spending, foreign military intervention, and the connections among these issues.

In response to our survey, MFS sent us a copy of its 1985 National Program, an action program designed to provide a framework for local organizations to work in a coordinated effort for disarmament, non-intervention, and social and economic justice. Major priorities for 1985 were the Campaign Against First Strike and the Pledge of Resistance (against United States invasion of Central America). Ongoing campaigns included in the National Program were the Deadly Connection Campaign (an educational campaign on the deadly connection between the nuclear arms race and policies of military intervention); Education about the Soviet Union; the Middle East Campaign; the Rainbow Coalition; Work Against Apartheid, and Strengthening the Network. Major actions planned for 1985 were the Spring Peace and Justice Mobilization (April 19–22) and the Commemoration of the Fortieth Anniversary of the Bombing of Hiroshima and Nagasaki (August 6–9).

## Jobs with Peace Campaign

Since its founding in 1978, the Jobs with Peace Campaign has spread to dozens of cities across the country. Jobs with Peace (JWP) is a national campaign which seeks to redirect our tax dollars away from excessive military spending in order to fund local jobs and social programs including quality education, public transportation, housing, improved health care, and other essential human services and socially useful industries.

According to one of its brochures, "This shift can be accomplished by reducing spending on nuclear weapons, foreign intervention and wasteful military programs."

Continuing this quotation:

> The Jobs with Peace Campaign is made up of people who are concerned about cutbacks and layoffs in education, severe restrictions in local services, our declining industrial base and the cost of a runaway military budget.
>
> Over 100 members of Congress, hundreds of city councils, labor unions, and community, religious, and peace organizations, and more than one million voters have endorsed Jobs with Peace.

The JWP campaigns across the country transfer the distant debate about the federal budget into local political issues. Local campaign work begins with education, and JWP has created some top-quality printed and audiovisual materials for classrooms, union halls, and community meetings which are used throughout the nation.

Examples of JWP resource materials include:

• *Crossroads:* a unique high school curriculum in use throughout the world. (Three 10-day curricula, one each for English, Social Studies, and Science.)

• *The Choice Is Clear: Jobs with Peace:* a fast-paced slideshow which facilitates discussion about the links between growing military budgets and economic decline.

• *Books, Not Bombs:* describes the effects of federal cuts in education. (Prepared in cooperation with the National Education Association.)

Jobs with Peace organizes among those most directly affected by high military budgets: those on low or fixed income, working people, and minorities.

Campaigners have written Jobs with Peace budgets for their respective communities which show the amount of tax dollars flowing out of the community into the military budget. These budgets go on to show the tremendous number of jobs which would result if there were a reduction in the military budget and a transfer of funds to domestic programs. This approach has been a convincing argument against the jobs blackmail of the military.

The organization also published an alternative Federal Budget for Jobs, Peace, and Justice, which it claimed would contribute greatly to creating jobs and meeting the human needs of the American people; preventing nuclear war; pursuing international cooperation, peace and human rights; and ensuring our nation's military security.

Highlighting its alternative Federal Budget JWP stated:

We can safely cut the military budget by $70.8 Billion! if we:

| Freeze the Nuclear Arms Race | Saving $29.9 Billion |
| Stop Arming for Foreign Intervention | " 13.4 " |
| Reduce Pentagon Waste | " 27.5 " |
| Total | " $70.8 " |

and

We can invest our tax dollars to rebuild our communities.

| Health and Human Services | Invest $19.9 Billion |
| Education | " 8.7 " |
| Housing | " 10.0 " |
| Public Infrastructure | " 10.0 " |
| Mass Transit | " 8.0 " |
| Energy | " 6.3 " |
| Economic Conversion | " 7.9 " |
| Total | " $70.8 " |

Local JWP campaigns have sponsored and passed referenda throughout the country calling for a transfer of federal budget dollars away from the military and toward underfunded domestic needs.

Due to common interests and objectives, JWP works in coalition with many other local and national organizations such as labor, peace, low-income, and third world groups.

## Peace with Justice Emphasis of the United Methodist Church

The 1980 General Conference of the United Methodist Church approved a special program on "Peace and Justice" and made its Board of

Church and Society responsible for designing, promoting, and providing resource materials for this special emphasis. Purposes of this program were:

- To make "peacemaking" an urgent claim on the United Methodist Church.

- To create a process that gives substance, structure, and force to the "peacekeeping" effort.

- To achieve a fellowship of God's people committed to peace and the creation of a peaceful world.

- To provide a possibility of building on peace efforts of the past and expanding those efforts in the church's next quadrennium.

In response, the Board of Church and Society prepared and distributed a wealth of materials to assist local congregations in implementing this special emphasis. Objectives outlined by the Board of C&S were listed under four headings as follows:

*A Faithful World.* To understand the concept of Shalom as it points to God's intention for a peaceful world; to identify areas in which God's intention is thwarted; and to apply the vision of Shalom in achieving disarmament, justice and security.

*A Disarmed World.* To understand war as the problem, not a method of solving conflicts; to expose the idolatry of the arms race; to examine roles of the military in national and international systems; and to achieve a world where human needs are given a higher priority than military expenditures.

*A Just World.* To understand that the overarching biblical message is one of freedom, justice and peace; to understand issues from the perspective of other peoples and cultures; to make informed ethical judgments in order to have an impact on foreign policy, particularly in regard to political or economic issues; and to understand world political and economic systems as they promote or thwart justice.

*A Secure World.* To understand that a secure world is achieved through equitable relations within and among peoples and nations rather than through economic exploitation, denial of human rights or military might; to enable United Methodists to know that they are peacemakers so that they will not leave peacemaking to national leaders; to make clear the commitment of the United Methodist Church to the United Nations; and to enable United Methodist agencies to see their peacekeeping and peace building role and to develop policies, priorities and problems to that end.

Along with these objectives, the outline provided related recommended goals and suggested strategies for achieving them.

In one of its booklets, entitled *The United Methodist Church and Peace,* the opening paragraph is a quotation from the Bishops' *Call for Peace and the Self-Development of People* as follows:

> Peace is not simply the absence of war, a nuclear stalemate or combination of uneasy cease-fires. It is that emerging dynamic reality envisioned

by prophets where spears and swords give way to implements of peace (Isaiah 2:1–4); where historic antagonists dwell together in trust (Isaiah 11:4–11); and where righteousness and justice prevail. There will be no peace with justice until unselfish and informed love is structured into political process and international arrangements.

Included in this study booklet is a discussion of the following issues: (1) Disarmament, (2) Democracy and Freedom, (3) the United Nations, (4) World Trade and Economic Development, (5) Military Conscription, Training, and Service, and (6) Peace Research, Education, and Action. There are also informative sections entitled: "Nuclear-Free Pacific," "In Support of the United Nations," and "Christian Faith and Disarmament."

Although the United Methodist Church and its predecessor denominations have not been considered to be among the "historic peace churches," they have strongly witnessed and acted for peace throughout their history. Evidence of this commitment to peace may be found in:

• The establishment of the Methodist-Episcopal Commission on World Peace in 1924.

• The declaration of the 1940 General Conference that "the Methodist Church, although making no attempt to bind the conscience of its individual members, will not officially endorse, support, or participate in war."

• The establishment of a Board of World Peace by the Methodist Church in 1940.

• The Methodist Church's Crusade for a New World Order in the 1940s.

• The Crusade for World Order of the Methodist Church in the 1950s.

• The present Board of Church and Society established (renamed) in 1972.

More information on the history of peace activities within the Methodist tradition may be found in Herman Will's book *A Will for Peace.* (See Bibliography.)

Although the 1980 action of the General Conference called for a Peace and Justice Program during 1981 through 1984, many conferences of the United Methodist Church indicated a desire to continue peace and justice as a priority during 1985 through 1988 (according to a July 8, 1983, issue of the *United Methodist Newscope,* the national weekly newsletter for United Methodist leaders).

In November of 1984, the Council of Bishops of the United Methodist Church unanimously approved a proposal for "a major two year intervention by the Council of Bishops to mobilize the church to witness and action in the face of the major threat to human survival in our time: the nuclear arms race"; and it authorized the preparation of "a study document and pastoral letter on the nuclear crisis." Their purposes were: (1) to state clearly their convictions about the issues of the nuclear crisis and a just peace; (2)

to evoke a full and fair discussion of these issues across the denomination, including the offering and discussion of alternative convictions; and (3) to urge United Methodists to do the things that work for peace.

This two-year study resulted in: (1) a Foundation Document, and (2) a Pastoral Letter, both entitled *In Defense of Creation: the Nuclear Crisis and a Just Peace*. Both were approved by the Council in May of 1985. Highlights of the *Foundation Document* included:

• A review of the biblical foundations for peacemaking.

• An examination of ethical traditions and their contemporary applications.

• A list of guiding principles for a theology for a just peace.

• A distinction between the primal issues of blast, fire, and fallout, and the consequent issues of long-term systemic effects on human institutions and behavior.

• A critique of the policy of deterrence.

• A plea for an ethic of reciprocity and mutual security.

• Beginning proposals for public policy.

• A call for Christians and churches to work for peace.

The *Pastoral Letter* was reprinted as an appendix to the Foundation Document. The following paragraph is quoted from the letter:

> Now, therefore, we ask you, our sisters and brothers, to join with us in a new covenant of peacemaking, to use the Bible together with our Council's Foundation Document as basic resources for earnest and steadfast study of the issues of justice and peace. We call upon each local pastor and lay leader to give leadership in a local church study of the issues surrounding the nuclear threat. We ask you all to open again your hearts, as we open our hearts, to receive God's gracious gift of peace; to become with us evangelists of shalom, making the ways of Jesus the model of discipleship, embracing all neighbors near and far, all friends and enemies, and becoming defenders of God's good creation; and to pray without ceasing for peace in our time.

## Presbyterian Peacemaking Program

A report entitled "Peacemaking: the Believers' Calling" was submitted to the One Hundred Ninety-Second General Assembly of the United Presbyterian Church, U.S.A., in 1980.

In 1983, the United Presbyterian Church, U.S.A. (Northern) and the Presbyterian Church, United States (Southern) voted to merge, the merger to be completed by 1988 as the Presbyterian Church, U.S.A. They immediately joined their efforts in peacemaking, and the One Hundred Ninety-Fifth General Assembly (1983) urged all local congregations in the combined Presbyterian Church, U.S.A., to consider making a commitment to integrate peacemaking into the life and mission of their local churches. A "Commitment to Peacemaking" statement was prepared and commended by the General Assembly for consideration and approval by local congregations. It follows:

### Commitment to Peacemaking

God's Covenant with creation is given as grace and peace. Peace (shalom) is the wholeness and community in which human beings are meant to live. Although all people are sinners, God continually renews the Covenant through our Lord Jesus Christ. God's peace heals, comforts, strengthens, and frees.

Responding to this good news, the church goes into the whole world to point to and become a part of God's peacegiving. God's peace is offered wherever there is brokenness — in individual lives, families, congregations, communities and nations. In God's Covenant, the world and the church experience wholeness, security and justice.

The 1983 General Assembly has affirmed in "Peacemaking: the Believers' Calling" that God's peacegiving in a broken and insecure world is central to the message of the gospel. Therefore people of faith engage in peacemaking not as a peripheral activity, but as an integral part of their congregational life and mission.

Responding to God's Covenant, the session of the _____ Church now commits itself to peacemaking during this decade. In fulfilling this commitment, we will:

- Help to provide worship that points to the reality of God's peacegiving.
- Encourage the members of the congregation to receive God's peace in their own lives and, through prayer and Bible study to seek it for today's world.
- Enable and equip members of the congregation to grow as peacemakers in their families, in the congregation and in the community.
- Help the congregation to work for social, racial and economic justice, and respond to people in the community who are caught in poverty, hurt by unemployment, or burdened by other problems.
- Encourage the congregation to support human rights and economic justice efforts in at least one area of the world, such as Central America, southern Africa, the Middle East, East Asia, East Europe, or Central Asia.
- Work to end the arms race, to reverse the world-wide growth of militarism, and to reduce tension among nations.
- Support financially the churchwide peacemaking effort through the Special Peacemaking Offering on World Communion Sunday, the Presbyterian Peacemaking Fund, or other means.

The Session will lead and support the congregation in this peacemaking response to God's Covenant. We will appoint a member or committee to be our contact with the presbytery peacemaking task force and with the Presbyterian Peacemaking Program to receive and distribute information and resource materials which will help us to fulfill this commitment.

The above commitment is signed by the Moderator and Clerk of the Session of the local church.

To help carry out the Presbyterian Peacemaking Program at the local level, the national office distributed copies of the 1980 "Peacemaking: the Believers' Calling." In addition, it published brochures and a notebook of suggestions for implementing their "Commitment to Peacemaking." One of the aids jointly produced by the two denominations before merger was an excellent booklet entitled "Peacemaking Skills." This included sections on Peacemaking in the Self, Peacemaking in the Family, Peacemaking in the Congregation, Peacemaking in the Community, and Peacemaking in the International Arena.

See reports on the peace programs and projects of the United Methodist Church and the United Church of Christ also in this chapter.

## University for Peace — Costa Rica

The creation of a University for Peace was proposed to the General Assembly of the United Nations by the President of Costa Rica, *Rodrigo Carazo,* in 1978. An offer from the Costa Rican government of 700 acres of land for such an institution accompanied the proposal. (The government had inherited the land from a Costa Rican philanthropist, *Cruz Rojas Bennet.)*

Upon receipt of positive reactions from member states, UNESCO, UNITAR, and the United Nations University, the General Assembly established an International Commission in 1979 to plan, organize, structure, and implement the University for Peace, in collaboration with the Government of Costa Rica.

The first meeting of the International Commission, held in June 1980, was presided over by the former President of Venezuela, Dr. Rafael Caldera. In July, the Commission held an International Seminar on "Education for Peace and Communications" in San Jose, Costa Rica.

In September 1980, the International Commission recommended to the Secretary-General of the UN that the University be created through an International Agreement and that it should be associated with UNESCO and the United Nations University.

Finally, in December 1980, the General Assembly of the UN approved the International Agreement and the University for Peace as an international center of higher learning for postgraduate studies, research, and the dissemination of knowledge aimed at training for peace.

Among the materials received in response to this survey were the following statements:

> The University for Peace is an international institution devoted to seek peace through education with humanistic purposes and according to the principles of the Charter of the United Nations and the Universal Declaration of Human Rights....
> The goal of the University is to contribute to the great universal task of educating for peace by engaging education, research, and the dissemination of knowledge to promote peace....

The epistemological axis of the University for Peace is peace, education for peace and human rights. Other problems which have a direct or indirect bearing on peace, such as environment, natural resources, technology, transnational corporations and others, will not be approached in a conventional or frontal fashion, but will be analysed in terms of their impact on peace.

As with the United Nations University, the Charter of the University for Peace provides for full autonomy and academic freedom. Students from all parts of the world are admitted after complying with requirements established by the Council of the University. It is authorized by the Council to grant master's degrees and doctorates.

The Charter of the University allows for concluding agreements with governments or similar organizations, with international or private organizations in the field of education, and in particular, with the United Nations University and UNESCO.

An area of 500 acres has been set aside to be preserved as virgin forest and to be used for programs in ecology and environmental education. Campus buildings are being placed on the remaining 200 acres.

The University's first students were admitted in 1985 when its first Master's course started, a course in Communications for Peace. Future Master's courses will be dealing with education for peace, human rights and peace, natural resources and quality of life, technology of the resolution of development problems, and Islamic studies for peace.

The following is a quotation from Rodrigo Carazo during his term as President of the University of Peace:

> If you desire peace, prepare for peace. The University for Peace must be the laboratory of the spirit of peace, the crucible in which we must form the new mentality of peace over the decades to come. For the twenty-first century shall be peaceful, or it shall not be.

This initiative by Costa Rica to establish a University for Peace was in keeping with its long pacifist tradition. (Costa Rica abolished its army in 1949, maintaining only a police force.)

## International Physicians for the Prevention of Nuclear War

The International Physicians for the Prevention of Nuclear War (IPPNW) was organized in 1980 by two physicians, one a Soviet, *Dr. Yevgeny Chazov,* and the other an American, *Dr. Bernard Lown,* to publicize the dangers of nuclear weapons.

The IPPNW is not a membership organization of individual doctors. Instead, it is a federation of affiliate organizations in over 40 nations (such as the Physicians for Social Responsibility in the United States).

The IPPNW's policy is set by an International Council representing all of the national affiliates. An Executive Committee, with co-presidents from the U.S. and U.S.S.R., carries out this policy through offices in Boston and London.

An open letter from Co-President Bernard Lown, dated November 1985, explains the unique role of physicians:

> We doctors have a solemn obligation to protect life. We must, by virtue of our professional oaths and codes of ethics, speak out against threats to life.
> And since the medical facts about nuclear war indicate that it is the greatest of all the threats to life and health, we are compelled to convey those facts to our patients — the peoples of the world.
> By speaking objectively and scientifically, as doctors, we are able to communicate with leaders and groups not reached by other avenues.

Accomplishments and recognitions of IPPNW to date include:
• The creation of an international medical movement which now includes a global network of over 135,000 physicians (through their affiliate organizations).
• The opening of communications with the Soviet Union through a uniquely bilateral emphasis. Soviets and Americans work together through IPPNW, avoiding one-sided political rhetoric.
• The dissemination of indisputable facts about the consequences of nuclear war, to both East and West, through professional articles, radio and TV broadcasts, newsletters, and books. *(Last Aid: the Medical Dimension of Nuclear War* is an example of IPPNW's dissemination efforts. It is a collection of essays by American, Japanese, Soviet, and Western European physicians and scientists. Their frequently repeated theme is that there will not be — cannot be — any effective medical response to the effects of nuclear war.)
• The beginning of a series of exchanges and visits co-sponsored by IPPNW, its American affiliate, (Physicians for Social Responsibility), and its Soviet counterpart. (First of such visits involved a group of U.S. doctors going to Moscow in 1984. In 1985, Dr. Yevgeny Chazov and three of his prominent Soviet colleagues visited several American cities, hosted by Dr. Bernard Lown and Dr. Sidney Alexander. Also in 1985 ten American physicians visited the U.S.S.R. to speak directly to the Soviet people, and another group of ten Soviet physicians visited several American cities.)
• Being instrumental in securing agreement from the Soviet Union to stop nuclear testing if the United States also agreed.
• Dr. Yevgeny Chazov of the U.S.S.R. Cardiological Institute and Dr. Bernard Lown of the Harvard School of Public Health, Co-Founders, and now Co-Presidents of IPPNW, received awards from the Beyond War organization in 1984 for their leadership in the work of IPPNW.
• The IPPNW received the UNESCO Peace Education Prize also in 1984. (This prize is awarded annually by UNESCO to the organization that most

"promotes actions aimed at constructing the defenses of peace in the minds of men.")

• The IPPNW received the 1985 Nobel Peace Prize. The Official Statement of the Norwegian Nobel Committee, dated 11 October 1985, follows:

> The Norwegian Nobel Committee has decided to award the Nobel Peace Prize for 1985 to the organization International Physicians for the Prevention of Nuclear War.
>
> It is the committee's opinion that this organization has performed a considerable service to mankind by spreading authoritative information and by creating an awareness of the catastrophic consequences of atomic warfare.
>
> The committee believes that this in turn contributes to an increase in the pressure of public opposition to the proliferation of atomic weapons and to a redefining of priorities, with greater attention being paid to health and other humanitarian issues.
>
> Such an awakening of public opinion as is now apparent both in the East and the West, in the North and in the South, can give the present arms limitation negotiations new perspectives and a new seriousness.
>
> In this connection, the committee attaches particular importance to the fact that the organization was formed as a result of a joint initiative by Soviet and American physicians and that it now draws support from physicians in over 40 countries all over the world.
>
> It is the committee's intention to invite the organization's two founders, who now share the title of president — Professor Bernard Lown from the U.S.A. and Professor Yevgeny Chazov from the Soviet Union — to receive the Peace Prize on behalf of their organization.

Future plans of IPPNW include:

• Strengthening its worldwide affiliates, especially in countries with the capacity to develop nuclear weapons.

• Further educating people and governments with reports on topics such as accidental nuclear war, long-term radiation effects, and the psychology of nuclear deterrence.

• More U.S./U.S.S.R. interchanges through joint research projects; formal exchanges between America's affiliate, Physicians for Social Responsibility, and its Soviet counterpart; and TV broadcasts via satellite to viewers in both countries.

• Continuing to press both the U.S. and the U.S.S.R. to declare an immediate, mutual moratorium on all nuclear explosions.

## Educators for Social Responsibility

The national office of Educators for Social Responsibility is located in Cambridge, Massachusetts. It was founded in 1981 by a group of educators and parents in Massachusetts seeking ways in which education could help prevent nuclear war. Its membership consists of parents, teachers, and administrators of elementary schools, middle schools, high schools, and universities. The ESR's motto is, "Educating for new ways of thinking in the nuclear age," and one of its brochures states its primary goals as follows:

> *In our classrooms* we are committed to teaching divergent points of view about the nuclear arms race to develop students' critical thinking skills. We are teaching the skills of cooperation and negotiation, the knowledge of our social, economic, and biological interdependence; and the ethics that will help ensure the survival of humanity.
>
> *In our communities* we are organizing for a more informed and widespread dialogue on the arms race, national defense policies, and new social and economic priorities.
>
> *In our professional associations* we are researching new ways to educate students for social responsibility and active citizenship.

The ESR now has a strong network of chapters throughout the country where members initiate local projects in nuclear age education. It also maintains a National Resource Center which provides consulting services to local chapters and supports teacher training, curriculum development and assessment, research, and implementation of a balanced curriculum in our schools. Other membership benefits include: a quarterly newsletter, curricula updates, chapter newsletters and local activities, and opportunities to participate in state, regional, and national programs.

The national office and local chapters of ESR work together in:

• Working with school systems and parent groups to plan and introduce new curricula and professional development programs.

• Offering workshops, in-service training programs, and institutes that present different points of view on nuclear arms issues and other controversial social issues.

• Developing and piloting grade-appropriate curriculum materials that present different points of view on nuclear arms issues.

• Assessing materials for educating adults and students about contemporary public issues such as security, war and peace, conflict, human rights, justice and freedom, and social consciousness and values.

• Sponsoring conferences in schools and communities around the country for the discussion of nuclear issues and education.

• Providing ESR resource persons for educational conferences and community programs.

Publications of ESR include new curricula for kindergarten through adult education, developed by and for educators; annotated bibliographies of educational materials; and *Forum,* a quarterly publication of new ideas, programs, and resources related to nuclear education.

In an open letter dated May 1985, Tony Wagner, ESR's Executive Director, stated:

> ESR's materials for teachers are very clear on how balanced presentations are part of the teaching and learning process. Young minds deserve

respect, not indoctrination. By helping young people think critically about controversial issues, ESR creates the basis of an informed and active citizenry, similar to that envisioned by the American philosopher and educator John Dewey....

We want to make education about the nuclear arms race, national security, and U.S.–Soviet relations part of what kids learn because they have the right and need to know it.

A letter dated December 15, 1986, from ESR's new Executive Director, Susan Alexander, gave a progress report on its U.S.–Soviet Education Project designed to enable future generations to think more fully and accurately about the Soviet Union and U.S.–Soviet relations in the context of our transformed nuclear world. The letter also encouraged financial support for "educating a generation for the challenge of peace," through its Fund for the Future.

A recent descriptive brochure from the Wisconsin Educators for Social Responsibility (a state affiliate of ESR) ended with a quotation from H.G. Wells: "Human history becomes more and more a race between education and catastrophe." Members of ESR are committed to making sure education wins this race.

## United Church of Christ's Peace Priority

In response to this survey, the Office for Church in Society (OCIS) of the United Church of Christ (UCC) sent us several items, including:

• An overview of its Office for Church in Society.

• A copy of its proposed pronouncement affirming the UCC as a "Just Peace Church."

• A copy of its Proposal to Action entitled "Organizing the UCC as a Just Peace Church."

• A draft copy of a proposed study guide entitled "A Just Peace."

• A copy of its June 1985 monthly newsletter captioned "UCC Peace Priority."

• A study guide related to the 1983 Pastoral Letter on War and Peace from the U.S. Catholic Bishops.

• A brochure about the UCC Peace Fund.

In 1981 the Office for Church in Society of the United Church of Christ appointed a Peace Theology Development Team. In 1983, the team was commissioned by the General Synod of UCC to prepare a study document on peace. As a result of this work, the General Synod declared the UCC a "just peace church" in June 1985. The team that drafted the proposal explained:

A Just Peace is our understanding of God's will for humankind. The definition of a "Just Peace" is based on the concept of peace expressed by the Hebrew word "shalom" as it is used biblically. The Old Testament scholar Von Rad explains that the word shalom carries the concept that we should utilize. He defines shalom as not some inner, personal, pietistic possession, but a communal well-being in which God's creation is justly ordered. It is a state of existence in which all aspects of God's creation play their individual roles harmoniously for the good of the whole.

In affirming the ucc to be a Just Peace Church, they also defined "just peace" as the interrelation of friendship, justice, and common security from violence, and they placed the ucc in opposition to the institution of war.

A Proposal for Action related to the above pronouncement called all in the ucc to recognize that the creating of a just peace is central to their identity as Christians and to their baptism into the Christian community. All ucc churches were asked to organize themselves locally, regionally, and nationally for a more effective peace witness.

The Fifteenth General Synod called for the development of four key components within local churches: (1) spiritual development, (2) just peace education, (3) political advocacy, and (4) community witness.

The study guide entitled "A Just Peace," first drafted in 1984, was sent to over 4,000 ucc members for reaction and constructive criticism. It proposed the church move beyond the historic Christian approaches to war and peace — pacifism, the "just war," and the "crusade" — to the biblical vision of shalom which links peace with justice.

The 1985 pronouncement embodied eight central ideas:

• Peace is possible.

• The meaning of a just peace is understood through the Bible, church history, and the voices of the oppressed.

• Nonviolent conflict is normal and is a reflection of diversity.

• Violence can and must be minimized if not eliminated.

• War can and must be eliminated.

• The state is based upon participatory consent and is primarily responsible for developing justice and well-being, enforcing the community's will and minimizing violence.

• International structures of friendship, justice and common security are necessary and possible.

• Unexpected initiatives of friendship and reconciliation can transform interpersonal and international relationships and are essential to restoring community.

Recognizing that peacemaking is a central task of the church, the Executive Council established a Peace Fund in 1983 to ensure a continuing peace ministry within the United Church of Christ.

The monthly publication of the Office for Church and Society of the United Church of Christ was renamed *Courage in the Struggle for Justice and Peace* in 1986. It addresses current issues such as "Sanctuary" and "Star Wars," and carries news of activities for justice and peace in local congregations and conferences as well as its denomination as a whole. Regular sections of the monthly are entitled: "Visions of a Just Peace," "News of the Network," "Peace Advocacy," and "Justice Advocacy."

## High Technology Professionals for Peace

High Technology Professionals for Peace (HTPFP) is an organization of scientists, engineers, and other technical workers concerned with the current threat of nuclear war. The HTPFP was founded in 1981 to provide information about the impact of various weapons systems on national security, the economy, the environment, and on our society in general. It conducts service, educational, and scientific projects, and promotes discussion of issues involving work in the "defense" industry.

The HTPFP provides an informal and supportive atmosphere in which to reconsider personal career decisions. It has also prepared brochures for distribution to students on professional development and specialization, the structure of the arms industry, and professional ethics. It also operates an employment agency for technical professionals seeking alternatives to weapons-related work. Scientists and engineers ranging from students to well-established professionals in the defense industry are served by this agency.

The HTPFP provides speakers for a lecture series which emphasizes the history and capability of nuclear weapons systems, and the relationship between pure research and military application. Speakers for community, campus, and church groups also cover topics such as civil defense, technical aspects of the arms race, professional drawbacks to defense employment, and nuclear proliferation.

The HTPFP cooperates with other peace groups and participants in major conferences and public events. It has co-sponsored forums on diversification and conversion of industry, and an interfaith conference concerned with counseling workers in defense industries.

Members of HTPFP provide legislators with technical analyses of weapons systems and related policy considerations. Research and analysis papers and special reports are published in HTPFP's newsletter, *Technology and Responsibility,* and the mass media.

Those HTPFP members who are also members of other peace organizations encourage discussion on arms control and professional ethics within their other groups.

The following statement is a quotation from one of HTPFP's brochures:

> Projects to inform and serve the technical community and the public must be accompanied by efforts to change national policies that stimulate the arms race and retard the development of nonmilitary technologies. HTPFP accordingly supports the Nuclear Freeze Campaign and similar initiatives which inform legislators of the popular support for arms control.

# Beyond War

Although Beyond War is now an autonomous educational movement, it grew out of a group of concerned San Francisco citizens who formed Creative Initiative in 1962. Its members committed themselves to work together to build a world in which all children could have the opportunity to live a peaceful life.

Creative Initiative, as a foundation, sponsored living-room discussions on global issues such as population control and natural resources depletion, and inspired local projects related to them.

In 1982, their focus shifted to facing the threat of nuclear war and the possibility of extinction of all life as we know it. The name given to this new focus was *Beyond War.*

Quoting from one of their brochures:

> Beyond War is an idea rather than an organization. There are already thousands of people working throughout the country to spread the ideas that:
> • Nuclear weapons have made us realize that all war is obsolete;
> • We live together on Earth—one interdependent, interrelated life support system;
> • We must change to a new mode of thinking about the planet's future;
> • Together we can build a world beyond war.

The UNICEF Charter includes the following statement: "War begins in the minds of men. Since this is so, the minds of men must be capable of ending war." In endorsing this statement, *Beyond War* acknowledges the critical role of human psychology in determining the destiny of our planet. Thus, Beyond War provides "an orientation toward a new way of thinking. . . ."

Again quoting from *On Beyond War,* August 1984:

> Forgetful of our common humanity and common mortality, are we not, we and the Russians, preparing to fight the wrong enemy with the wrong weapons?
> Are we not like two drunks brawling in a bar, mindless of the fact that the building itself is on fire?
> Are we not co-tenants of a planet beset by hunger, disease, illiteracy, rampant population growth, erosion of topsoils, desertification, massive destruction of tropical rain forests, accumulation of nuclear and toxic wastes, acid rain, and accelerating extinction of plant and animal species?
> Are these symptoms of planetary degradation—all of them quite indifferent to military force—not a common enemy to us and to the Russians? These and war itself?
> Can we not set aside ideological differences to make common cause against a common enemy, using the weapons of intelligence, open-mindedness, creativity, and love of our fellow humans and other fellow species of our planetary home?

Obsessed with the will-of-the-wisp of military security, which we chase at the expense of social, economic, and ecological life-support systems that are just as vital to the security of nations, are we and our Soviet rivals not forgetting that:

- the best guarantor of one's security is the security of others, including the adversary's;
- the best guarantor of one's prosperity is the prosperity of others;
- there can be neither security nor prosperity in an over-militarized, dehumanized, economically chaotic, and ecologically devastated world?

In 1946, Albert Einstein warned:

The unleashed power of the atom has changed everything save our modes of thinking, and we thus drift toward unparalleled catastrophes.

To help change our way of thinking, Beyond War families are uprooting themselves to move to other parts of the country for a year to spread the word about this need to change. Through formal and informal presentations to large and small groups of listeners, these families are stressing that the annihilating capacity of the world's nuclear arsenal makes war obsolete. They emphasize that all of life on earth is interdependent, and that a new mode of thinking—an expanded identification with all humanity—is required to take us beyond war.

Before returning home, these teams have trained other families to carry on their educational effort to change the nation's thinking. Beyond War presentations do not focus on legislative or administrative action, and they shun partisanship.

Beyond War does not restrict its activities to living-room discussions and luncheon speakers. It presents its Beyond War Award annually to honor a group or individual who has made an outstanding contemporary contribution toward building a world beyond war.

In 1983 the National Conference of Catholic Bishops (U.S.A.) was its first recipient of the award for drawing worldwide attention to the fact that we must "summon the moral courage . . . to say 'no' to weapons of mass destruction."

The Physicians for the Prevention of Nuclear War organization was the recipient of the 1984 Beyond War Award for educating the world that nuclear war is not survivable. (See report on IPPNW in this chapter.)

The 1985 Beyond War Award went to the six leaders of the Five Continent Peace Initiative: Raul Alfonsin, President of Argentina; Rajiv Gandhi, Prime Minister of India; Miguel de la Madrid, President of Mexico; Julius Nyerere, President of the United Republic of Tanzania; Olof Palme, Prime Minister of Sweden; and Andreas Papandreou, Prime Minister of Greece. (See report on Parliamentarians GLOBAL ACTION in Chapter 4.)

In 1986, the award went to the Contadora Group (Colombia, Mexico, Panama, and Venezuela) for its efforts beginning in 1983 to bring about a negotiated peace in Central America. (As the Contadora process for resolving conflicts in Central America became recognized as the one viable alternative to war and violence, the initial group of four has been joined by a support group of four other Latin American nations: Argentina, Brazil, Peru, and Uruguay.) Leaders accepting the award were Virgilio Barco Vargas, President of the Republic of Colombia; Miguel de la Madrid Hurtado, President of the United States of Mexico; Eric Arturo Delvalle, President of the Republic of Panama; and Jaime Lusinchi, President of the Republic of Venezuela. In the closing of the awards ceremony, Beyond War leaders pledged continued support for the Contadora process.

The Beyond War movement has utilized live "spacebridge" teleconference technology for its awards programs; e.g. linking Moscow and San Francisco for the 1984 IPPNW award, the six nations of the Five Continent Peace Initiative for its 1985 award, and four United States cities with the four capitals of the Contadora Group in 1986. These award programs were viewed by millions around the world.

The same "downlink" closed circuit technique was used by Beyond War in October of 1985 to bring together more than 15,000 people who had trained as leaders of Beyond War discussion groups for a nationwide update on programs and plans for the future.

In line with their pledge of continued support for the Contadora process, an eleven-member task force spent four weeks in Central America during February and March of 1987. They traveled in five countries to gain first-hand knowledge about the problems and needs of peoples there. Reports of their experiences were relayed by electronic mail to Beyond War networkers nationwide.

They found Costa Rica to be an exception due to relative stability and prosperity resulting from 100 years of democracy; but found Guatemala, Honduras, El Salvador, and Nicaragua to be in deep social, economic, and political crisis. Two-thirds of the people live in poverty, 40 percent have no access to health care, and 60 percent have no potable water or sanitation. Matthew Weil, a member of the task force, published an article in a special issue of *On Beyond War* entitled "Central America: The Way Is Clear." His closing paragraphs were:

> Underpinning the violence, justifying the neglect, there is only blame. The poor blame the rich, the civilians blame the military, El Salvador blames the communists, and the guerrillas blame the oligarchy. Honduras blames Nicaragua, Nicaragua blames Honduras. Above all, almost everybody blames the U.S. For many, the blame alone is sufficient and excuses inaction. Central America is pervaded by a sense of impotence. Blame polarizes. Violence degrades the entire — social, economic, environmental. The problems, viewed from within, appear so monumental as to defy solution.
>
> For the United States and for Central America, the way is clear. Renounce violence as a means of resolving conflict and renounce blame. We

must accept the responsibility for constructive action. The choice is theirs — and ours — to make.

Upon their return, the 11-member task force was joined by 27 other Beyond War workers from 14 states who took a week off from their jobs and their families to travel to Washington, D.C. From April 5 through 11, they met with members of Congress, think tanks, policy makers, labor unions, nonprofit foundations, and public organizations. The task force talked with congresspersons or their aides in a total of 110 offices of the House and 54 Senate offices, as well as meeting with 164 organizations and prominent individuals. Their combined efforts represented 3,000 person-hours.

They worked in teams of three, each team including one person who had been on the task force in Central America. Other team members included business people, lawyers, doctors, engineers, liberals, and conservatives from all regions of the country. They averaged about six meetings per day; and while their presentations varied with their personal diversity, one theme was common to all: the need to clarify our nation's principles and then to act consistently.

With the aid of basic charts, each meeting began with the proposition that nuclear weapons have changed the environment forever. They have rendered war obsolete. Then, using Central America as an example, they argued that war is not working as a solution to the problems there. Finally, they proposed that the United States has an opportunity to support an alternative to war in Central America — to lead the way in discovering appropriate international conduct in the nuclear age. In each meeting, they raised a central question: How can the people of this country participate in defining a set of principles to guide United States foreign policy?

Another nationwide "downlink meeting" was held in April to share the experience of both task forces with local networkers. They in turn made video tapes for further sharing at later dates and places.

The monthly newsletter, *On Beyond War,* keeps participants abreast of the fast-moving developments of the movement to build a world beyond war.

## Institute for Space and Security Studies

The Institute for Space and Security Studies was founded in 1982 by Dr. Robert Bowman, Lt. Col., USAF, ret., and former director of "Space Wars" research for the United States Air Force. The Institute is an independent organization "devoted to research and educational activities in science and strategy related to space and other high-technology areas important to national security and the maintenance of peace."

The primary goal of the Institute is to prevent nuclear war; and it warns:

- An arms race in space greatly increases the danger that such a war will occur.
- The ABM system proposed by the Star Wars program could offer no real protection.
- The deployment of such a system would violate several treaties including the ABM treaty, the only treaty ratified by the United States Senate in over a decade.
- If both superpowers deployed such systems, each side's "defense" system could destroy those of the other side at the speed of light without any warning.
- The incentive to "go first" would be so strong that the onset of war would be inevitable.

On the positive side, the Institute believes "we *can* prevent an arms race in space!" Dr. Bowman, now President of the Institute, has been speaking with authority against deployment of the proposed ABM system (Star Wars) to a wide range of audiences throughout the nation, and public support for Star Wars has been waning. Dr. Bowman has helped us realize that "there is no longer any such thing as *national* security. There is only *common* security."

An article in the April 1986, issue of *Jobs with Peace News* quoted Dr. Bowman as saying:

> Even if a totally impregnable, invulnerable "Star Wars" system could be employed — one capable of destroying all ICBMs in flight — it would be of little or no strategic value, because it could not prevent nuclear weapons from being delivered by other means.

Newspapers throughout the country have quoted Dr. Bowman's statement that:

> Star Wars has nothing to do with defense. It is a blatant attempt to regain absolute military superiority through development of new offensive weapons, disguised as defense.

Major achievements of the Institute have been:
- Getting Congressional restrictions on the testing of anti-satellite (ASAT) weapons against space targets.
- Getting the Pentagon to delay the scheduled first test of the advanced ASAT system.
- Working out, with Soviet space experts, the details of a treaty in the interest of both sides.
- Making space weapons an election year issue.
- Getting the Administration to discuss space weapons in "umbrella" arms talks with the Soviet Union.
- The moratorium on ASAT testing against targets in space by both the United States and the Soviet Union.

• Wide positive media coverage including requests to appear on major TV broadcasts.

• Requests for Dr. Bowman's testimony at Congressional hearings on issues of space and security.

• Involvement of international scientists.

• Publishing of research papers, issue papers, and newsletter, *Space and Security News.*

# Peace PAC

Peace PAC for the Prevention of Nuclear War was organized in 1982 as an affiliate of the Council for a Livable World, previously founded in 1962 by nuclear scientists concerned with the menace of nuclear war. (See page 102 for report on CLW.) Since its inception, CLW has provided millions of dollars to candidates for the United States Senate.

Recognizing the increasing importance of the House of Representatives on such issues as measures to freeze and reduce nuclear arms and military spending, the Council for a Livable World helped organize Peace PAC to support candidates for the House.

To launch Peace PAC the CLW provided operating expenses so maximum contributions could be made by Peace PAC to deserving candidates in critical House campaigns.

Candidates are selected for support in the following manner:

• Peace PAC's research staff reviews congressional races throughout the country to identify candidates deserving support, regardless of party.

• Candidates are also recommended by Peace PAC contributors and by cooperating organizations.

• Candidates must be politically viable, incumbent or challenger. They must demonstrate the capacity to run a credible campaign.

• To be selected for support by Peace PAC candidates must support measures to freeze the nuclear arms race, reduce the number of nuclear weapons and diminish the risk of nuclear war. They must also have demonstrated leadership on arms control and military spending.

• Peace PAC's Board of Directors makes the final decisions for support. The Board represents a wide range of political and scientific experts.

By election day, 1984, over 15,000 men and women had joined in support of Peace PAC's political and legislative efforts in the House of Representatives, compared with 6,000 in 1982.

Peace PAC's January 1985, Election Report highlighted four 1984 successful Peace PAC candidates: Les Aucoin of Oregon's First District, George Brown of California's Thirty-Sixth District, Bruce Morrison of Connecticut's Third District, and Frances Farley of Utah's Second District. The Election Report also included a clear and concise statement on the "Legislative Outlook for Nuclear Arms Control."

Peace PAC experts work in the House constantly, providing legislators with information on upcoming votes, as well as expert advice on weapons systems and military policy.

Peace PAC supporters throughout the United States are called when a member of Congress needs to be lobbied from the grass roots. In addition, 5,000 supporters have volunteered to call their Representatives when votes are needed on critical arms control appropriations.

A record of votes by Representatives on selected nuclear arms issues is distributed regularly to supporters, other peace groups, and the media.

Peace PAC also provides a Nuclear Arms Control Hotline which carries taped messages from its Washington lobbyists about what is happening in Congress and what action is recommended for grass-roots activists.

## Civilian-Based Defense Association

The Association for Transarmament Studies (ATS) evolved from the Omaha (NE) Peace Association in 1982. Then, in October 1987, it changed its name to Civilian-Based Defense Association (CBDA).

Members of CBDA strongly advocate a planned, nonviolent, civilian-based defense as a possible alternative to war. Quoting from an early ATS brochure:

> The destructiveness of modern war, the possibility of annihilation and the billions spent on the military are a concern for everyone, yet we cling to preparations for war as the only way to defend our way of life against invasion or repression.
>
> As long as people see no adequate substitute for violent sanctions there is no chance of war being renounced or abandoned.
>
> If we do not want to rely on violent sanctions, it is necessary to find a substitute. There may well be a nonviolent alternative by which people can defend liberty, their institutions and their society against military attack at least as effectively as can be accomplished by military means. One substitute, a nonviolent counterpart, could be a civilian-based defense.

The stated objective of CBDA is to facilitate more widespread study, discussion, and research in developing the concept of "transarmament."

The term "transarmament" was coined to convey "the idea that a nation accustomed to defense by military means might, for pragmatic reasons, lay aside military defense and choose in its place a defense system utilizing prepared, but nonviolent, civilian struggle to preserve the society's freedom, sovereignty and constitutional system against internal coup d'etat and external invasions and occupations." As a process, transarmament "would be the change-over from one defense system to a fundamentally different one, in our case, from conventional military or nuclear defense to civilian-based defense."

The brochure explains "civilian-based defense" as "planned nonviolent action by a society against a power considered illegitimate." The CBDA uses the term "civilian-based defense" primarily in a situation where an attempt is being made, from abroad or from within a country, to establish illegal control. It believes an invader or an attempted coup d'etat could be resisted effectively by nonviolent means through the institution of a national civilian-based defense campaign. (The CBDA prefers to use the term "nonviolent struggle/action for social change" to describe efforts to resist one's own government or an oppressive domestic social system.)

Continuing to quote:

> Civilian-based defense (CBD) is a projected nonviolent defense strategy based upon action by civilians. It could be an alternative or a supplement to military defense, a system with the potential to be as or more effective than traditional defense systems. CBD would attempt to defeat military aggression by using the resistance of large numbers of civilians to make it impossible for the invader or usurper to establish and maintain political control over the state — to protect their social and political institutions.
>
> This defense concept has been under development for several decades. Gandhi was one of the pioneers. A vast history exists of people who, refusing to be convinced that the apparent "powers that be" were omnipotent, defied and resisted powerful rulers. Recently, significant progress has occurred in Europe with investigation of civilian-based national defense being undertaken by the governments of Sweden, Switzerland, the Netherlands, Norway and Denmark as a complement or replacement for their military systems of defense.

The Civilian-Based Defense Association "believes that research and investigation must be carried out in order to judge the workability of civilian-based defense and to relate CBD to the defense problems of specific countries.

An oft-quoted statement by Albert Einstein warns, "The unleashed power of the atom has changed everything save our modes of thinking, and we thus drift toward unparalleled catastrophes."

Gene Sharp's response to this statement is, "The nonviolent technique of struggle may provide one of our last hopes for effective reversal of the current direction."

The CBDA publishes a quarterly newsletter, *Civilian-Based Defense: News & Opinion*. On the back page of its March 1987 issue were listed the following publications and resources available from CBDA:

- Introductory packet on CBD.
- Audio tape (radio interviews with Gene Sharp).
- "Defending America Without War" by Liane Norman (discussion guide).
- "Gandhi as a Political Strategist" by Gene Sharp.
- "Making Abolition of War a Realistic Goal" by Gene Sharp.
- "Making Europe Unconquerable" by Gene Sharp.

- "National Security Through Civilian Based Defense" by Gene Sharp.
- "The Politics of Nonviolent Action" by Gene Sharp: Part 1, "Power and Struggle"; Part 2, "The Methods of Nonviolent Action"; Part 3, "The Dynamics of Nonviolent Action."

## Psychologists for Social Responsibility

Psychologists for Social Responsibility (PsySR) was organized in 1982 to join with other independent organizations such as Educators for Social Responsibility, Lawyers for Social Responsibility, Engineers for Social Responsibility and Physicians for Social Responsibility in working for peace.

Its founders envisioned PsySR becoming an educational, idea-generating organization having the unique opportunity to disseminate the fruits of psychologists' efforts in peace work and to encourage their efforts.

The first issue of PsySR's newsletter, published in the summer of 1982, proposed its agenda for the near future and invited disagreements, suggestions, and ideas. In line with organizational goals and objectives, PsySR planned to:

- Promote a public forum to discuss alternatives to current policies with high medium exposure; and private meetings and brainstorming sessions culminating in press releases or other publications which propose alternatives to current policies.
- Develop strategies based on psychological principles to combat denial among the citizens of our country to make sure we are "never lulled to sleep again."
- Establish contact with psychologists abroad, especially those in the Soviet Union and in Warsaw Pact nations.
- Make a commitment to publish, as psychologists, lay and professional articles on the topic of nuclear warfare.
- Encourage its members to do research on nuclear warfare.
- Continue making the results of its work for peace available to those in positions of power, from city council people to United States Senators and the President of the United States.
- Hold firm to its opposition to both war and surrender to totalitarianism and in its search for viable alternatives.

In an open letter from PsySR dated October 13, 1983, readers were alerted to the upcoming showing of the TV film "The Day After," which portrayed Kansas City and its surroundings after a simulated nuclear war between the U.S. and the U.S.S.R. In this same letter, it stated:

Around the country PsySR's are fitting activities to local circumstances: joining with other groups, or acting as a unit. In NYC PsySR will rent a hall with a widescreen TV for communal viewing and discussion. National PsySR will be represented on an inter-discipline Task Force for a press conference about the effects of nuclear threat on children.

PsySR's eight-page quarterly newsletter documents an active and growing organization. Its Spring 1984 masthead stated, "Dedicated to reversing the arms race and building a durable peace." Most issues of the newsletter report on activities around the country and around the world, and on their Curriculum, Legislative, and Research Task Forces. They also report on new resources (books, audio-visuals, and other materials). Their Winter 1987 issue had a lead story on "Psychological Techniques Used in *Amerika*" (the controversial TV mini-series).

In the spring of 1986, as they were about to begin their fifth year of operation, the editors of the PsySR newsletter reviewed some of their activities since being founded by *Alex Redmountain.* Following his proposed ten-point agenda as laid out in the first issue of the newsletter in the spring of 1982, this review included:

• Re: marching in support of the UN Conference on Disarmament, PsySR joined with thousands of others in both 1982 and 1985.

• Re: State and Municipal Directors organizing local chapters, PsySR now has a nationwide representative Steering Committee which oversees the major policy thrusts of PsySR with an OpCom to oversee the day-to-day process.

• Re: State and Municipal Committees of psychologists to recruit local members and network with other local anti-nuclear groups, PsySR had (in 1986) sixteen active local and/or state groups, and thirteen additional states with PsySR contacts. Many were working with other local groups.

• Re: Public forums, private meetings, and brainstorming sessions, PsySR has had a variety of public meetings, conferences, speakers' bureaus, expert testimony, and facilitation of group processes. Audiences have ranged from colleagues to other peace activists, to groups watching the TV show "The Day After," to Congressional staffs and advisory committees. Brainstorming has happened primarily within psychological groups.

• Re: strategies to make sure we are never "lulled to sleep again," PsySR is actively engaged in discussions at the local and national levels on how to combat denial and how to communicate effectively to decision makers on how to use psychological skills to reduce international tension, and how to educate the general public on the psychological aspects of the arms race.

• Re: contacting psychologists abroad, especially in the Soviet Union and Warsaw Pact nations, PsySR (in 1986) had members in Canada, England, Indonesia, Italy, Japan, Nicaragua, Sweden, Swaziland, Switzerland, and West Germany.

• Re: publishing articles on nuclear warfare, PsySR members have published numerous articles on the psychological aspects of the nuclear issue and PsySR has published a bibliography of such resources.

• Re: doing research, PsySR's Research Task Force is publishing a directory of people engaged in research on various aspects of the nuclear threat.

• Re: making its expertise available to those in positions of power, PsySR is providing legislators with information on conflict resolution, underlying psychological issues involved in the arms race, and how enemy images are constructed.

• Re: holding firm on their opposition to both war and surrender to totalitarianism, and seeking viable alternatives, the Steering Committee of PsySR renewed its commitment to "preventing a nuclear war and building a durable peace" by approving the following policy statement:

> ...we support alternatives to exclusively military solutions of political problems. Rather than national confrontations, we look for ways to confront issues, and move from adversarial to cooperative models. We promote activities which reduce world tensions and create a psychologically more favorable climate for survival.

The Fall 1984 issue of PsySR's newsletter reprinted the following quotation from Norman Cousins:

> No greater fallacy exists in the modern world than that the individual in a free society is helpless. If anything, he exercises his power without being aware of it. Vast sums are spent to find out what he thinks or is likely to think. No major move can be made without him.

## U.S. Committee *Against* Nuclear War

Since its inception in 1982, the U.S. Committee *Against* Nuclear War has grown to over 30,000 concerned citizens, and it has reached more than one million concerned arms control advocates with issue updates.

Its efforts to reverse the arms race have had positive results. For example, the U.S. Committee launched a grass roots lobbying campaign that reached a half-million Americans and got them involved in the struggle to get the Freeze passed in the House of Representatives. As a result, the House approved the Nuclear Freeze Resolution in May of 1983.

The Committee initiated special candidate contributions to opponents of the MX Missile System—Representatives and Senators who feared that their opposition to the MX would cost them their careers.

The U.S. Committee alerted thousands of activists, politicians, and journalists to the dangers of new nuclear missiles in Europe. This rallied support behind a congressional resolution to delay the missiles until negotiations could be successful.

During the 1984 election, the U.S. Committee *Against* Nuclear War

# U.S. COMMITTEE AGAINST NUCLEAR WAR

## OFFICIAL CONSTITUTIONAL PETITION
### TO THE CONGRESS AND THE PRESIDENT OF THE UNITED STATES

*Petition of:*

*Your Contribution of $25 will help our campaign greatly. E.J.M.*

I exercise my rights under the First Amendment to the U.S. Constitution to "petition the government for a redress of grievances."

1) I petition the President to immediately drop his Star Wars plan, and adhere to all agreements for peaceful use of space. I ask that the Congress not approve any funds for such a Star Wars plan as long as the Soviets do not build such a system.

2) I petition the President and the Congress to stop the construction of any new MX missiles or other first-strike nuclear weapons. The U.S. should not build weapons which will only make nuclear war more likely.

3) I petition the President to enter into negotiations with the Soviet Union for a mutual, verifiable Nuclear Freeze. I urge the Congress to enact legislation demanding a Nuclear Freeze.

4) I petition the President and the Congress to stop wasting money on Pentagon boondoggles and start using our national resources to help people—not defense contractor profits.

Respectfully submitted,

_____ (your signature) _____ (date)

NW-OF-16

CONGRESSMAN MARKEY, HERE IS MY CONTRIBUTION TO STOP STAR WARS AND THE MX.

As a Participating Member, I want to support the U.S. Committee and its efforts to halt the arms race. With crucial Congressional hearings just weeks away, I want the Congress and the President to know where I stand. Please keep me informed of the impact of this citizen campaign on our nation's leaders!

$20 __ $25 __ $35 __ $50 __ $100 __ $250 __ Other $ __

IMPORTANT: Return the ENTIRE PETITION FORM to U.S. Committee Headquarters in the enclosed envelope. Send your petition TODAY, so that we can present the petitions to President Reagan at this critical time.

Please make checks payable to: U.S. Committee Against Nuclear War Washington, D.C. 20070-2026
The Federal Election Commission requires us to request the following:
Occupation _____
Name of Employer _____
Location of Employer _____
Paid for and authorized by the U.S. Committee Against Nuclear War. A copy of our report is filed and available for purchase from the Federal Election Commission, Washington, DC.

*Petition to Congress and the President of the United States, circulated in 1985 by the U.S. Committee Against Nuclear War.*

helped about 60 candidates for the House and Senate, with a resulting 80 percent victory record.

In a 1984 open letter, the U.S. Committee *Against* Nuclear War pointed out that when it was just getting underway in 1983, the nuclear arms race already had a 38-year headstart of unchecked momentum in Congress. It referred to 1983 as the turning point: the Freeze won in the House; the building of the MX missile was slowed. European missiles were protested, and the public rallied to the cause of disarmament.

In another open letter dated August 6, 1985, signed by Congressman Ed Markey, the U.S. Committee asked for support in stopping the U.S. Strategic Defense Initiative (SDI) or "Star Wars" as an escalation of the arms race, and to halt further production of the MX missile.

Also in 1985, the U.S. Committee circulated a petition to Congress and the President of the United States, calling for a variety of measures to halt the nuclear arms buildup (see copy of that petition, above).

# World Citizen, Inc.

World Citizen, Inc. (WCI), was founded in Minneapolis, Minnesota, in 1983 by a group of teachers, parents, and business leaders from the Twin Cities (Minneapolis, St. Paul). Its primary purpose is to encourage young people to learn about local, regional, national, and international affairs, and to keep this global perspective in mind as they deal with others. The ultimate goal is a peaceful, healthy world, and the survival of the Human Family, which includes everyone across the oceans as well as across the street.

In a recent brochure, the mission of World Citizen, Inc., is emphasized as follows:

> The mission of World Citizen Inc. is to develop in young people a global perspective by encouraging the use of global education resources in school and community youth groups. World Citizen's goal is that young people recognize the unity of the Human Family and reflect that understanding in their association with others.

World Citizen, Inc., encourages the formation of World Citizen Clubs for youth in grades five through twelve. These clubs have proven to be most effective in introducing a global perspective for future business, education, and governmental leaders.

A wide variety of World Citizen Club activities result in constructive global education — activities such as movies, speakers, discussions, peace projects, and helping students in Third World countries.

Again quoting from WCI's brochure:

> A long-range goal is for every subject, kindergarten through 12th grade, to have a global perspective designed into its course of study.
>
> The teachers, parents and business leaders who launched WCI are ultimately striving for a world without war, with free trade and jobs for all, and with a strong, effective United Nations. Societies around the world are constantly changing and young people must learn how to deal with changes locally, nationally and internationally in this interdependent world. In effect, they need to become World Citizens who are striving for a peaceful, healthy world.

World Citizen, Inc., provides consultants for any school or youth group in forming a World Citizen Club. It is a valuable resource and guidance center for leaders interested in forming such clubs. They may contact WCI for global education materials and curricula suggestions and lesson plans. Among those listed are:

• *Alpha or Omega,* a fifteen-minute film written by and starring John Denver that illustrates Human Family concepts and world citizenship.

• *Spaceship Earth,* a fifteen-minute film written by and starring fourteen Minneapolis public school World Citizen Club members that explains

complex world problems in simple terms. It comes complete with a teacher's guide.
- Materials from Global Education, Minneapolis.
- A newsletter, *World Citizen News,* written by student reporters contributing global education activity ideas and information from their respective clubs.

## Institute on Global Conflict and Cooperation

The Institute on Global Conflict and Cooperation (IGCC) is an interdisciplinary multicampus research unit of the University of California which was formally established by the Regents of the university in 1983.

The twofold focus of IGCC is concerned with: (1) conflict situations which are sufficiently severe to threaten escalation into a large-scale war; and (2) various forms of international cooperation to meet problems which threaten world peace. The main, but not exclusive, emphasis is on threats of and avoidance of nuclear war.

The mission of IGCC is to enlarge the capability of the university to contribute to international cooperation and security by promoting and sponsoring activities best carried out by a university. The IGCC makes possible the exploration of ideas and the teaching of subjects previously not adequately included in the university's program.

The Institute's programs focus on the causes of conflict as well as relevant ideas, institutions, policies, and mechanisms for eliminating, reducing, or managing conflicts that might lead to global war.

In one of its brochures, IGCC explains that its work is divided between individual projects supported by small grants made in response to proposals generated by University of California faculty, students, and staff in a normal solicitation process, and other activities planned and initiated by the Institute's central office.

The Institute supports the following programs: research and education projects; dissertation fellowships; IGCC Central Projects; summer seminars on global security and arms control; IGCC lectureships; a media library; and Peace Research Workshops.

The IGCC is administered by an Advisory Panel and a Steering Committee. It also has a director and maintains a Central Executive Office on the University of California–San Diego campus. Liaison officers are also located on each of the University of California campuses with programs located in Berkeley, Davis, Irvine, Los Angeles, Riverside, San Diego, San Francisco, Santa Barbara, and Santa Cruz.

## National Peace with Justice Week

The National Peace with Justice Week is the nation's largest religious witness for peace and justice. It began as a one day "Peace Sunday" and soon expanded to a full week of activities nationwide in 1983 (resulting from action taken by the Governing Board of the National Council of Churches of Christ in the U.S.A. in May of 1982).

The National Peace with Justice Week is now sponsored by the following "Inviting Organizations" which welcome others in joining their coalition:

- Baptist Peace Fellowship
- Baptist Peacemaker
- Brethren Peace Fellowship
- Catholic Peace Fellowship
- Church Women United
- Clergy and Laity Concerned
- Disciples Peace Fellowship
- Episcopal Peace Fellowship
- Evangelicals for Social Action
- Fellowship of Reconciliation
- American Friends Service Committee
- Jewish Peace Fellowship
- Las Hermanas
- Leadership Conference of Women Religious–Executive Committee
- Lutheran Church Women
- Lutheran Peace Fellowship
- Methodist Peace Fellowship
- National Association of Black Catholic Administrators
- National Campus Ministry Association
- National Conference of Catholic Bishops
- National Council of the Churches of Christ in the U.S.A., in-

cluding: American Baptist Church, Progressive National Baptist Convention, Inc., Church of the Brethren, Southern Christian Leadership Conference, National Farmworker Ministry, Philadelphia Yearly Meeting of the Religious Society of Friends, Global Ministries (Women's Division and World Division), Union of American Hebrew Congregations, New Jewish Agenda, American Lutheran Church, African Methodist Episcopal Zion Church, United Methodist Church General Board (Church and Society), Religious Task Force/Mobilization for Survival, Pastoral Care Network for Social Responsibility, Pax Christi (U.S.A.), New Call to Peacemaking, Presbyterian Church (U.S.A.), Riverside Church Disarmament Program, Sojourners, Unitarian Universalist Peace Network, Unitarian Universalist Service Committee, United Church of Christ, United Ministries in Education, World Peacemakers, and World Student Christian Federation (North America).

Following its positive experience of 1983, the second annual National Peace with Justice Week in 1984 expanded to include more than 20,000 local congregations and religious communities in all 50 states as they engaged in worship programs and actions for peace and justice.

The packets of materials prepared each year for local peace with

justice efforts are evidence of a well-organized promotion for peace. The packets contain posters and excellent materials bearing titles such as:
- "A Call to Common Witness and Action."
- "Organizer's Booklet."
- "Organizing Before, During, and After Peace with Justice Week."
- "Justice Will Bring Peace in the Home."
- "Justice Will Bring Peace in Our Community."
- "Justice Will Bring Peace in Our Nation."
- "Justice Will Bring Peace in Our World."
- "Youth Activities Calendar for Peace with Justice Week."
- "Cross Section of Peace with Justice Week Events Occurring Across the United States [the previous year]."
- "Working with the Press."
- "Justice Will Bring Peace: A Worship Theme [together with suggested Litany for Peace with Justice]."
- "Peace with Justice Week Speaker Resource Guide."
- "Resources and Inviting Organizations."
- "Graphics for Peace with Justice Week."

Packets and posters are available in both English and Spanish.

The 1987 Peace with Justice Week Organizers' Booklet included suggestions for (1) Proclaiming the jubilee in the home, in the community, in the nation, in the world; (2) tips on organizing for peace and justice; (3) an extensive list of resources recommended by the various inviting organizations; (4) additional resources and speakers; (5) a guide for intergenerational activities; (6) suggestions for advocacy and involvement; (7) worship materials and bulletin inserts; (8) ads and graphics; and (9) an attractive poster.

Also, on the 1987 order form were separate booklets containing activity suggestions, entitled: (1) "Campus Guide," (2) "Celebration Guide" (ideas for Peace with Justice fairs), (3) "Worship Suggestions," and (4) "Youth and Family Guide."

One recent sheet on organizing makes the point that

> the many issues of peace and justice cut across religious and sex boundaries; thus it is necessary to build bridges between different organizations and communities. For example, it is vital to recognize the arms race as not only a threat in creating mass destruction, but also as a cause of current misery since funds go to armaments and not to basic human needs. This displacement of funds hits women, youth, the elderly, the handicapped and persons of color particularly hard.

The theme papers on Peace with Justice in the home, community, and nation are excellent as aids to learning to live and work peacefully together at these levels as foundations for attaining peace with justice on a world level.

In announcing plans for the 1987 Peace with Justice Week, organizers prepared the following statement for use in local newsletters:

OUACHITA TECHNICAL COLLEGE

This year, from World Food Day to World Nations Disarmament Day, October 16–24, faith communities across the United States will be celebrating the Fifth Anniversary of Peace with Justice Week. The theme of the Week in 1987 arises from the biblical understanding of Jubilee: a call to set things right. Leviticus 25 cries out to people of faith to "...proclaim liberty to all the inhabitants of the land ... it shall be a Jubilee for you...." The cry is to live out God's vision of Shalom for all peoples and for Creation itself.

## Unitarian Universalist Peace Network

Time and again, Unitarian Universalists have rallied to promote peace and justice. They have raised the banner as abolitionists, suffragists and civil rights and peace activists. In 1985 they brought together the strengths of six Unitarian Universalist organizations to launch a new effort to end the nuclear arms race and promote peace. The six organizations brought together in this Unitarian Universalist Peace Network were the Unitarian Universalist Association, the Peace Fellowship, the Service Committee (See Chapter 2), the United Nations Office, the Womens Federation, and the International Association for Religious Freedom.

In the first issue of their journal, *The Peace Activator,* dated March 15, 1985, they outlined their plan of action:

Together we will:
- Build an effective Rapid Action Alert Network to communicate our concerns to our elected representatives. Your pledge to call other Unitarian Universalists and your representatives can make a difference.
- Strengthen peace work among Unitarian Universalists and in interfaith communities through the Fund for Peace grants program. [See report on Fund for Peace in this chapter.]
- Establish programs to assist congregations, clusters, units and districts in the development of effective peace programs, conferences and workshops.
- Distribute information, action alerts, printed and audio-visual resources in the publications of all sponsoring organizations. *The Peace Activator* will provide a useful forum for information and networkings.
- Establish a strong Unitarian Universalist participation in interfaith and international peace programs.

To assist participants in the network, its leaders have prepared an *Issue/Action Briefing Packet* containing announcements of the peace programs of its sponsoring organizations, an attractive multicolor Peace Network Poster, current briefing papers on arms race issues, and a list of new resources and action ideas.

In its brochure, the Network asks participants to share news items of their peace activities; their peace-oriented religious education materials;

and their peace-oriented worship materials, including sermons, readings, poetry, drama and dance. In closing, the brochure makes the charge that

> together we can create a powerful, synergistic web of shared resources — a network of positive action for peace.

## Wisconsin Institute for the Study of War, Peace, and Global Cooperation

The Wisconsin Institute for the Study of War, Peace, and Global Cooperation is a consortium of 21 institutions of higher learning in the state of Wisconsin. It was founded in 1985 to enable its member institutions to coordinate mutually beneficial activities and pursue common sources of funding for these activities.

According to its 1985–86 program brochure:

> The mission of the Institute is to encourage and legitimize research and teaching on the roots of organized violence, on security issues, and on the factors necessary for a just global peace; to develop and maintain a resource base for peace studies; and thereby to increase the probability of the survival and enhancement of life in the nuclear age.

To carry out its mission, the Institute promotes the development of innovative and interdisciplinary teaching programs, curricular strategies and resources for education in domestic and international conflict. This promotion is done:

- By providing curricular assistance to participating institutions.
- By organizing conferences, symposia, and summer workshops.
- By seeking funding from individual public and private foundations and other agencies to support its operations and programs.
- By allocating funds (as available) for teaching and research grants to faculty, released time for faculty and staff, and financial support for undergraduate and graduate student projects.
- By providing in-service consultant and professional services to primary and secondary schools in Wisconsin.

The Institute is receptive to both traditional and nontraditional teaching and study, and provides a forum where all viewpoints may be expressed and considered.

Also, the Institute is dedicated to enabling scholars, teachers, and the public to improve their understanding of war, peace and justice, but it does not seek to prejudice judgments about these issues with any particular ideology. It believes that, using reason, humanity can avert the catastrophe of a nuclear war.

The Institute's brochure also includes information about its Teaching Resource Center, centrally located at the University of Wisconsin–Stevens

Point, as well as announcements of its annual conference and the dates, locations, and speakers for its four Campus Visitor Programs for the year.

Membership in the Wisconsin Institute for the Study of War, Peace, and Global Cooperation is open to any public or private accredited institution of higher learning in the state. In 1985–86, its membership included Beloit College (Beloit); Carroll College (Waukesha); Carthage College (Kenosha); Lawrence University (Appleton); Marian College (Fond du Lac); Northland College (Ashland); Ripon College (Ripon); St. Norbert College (DePere); Viterbo College (La Crosse); and the University of Wisconsin at Eau Claire, La Crosse, Madison, Milwaukee, Oshkosh, Parkside, Platteville, Stevens Point, and Whitewater, plus UW Centers, Extension, and System.

# 4. Structural Approaches

*Examples of Organizations Promoting Peace Primarily Through World Unity, Organization, Federation, Citizenship, Justice, Law and Order*

As described in Chapter 1 on Historical Approaches, proposals for peace, cooperation, and prosperity among nations have been advocated for centuries. Four good examples of actual implementation of such proposals were the Greek Achaean League, the European Hanseatic League of the Middle Ages, the Iroquois League of Nations in North America, and the Articles of Confederation (1777) and Constitution (1788) of the United States of America. Other federal unions followed such as Switzerland, Canada, Argentina, and Mexico. Another good example in more recent times is India's federation of its many states with their diverse languages and religions.

Thus, the educational organizations described in this chapter have a rich background on which to base their efforts in advocating institutional and structural changes needed for the substitution of a system of just international law for the war system in dealing with international and global problems. Some of them stress support of the United Nations, but urge several "reforms" to make it more effective as a peace keeping body. Others believe the UN places too much emphasis on protecting national sovereignty. Some see nationalism as one of the primary causes of war and advocate one "world government of world citizens" with a primary goal of protecting their rights as defined in the UN's Universal Declaration of Human Rights. Some believe the time is ripe to follow the example of the founding fathers of the United States Constitution at the global level by forming a federation of nations to manage global affairs. One organization has already drawn up a proposed Constitution for the Federation of Earth and has had three sessions of a Provisional World Parliament that has passed several bills of legislation concerning global issues that transcend national boundaries.

To enable the proponents of these different approaches to communicate and support each other, a World Government Organization Coordinating Council was formed in 1977 (renamed World Government Organization Coalition in 1987). (See report on WGOC in this chapter.)

# Campaign for World Government

In response to this survey, The Campaign for World Government sent a wealth of materials and claimed to be the oldest world federalist organization. The main points of its blueprint for governmental or unofficial action to organize the world were drawn up in 1924. These were revised and published in 1937. Its plan for governmental action called for the heads of state to "invite a small group of experts on voting methods to formulate the best practical method for the democratic election in all countries alike of delegates to a World Constitution Convention." Upon adoption of their committees' reports, delegates to the Constitution Convention were to be elected.

If governments failed to act, the plan called for internationally minded individuals to be chosen as delegates by methods recommended by an unofficial Committee of Experts; and these unofficial delegates were to meet in an unofficial World Constitution Convention to draw up a federal constitution. All nations were to be urged to adopt this World Constitution.

This plan also included a section on tentative operating plans for the Federation of Nations and a meeting on Federal Commissions to be organized.

The work of Campaign for World Government, Inc., was suspended during World War II, but its members again pushed for a federalist form of world organization instead of the loose association proposed for a United Nations at Dumbarten Oaks. They circulated the following petition:

> We the undersigned people of the United Statse, believing as we do that just government rests on the consent of the governed, respectfully urge that you establish a world legislative body to which we can elect our own representatives.
>
> The sovereignty which belongs to us, the people, we now wish to redivide, giving to a higher world level of government — which we continue to control through our representatives — the power to decide questions of world-wide concern.
>
> If democratic international machinery capable of resolving the economic and political problems which menace the general welfare of our ONE WORLD is not established in San Francisco, it will remain for us to organize it in order to secure for ourselves and our children the blessings of peace, prosperity, and freedom.

In their literature, they pointed out that one of the problems of the UN was that it still attempted to protect national sovereignty. They emphasized that no nation can be truly sovereign when there is no system of control over the actions of other nations. There can be no protection against nuclear weapons and their effects. "We are all hostage under the threat of a nuclear holocaust."

A 1983 flyer distributed by the Campaign for World Government points out that true sovereignty belongs to the people, and it recommends a "re-allocation of our rightful powers. We would continue our loyalty to the nation, and it would continue to manage national affairs. Under a [world] constitution subject to popular ratification, we would elect representatives to a world body to manage world affairs on our behalf — to enact real laws to be independently enforced world-wide (but only within granted jurisdiction) on *individual citizens* by civilian authorities."

Continuing their crusade, members of the Campaign for World Government circulated questionnaires to all 1980 and 1984 candidates for the United States Senate and House. The 1984 questions were as follows:

1. Do you believe that the UN structure is adequate to provide for peace among nations?

2. Will you work for the election — rather than the appointment, as now — of the U.S. delegation to the UN?

3. Will you urge the President and the U.S. delegation to work for basic UN reform toward world government?

4. Will you work to extend the area of government in the world, in accord with President Lincoln's quotation calling for government "of the people, by the people, and for the people"?

5. Will you work to establish a universal, democratic federal world government with civilian law enforcement on individuals, as in the U.S. federal system?

6. Would you urge the President to send a U.S. delegation to a world constitutional convention to establish a world government, as referred to here?

The strongest favorable responses were for reform of the UN and for extending the area of government by consent of the governed over world affairs. Overall replies were fairly evenly divided between Democrats and Republicans, with about 20 Libertarians and members of other minority parties. Fifteen incumbent members of Congress replied.

## United Nations Association — USA

The League of Nations Non-partisan Association, founded in 1923, changed its name to the American Association for the United Nations in 1945. A National Committee for UN Day was formed in 1949; and in 1965, the association and the committee merged as the United Nations Association of the United States of America (UNA-USA). It is the largest nationwide, private, nonpartisan organization in the United States concerned with international affairs. It is one of 60 UN associations in nations throughout the world, all interested in helping the United Nations succeed in living up to its charter. For example, a January 1985 UNA-USA letter to its members informed them:

> In January, UNA-USA will host a high-level Soviet-American meeting to discuss ways of bolstering East-West cooperation in the non-proliferation effort. The Soviet UN Association has agreed to publish a joint statement on the topic with UNA-USA this summer on the eve of a potentially divisive Review Conference of the Non-Proliferation Treaty. The Soviet and American Associations will also produce a joint statement on ways of strengthening UN peace and security mechanisms — the subject of this year's multilateral project — to commemorate the UN's 40th anniversary.

The UNA-USA conducts programs of research, study, and information to:
- Heighten public awareness of global issues and the relationship of these issues to the United Nations system.
- Encourage, where appropriate, multilateral approaches in dealing with international issues.
- Build public support for constructive U.S. policies on matters of global concern.
- Enhance the effectiveness of the United Nations and other multilateral institutions.

The UNA-USA carries out its program through a network of national and community organizations. This network is composed of 175 UNA-USA chapters and divisions throughout the country, and over 130 affiliated national organizations. The citizens who participate in UNA-USA's programs come from business, labor, and academia. Many have held senior positions in the United States government or the United Nations.

The UNA-USA also provides information and education services on UN-related matters and international affairs for student groups, model UNs, the media, Congress, and policy-making groups.

More specifically, UNA-USA:
- Publishes the highly acclaimed periodical *The Interdependent*.
- Invites hundreds of editors to the United Nations each year for on-the-record, behind-the-scenes briefings.
- Briefs members of Congress on the effects of their votes dealing with the United Nations, helping them to make informed decisions.
- Brings together diverse groups of experts to formulate policy recommendations on the most challenging international problems facing America.
- Guides year-round programs on international issues in the 175 local UNA chapters, and helps over 1,200 communities observe UN Day.
- Analyzes the United Nations agenda in advance of each General Assembly session in a publication considered indispensable by governments, journalists, and educators.
- Works with over 130 national organizations, helping them to keep their membership aware of global issues.

• Prepares resource materials for thousands of students attending model United Nations conferences each year.

• Examines United States foreign policy as it affects the United Nations and makes recommendations for government action.

• Participates with some 60 other nations in a World Federation of United Nations Associations.

The publication list of UNA-USA includes information on the UN; fact and information sheets on key issues; policy studies reports; Economic Policy Council reports; a Policy Studies book series; reports on the Multilateral Project; and education/curriculum materials. These UNA-USA materials remind us that "global problems are increasing in magnitude and complexity." Problems such as the arms race and the threat of nuclear war, energy, human rights violations, hunger and malnutrition, inflation, job insecurity, pollution of the environment, and population growth are all related and interdependent. No one nation can deal with these problems on its own. All nations must work together in cooperation to solve them.

For the past four years, the UNA-USA's Multilateral Project has sponsored a series of national studies. The program's purpose is to involve a broad range of citizens in analyzing and shaping United States foreign policy on global issues. The 1983–84 study focused on the danger of the spread of nuclear weapons. The 1984–85 study was on the role of the United Nations in maintaining international peace and security. In 1985–86, 90 communities participated in a study on the prospects for international cooperation in outer space. The 1986–87 study was on Food: Seeking Global Solutions to Chronic Hunger. The conclusions and recommendations from these studies have influenced policy in the capitals of other nations as well as Washington, D.C.

In August 1987, UNA-USA was one of 25 co-sponsors of an International Bicentennial Symposium on Strengthening the United Nations held in Philadelphia, Pennsylvania. (For more information on the Symposium, see the following section on the World Federalist Association.)

## World Federalist Association

Although the present World Federalist Association (WFA) was not established until 1975, its predecessor, the United World Federalists, was founded in 1947 when five organizations merged in a convention held in Asheville, North Carolina. Merging groups were: (1) Americans United for World Government, (2) the Massachusetts Committee for World Federation, (3) the Student Federalists, (4) World Citizens of Georgia, and (5) World Federalists, U.S.A. In 1969, the name was changed from United World Federalists to World Federalists, U.S.A., continuing to include a lobbying function (i.e., not tax deductible). Then, in 1975, the present tax-deductible World Federalist Association was formed to continue the non-political programs; and the Campaign for UN Reform was established to take over the political and electioneering activities.

The WFA and its predecessors have been a positive force for four decades in advocating the substitution of world law for war as a method of settling international conflicts. The following Statement of Goals and Beliefs appeared in the June 1985 issue of the *World Federalist* newsmagazine:

> The goal of the World Federalist Association is the abolition of war through the development of enforceable world law. Achievement of this goal requires the establishment of a federal world government with powers adequate to keep the peace and to assist in the promotion of a just world community. In such a federation, international conflicts would be resolved by political and judicial means rather than by violence, while national governments would continue to manage their own internal affairs.

By way of amplification, it continues:

> World federation is not a new or radical idea. It is simply an extension to the global level of the federal principle, now used in many nations. That principle was adopted by those who framed the U.S. Constitution, thereby providing thirteen states — actually thirteen small, independent nations — with an effective federal government. Those states replaced the inadequate Articles of Confederation with the Constitution. Similarly, the nations of today need to transform the present weak United Nations system into — or replace it with — a truly effective global institution or family of institutions having the authority to maintain world peace and to resolve conflicts among nations, and the capacity to promote a more just world society.
>
> While the abolition of war is our supreme goal, we believe that a world federation should be given not only adequate powers to keep disputes between nations from erupting into war, but also sufficient powers to deal with those other urgent global problems that clearly are not manageable by nations acting separately in an ungoverned world. Those problems include international air piracy, terrorism, narcotics trade, pollution that crosses national boundaries, and orderly management of non-national areas: the oceans, the polar regions, and outer space. Such a federation must have limited but adequate sources of revenue. It must be able to enforce decisions on the individual lawbreaker rather than go to war with the lawbreaker's nation. It must be able to banish all nuclear and other weapons of mass destruction. It must be able to establish a world peacekeeping force which would replace national military establishments capable of conducting international war. At the same time any infringement on human rights by the world government must be prevented by a federal Bill of Rights.
>
> As steps toward achieving our goals, World Federalists support efforts to reform and strengthen the U.N. system and/or to hold a convention to draft a federal world constitution, and also to create new global institutions such as the International Seabed Authority and a World Disarmament Authority. In addition, in order to bring the world closer together, we support efforts to strengthen programs — international,

national, and regional—to resolve conflicts peacefully, to protect the global environment, to promote respect for human rights, and to raise the living standards of the world's people. We also seek to gain acceptance of the concept that each individual is a citizen of the world as well as a citizen of his or her own city, state and nation.

While the precise details of the world federation we seek remain to be determined, we agree that the abolition of war and the achievement of a more just and livable society require a world federal system with the powers necessary to attain these ends. The mounting threats to all of humanity require immediate action toward this goal.

We seek to join with others in the United States and throughout the world in raising the consciousness of the human family to the idea that war can be abolished and greater justice achieved through world law. We must work together to persuade national leaders to accept world federation before it is too late. Unless immediate steps are taken toward a lawful world, the hostile anarchy which now exists among powerful armed and non-lawabiding national states will lead to further mass violence that may well prove to be irreversible, and that could even lead to the destruction of human civilization.

The WFA (USA) and 35 similar organizations in 31 countries are joined together in the World Association for World Federation (formerly the World Association of World Federalists, and also called the "World Federalist Movement" for a short time, 1986–87). The WAWF is headquartered in Amsterdam, the Netherlands. Allied with them is an international group of members of parliaments in 36 countries calling themselves "Parliamentarians GLOBAL ACTION."

In recent years, WFA (USA) has experienced considerable growth under the leadership of its President, Norman Cousins, and its Executive Director, Walter Hoffman. There are some 90 local units in all parts of the nation, and several affiliated and networking groups.

The WFA has taken the initiative in introducing and securing sponsors for congressional resolutions which promote the concept of a fully disarmed world under a global security system. For example, the U.S. and the U.S.S.R. agreed to such an approach in 1961 in their "Joint Statement of Agreed Principles for Disarmament Negotiations," referred to as the McCloy-Zorin Agreement. Unfortunately, this agreement was shelved for almost two and a half decades. However, it was resurrected in H. Con. Res. 36, a Concurrent Resolution dated January 24, 1985.

It was good to note that the WFA is active in numerous coalitions which support peace and world order. Two examples of jointly supporting such measures were concerned with the nuclear freeze resolution and the creation of a National Peace Academy. Efforts for the latter resulted in authorization and modest funding for a United States Institute of Peace.

The WFA has been called on frequently to assist educational organizations in the development of curriculum materials on the development of world order for both secondary schools and colleges. It offers a National Speakers Bureau, and it is organizing a group of international legal authorities to serve as "watchdogs" over blatant violations of international law. When fully operational, this body will have the potential of much needed, authoritative support for the use and respect of law as a means for regulating relations between and among nations, as opposed to the killing and violence of war.

In 1986, WFA distributed its educational pamphlet on *Creative Solutions to Meet Six Current Crises;* namely, the Arms Race, Central America, International Terrorism, South Africa, Transnational Pollution, and the UN Funding Crisis. All of these problems underline the need for "world peace through law with justice," the goal of WFA; and efforts to solve these current problems will move the world step by step toward the achievement of that ultimate goal.

To highlight the need for enforceable world law, WFA filed a lawsuit on September 23, 1986, in federal court to enforce the judgment of the world court which held that United States aid to the Nicaraguan contras is a violation of customary international law.

In June 1987, the Executive Committee of WFA adopted a new three-year plan. The plan incorporated "three current strategies for achieving intermediate steps toward world federation." These were: (1) "Structures for Peace" Networking Strategy; (2) U.N. Reform Political Action Strategy; and (3) Bicentennial/World Federation Public Education Strategy.

The carefully detailed plan included a statement of rationale for each strategy, and goals and action plans under each strategy for each of the three years of the plan (1987–90). Also included were plans for increasing youth membership and overall membership, for increasing the number of chapters, and for financial development. Anticipated additional personnel and increases in budgetary items were also included.

On August 6 through 9, 1987, an International Bicentennial Symposium on Strengthening the United Nations was held at Independence Hall and the University of Pennsylvania in Philadelphia. Initiating sponsors of the symposium were the Common Heritage Institute of Villanova University, the World Federalist Association (U.S.A.), and the World Association of World Federalists. Co-sponsors were:

- American Association of University Women
- American Movement for World Government
- Baha'i International Community
- Campaign for UN Reform
- Council on International and Public Affairs
- Clergy and Laity Concerned
- En Verden
- FN-Forbundet
- Friends Peace Committee
- Global Education Associates
- Gray Panthers
- Institute for Defense and Disarmament Studies
- International Affairs Association, Univ. of Pennsylvania

- International Peace Academy
- Pax Christi, U.S.A.
- Peace Research Institute of Dundas
- Philadelphia World Federalists
- Planetary Citizens
- Promoting Enduring Peace, Inc.
- Society for International Development
- United Church of Christ — Office of Church in Society
- Unitarian Universalist UN Office
- United Nations Association — U.S.A.
- Women's International League for Peace and Freedom
- World Without War Council

The stated purpose of the symposium was to focus scholarly and public attention on a single hypothesis: "In order to secure peace it is essential to restructure and strengthen the United Nations so that it has the power, authority and funding to maintain peace and to promote economic and social progress and respect for human rights." Participants from around the world were not required to agree with this hypothesis but were asked to consider it. As they did so, participating scholars, public figures and opinion leaders asked what lessons could be learned from the origin and operation of the United States and other federal systems and the European Community, and from the history of the United Nations. They asked how and why the American founding fathers and the founders of other federal systems agreed to restructure their national institutions and how and why they were able to win public support for their bold reform proposals. The participants tried to apply these lessons to the problems of restructuring and strengthening the United Nations.

The program of the symposium began at Independence Hall and ended at the Pavilion on Independence Mall. All other plenaries and seminars were held on the campus of the University of Pennsylvania. Plenary speakers included dignitaries from around the world speaking on their respective region's perspective on strengthening the United Nations; e.g., perspectives from Africa, China, Europe, Japan, Latin America, the Soviet Union, and Third World nations. Plenary speakers also included politicians, representatives from missions to the United Nations, from the media, the Common Heritage Institute, and the World Federalist Association.

Small group seminar topics included Arms Control and Disarmament; Federal Systems; Strategies for Strengthening the UN; Financing the UN; Representation and Decision-Making; Social, Economic and Environmental Issues; Human Rights; and Conflict Resolution.

The finale of the symposium was a public rally at the Pavilion on Independence Mall at which all in attendance were invited to sign the "Declaration of Philadelphia" and urged to present it to leaders of their respective governments as a means of securing their support of measures enabling the United Nations to fulfill its declared purposes. The text of the Declaration read as follows:

LIBRARY/LRC
OUACHITA TECHNICAL COLLEGE
P.O. BOX 816
MALVERN, ARKANSAS 72104

### The Declaration of Philadelphia

*Preamble*

Meeting on Independence Mall during the Bicentennial of the Constitution of the United States, we ask men and women of every nation, color, creed and ideology to sign this Declaration of Philadelphia, to present it to leaders of their governments and to ask these leaders to support measures which will enable the United Nations to fulfill its declared purposes.

We the people of the world demand that bold and imaginative action be taken to redeem the bright promises proclaimed in the United Nations Charter more than forty years ago. We urge our leaders to approach that job with the boldness and imagination which the American Founding fathers showed in Philadelphia 200 years ago as they sought to ensure peace and justice for the United States.

In San Francisco the United Nations was dedicated to maintaining peace and security, to encouraging arms control and disarmament, and to promoting economic and social progress and respect for human rights. But it was not given the means to carry out these high purposes.

Succeeding Generations have not been saved from "the scourge of war." The world has seen many "conventional" wars since World War II. It has seen a suicidal arms race which threatens to bring about a devastating nuclear war.

National governments are spending a million dollars a year on armaments in a vain effort to assure national security. But that arms race only encourages enmity between nations and interference in each other's affairs. It causes a scandalous misuse of resources urgently needed to provide for the basic needs of the human family, its need for food, shelter, health care, employment and a healthy and wholesome environment.

To turn the world away from war and want and toward peace and justice we urge public officials and private citizens to demand action leading to the restructuring and strengthening of the United Nations. It must be given power, authority and funding to fulfill its great purposes. We believe that a truly effective United Nations will enable nations and their peoples to live together in peace and enjoy a more secure, more prosperous and more satisfying life, with what ever form of national government they choose.

We ask people everywhere to join us in this effort to enable the United Nations to carry out its noble purposes.

# World Government of World Citizens

The World Government of World Citizens was founded in 1953 by *Garry Davis* in his Ellsworth (Maine) Declaration.

As a United States bomber pilot over Germany in World War II, Davis became deeply concerned over national governments requiring members of the human family to make war against each other. At the end of the war, he wrestled with the question of what he as an individual could do to replace the outdated system of dividing the world into sovereign nations with a "one-world" system.

To demonstrate his conviction against nationalism, Garry Davis presented himself at the United States Embassy in Paris on May 25, 1948, to renounce his United States citizenship and declare himself to be a citizen of the world. When, seven months later, the United Nations proclaimed its Universal Declaration of Human Rights on December 10, 1948, Davis saw in it a call for a world government to protect those rights. (See Appendix D for UN's UDHR.)

In 1949, Davis and enthusiastic supporters in Paris established an International Registry of World Citizens. Over the past 39 years, it has raised the consciousness of tens of thousands of people to their responsibilities as members of the world community. There are now over 750,000 registered world citizens, and national world citizen registration centers have been established throughout the world.

His renunciation of national citizenship led Davis to experience first-hand the plight of stateless people everywhere. Without proof of his identity, several countries jailed him (in violation of the UN's Declaration of Human Rights) for not leaving their borders to go into other countries equally unwilling to accept him without a nationally issued passport. In an attempt to meet this problem and demonstrate the need for such a document, Davis fashioned his own World Citizen's Passport.

In his Ellsworth Declaration, Garry Davis stated that his affirmaton of world sovereignty was based on three basic laws:

1. There is but *One Deity* or Ideal, Goal, Vision, Absolute, Origin, Source, Mind, Spirit, Reality, Understanding, Wisdom, Truth, and so on unitively conceived and intuitively, that is, by conscience, perceived, of which I am a living and integral part, as is all mankind; and

2. There is but *one world,* which is ideologically or intellectually, as my and mankind's natural home, despite social groupings such as tribal, communal, regional, geographical, cultural, historical, ancestral, lingual, or professional and which constitutes my total social environment or community; and

3. There is but *one physical human family,* which is instinctively felt by common fundamental needs and wants, despite color, race, sex, birth, property, economic, or other physical status, and thus one common citizenship. . . .

Further, I am convinced that the full recognition of these three fundamental or Prime Laws constitute a spiritual, social, and physical trinity, in that the first represents personal or individual freedom; the second, social or communal justice or fairness; and the third, physical security and well-being, upon which the rational organization of human society must be based for the increased happiness of all.

Following his 1953 Ellsworth Declaration of a World Government for World Citizens, Davis established a World Service Authority in 1954, headquartered in Basel, Switzerland, with district offices in London and Washington, D.C., to serve as the administrative agency of the World Government. Today, the WSA operates from offices in Washington, D.C.,

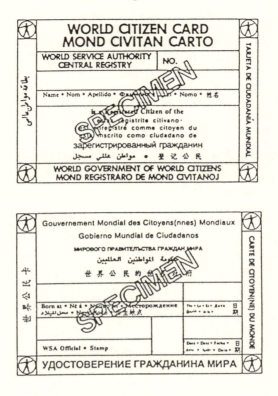

*World Citizen Card (sample).*

from which it issues all World Government documents. The World Passport has gone through seven editions and is printed in seven languages: Arabic, Chinese, English, Esperanto, French, Russian, and Spanish. Over 250,000 World Passports have been issued worldwide; and it has been recognized by over 100 nations on a case-by-case basis. Six nations have given it *de jure* recognition.

The WSA Passport had a precedent in the Nansen Passport issued to refugees in the aftermath of World War I by the Nansen Office for Refugees mandated by the League of Nations. Nansen, Norway's representative to the League of Nations, convinced his fellow delegates of the need for an international identification and travel document for stateless refugees.

Besides a World Passport, the WSA issues World Identity Cards, World Birth Certificates, the World Citizen's Registration Card, the World Marriage Certificate, and the World Political Asylum Card.

Documents of the WSA have a practical and a symbolic value. For many, they are valuable additions to whatever identity documents already held. A World Citizens' Legal Fund is also available to help defray legal expenses in human rights violations cases.

The Credo of a World Citizen is as follows:

A World Citizen is a human being who lives intellectually, morally and physically in the present.

A World Citizen accepts the dynamic fact that the planetary human community is interdependent and whole, that humankind is essentially one.

A World Citizen is a peaceful and peacemaking individual, both in daily life and contacts with others.

As a global person, a World Citizen relates directly to humankind and to all fellow humans spontaneously, generously and openly. Mutual trust is basic to his/her life style.

Politically, a World Citizen accepts a sanctioning institution of representative government, expressing the general and individual sovereign will in order to establish and maintain a system of just and equitable world law with appropriate legislative, judiciary and enforcement bodies.

A World Citizen brings about better understanding and protection of different cultures, ethnic groups and language communities by promoting the use of a neutral international language, such as Esperanto.

A World Citizen makes this world a better place to live in harmoniously by studying and respecting the viewpoints of fellow citizens from anywhere in the world.

The Pledge of Allegiance of a World Citizen is as follows:

I, the undersigned, do hereby, willingly and consciously, declare myself to be a Citizen of the World. As a World Citizen, I pledge my planetary civic commitment to WORLD GOVERNMENT, founded on three universal principles of One Absolute Value, One World, and One Humanity which constitute the basis of World Law. As a World Citizen I acknowledge the WORLD GOVERNMENT as having the right and duty to represent me in all that concerns fundamental human rights and the General Good of human-kind and the Good of All.

As a Citizen of World Government, I affirm my awareness of my inherent responsibilities and rights as a legitimate member of the total world community of all men, women, and children, and will endeavor to fulfill and practice these whenever and wherever the opportunity presents itself.

As a Citizen of World Government, I recognize and re-affirm citizenship loyalties and responsibilities within the communal, state, and/or national groupings consistent with the principles of unity above which constitute now my planetary civic commitment.

_____

Signature of World Citizen

The WSA is organizing World Citizen political parties, continues to register world citizens, and coordinates many other world activities begun in 1948. For example, it is now operating an Intra-global Postal Service.

In a recent open letter from Garry Davis as WGWC World Coordinator, he pointed out that all of us are already world citizens and invited us to register as citizens of the World Government of World Citizens. He emphasized that such registration would *not* require giving up our nationality. However, those who register will be joining a growing number who are committed to establishing social, economic, and political justice throughout the world in accordance with the fundamental moral code of all major religions.

The letter went on to explain that the registered World Citizens will "have an opportunity to help evolve just and democratic *World laws* to be enacted eventually by an elected *World Parliament,* administered by a *World Executive* controlled by a *World Court* and enforced by a *World Peace Force.*"

The World Government of World Citizens has a four-phase Master Plan:

• Phase 1. To build and identify its constituency.

• Phase 2. To politicalize its new world constituency by means of a new political party transcending the nation-state while fielding candidates at all levels.

• Phase 3. To consolidate: convening a world constitutional convention from which will come a world parliament and additional organs of government; the establishment of a world bank and the introduction of a world monetary unit; the dismantling of nuclear and conventional armaments as the economy regears to peacetime production.

• Phase 4. To operate as a fully functioning world government integrated with national and local units; with total elimination of armaments; with protection of the environment and the planet on which our lives depend.

As the operating structure of the World Government of World Citizens has been evolving, the following have accepted responsibilities as World Coordinators of twelve commissions: Syd Cassyd, for Communications; Stafford Beer, for Cybernetics; Yehudi Menuhin and Katherine Dunham, for Culture; William Peck, for Design-Science; Louis Kelso, for Economics; Guru Nitya Chaitanya Yati, for Education; Badi Lenz, for Forestry; Michio Kushi, for Health; Theodore Welles, for Oceans; Isaac Asimov and Carol Sue Rosin, for Space; Georgia Lloyd, for Women; and John Steinbrock, for World Political Asylum.

The statute for a World Court of Human Rights for the World Government Judicial System was written in 1972 for the Commission for International Due Process of Law and was established in 1984. It now awaits a world judicial commission and then the appointment of fifteen world judges and proper funding to begin its role of defending individuals against human rights violations.

Many cities and even states are now recognizing world citizenship as a new level of politics. Declaring a city to be "worldly" is called "mondialization," from the French word "monde," meaning "world." It began with Cahors, a city of 50,000 in France, in 1949 and has spread through the world. Minneapolis was the first United States city to "mondialize" in March 1968.

Minneapolis was followed in its mondialization by St. Paul, Minn.; San Pedro and Los Angeles, Calif.; St. Louis and Kansas City, Mo.; Richfield and Akron, Oh.; Eugene, Ore.; Racine, Wis.; and many others. The states of Iowa, Minnesota, and Illinois have made declarations of world citizenship as well. Minnesota's Declaration of Mondialization read as follows:

> WHEREAS, in recognition of the greatly increased interdependence of the world in this age of nuclear power, pollution, hunger, and
> WHEREAS, realizing that the common interests of man can only be met through world cooperation, and
> WHEREAS, seeking to free mankind from the curse of war and to harness all available sources of energy and knowledge to the service of man's needs, and
> WHEREAS, aware that we can best serve our city, county, state, and nation when we also think and act as world citizens
> NOW, THEREFORE BE IT RESOLVED, THAT WE THE Governor and Legislative Leaders of Minnesota, recognize the sovereign right of our citizens to declare that their citizenship responsibilities extend beyond our state and nation. We hereby join with other concerned people of the world in a declaration that we share in this world responsibility and that our citizens are in this sense citizens of the world. We pledge our efforts as world citizens to the establishment of permanent peace based on just world law and to the use of world resources in the service of man and not for his destruction.

[Note: The signature was Wendell Anderson's, dated March 26, 1971.]

In 1986, Garry Davis ran for Mayor of Washington, D.C., as an independent on a World Citizen platform. In his campaign he stressed that world law alone could protect that target city.

On January 19, 1987, Garry Davis, in a speech at Middlebury College, Middlebury, Vermont, announced his candidacy for the office of President of the United States on a World Government platform. The speech was entitled "World Peace Through World Government," and in it he pointed out that today's world leaders are opposed to any relinquishment of national sovereignty; and thus, "we are obliged to field our own candidate." (See Appendix E for World Government Platform of Garry Davis as a candidate for President of the United States.)

## World Constitution and Parliament Association

The World Constitution and Parliament Association (WCPA) was founded in 1958 by *Margaret* and *Philip Isely* and a group of like-minded persons dedicated to world peace. It is headquartered in Lakewood, Colorado, U.S.A., and is now a worldwide organization based on individual memberships, national branches, local chapters, and a section for members of national parliaments. The WCPA has individual members in 60 countries and national branches in 15.

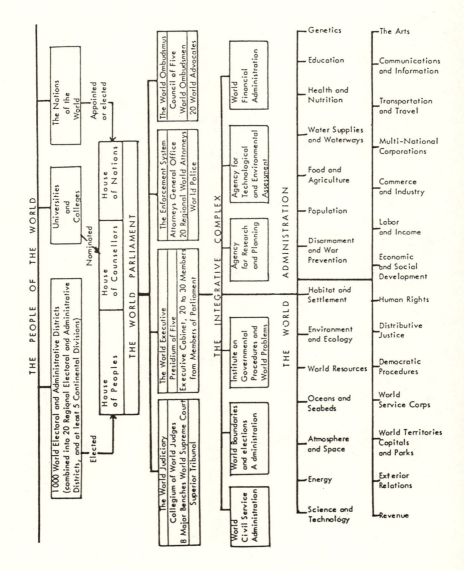

THE PEOPLE OF THE WORLD

1000 World Electoral and Administrative Districts (combined into 20 Regional Electoral and Administrative Districts, and at least 5 Continental Divisions)

Universities and Colleges

The Nations of the World

Elected

Nominated

Appointed or elected

House of Peoples

House of Counsellors

House of Nations

THE WORLD PARLIAMENT

The World Judiciary
Collegium of World Judges
8 Major Benches World Supreme Court
Superior Tribunal

The World Executive
Presidium of Five
Executive Cabinet, 20 to 30 Members
from Members of Parliament

The Enforcement System
Attorneys General Office
20 Regional World Attorneys
World Police

The World Ombudsmus
Council of Five
World Ombudsmen
20 World Advocates

THE INTEGRATIVE COMPLEX

World Civil Service Administration

World Boundaries and elections Administration

Institute on Governmental Procedures and World Problems

Agency for Research and Planning

Agency for Technological and Environmental Assessment

World Financial Administration

THE WORLD ADMINISTRATION

- Genetics
- Education
- Health and Nutrition
- Water Supplies and Waterways
- Food and Agriculture
- Population
- Disarmament and War Prevention
- Habitat and Settlement
- Environment and Ecology
- World Resources
- Oceans and Seabeds
- Atmosphere and Space
- Energy
- Science and Technology

- The Arts
- Communications and Information
- Transportation and Travel
- Multi-National Corporations
- Commerce and Industry
- Labor and Income
- Economic and Social Development
- Human Rights
- Distributive Justice
- Democratic Procedures
- World Service Corps
- World Territories Capitals and Parks
- Exterior Relations
- Revenue

An information sheet received from WCPA listed seven objectives and actions of the organization as follows:

1. WORLD GOVERNMENT: The comprehensive objective, to be achieved in progressive stages, is a *democratic, non-military, federal world government* which can solve world problems peacefully and administer those affairs which transcend national boundaries for the benefit of humanity everywhere.

The World Government will have a representative World Parliament to enact world legislation, with one chamber elected by the people; a World Executive responsible to the Parliament, with authority to implement world legislation directly; a World Judiciary with mandatory enforcement of decisions; and such other organs as are desirable and necessary for the adequate and effective solution of world problems and management of global affairs.

2. EARTH CONSTITUTION: To achieve a democratic World Government, the WCPA works for the ratification, or provisional ratification, of the *Constitution for the Federation of Earth*. Ratification is sought by national parliaments, national governments, local and state governments, universities and colleges, and by individuals and popular referendum. The Earth Constitution was prepared at two drafting sessions of a World Constituent Assembly, held in 1968 at Interlaken, Switzerland, and Wolfach, West Germany; and in 1977 at Innsbruck, Austria, with about 200 delegates from all continents; then reinforced at a third session at Colombo, Sri Lanka, in 1979.

3. PROVISIONAL WORLD PARLIAMENT: Until the Earth Constitution is ratified by at least 25 countries, the WCPA *helps to organize sessions of a Provisional World Parliament,* which is organized under the terms of Article 19 of the Constitution for the Federation of Earth.

The Provisional World Parliament has adopted eight world legislative measures to deal with major world problems, at its first two sessions which were held at Brighton, England, September, 1982, and at New Delhi, India, March, 1985. The third session is scheduled for Miami Beach, Florida, June, 1987. When the Earth Constitution is ratified by 25 countries, the Provisional Parliament will be supplanted by a fully functioning World Parliament elected and composed as specified in the Constitution for the Federation of Earth.

4. WORLD LEGISLATION: As part of the process of the emergence of World Government, the WCPA works for the ratification and step-by-step implementation of the world legislation enacted by the Provisional World Parliament, including:

Bill #1, to outlaw nuclear weapons and other weapons of mass destruction, and to establish a World Disarmament Agency.

Bill #2, for a World Economic Development Organization, which will establish a new global system of finance and credit, and help begin the "new world economic order."

Bill #3, for ownership, administration and development of the oceans and seabeds of Earth (from 20 km offshore) as the common heritage of the People of Earth.

*Opposite: Diagram of World Government under the Constitution for the Federation of Earth.*

Bill #4, for a Graduate School of World Problems, as part of a World University System.

Bill #5, for Provisional District World Courts.

Bill #6, for an Emergency Earth Rescue Administration to bring carbon dioxide levels under control, save the environment, and prevent universal starvation as a result of global climatic catastrophe.

Bill #7, for a World Government Funding Corporation, to finance the entire program.

Bill #8, for a World Commission on Terrorism.

And all World Legislation to be enacted by the Provisional World Parliament at subsequent sessions.

5. PROVISIONAL WORLD CABINET: As a further step towards an operating World Government, the Provisional World Parliament will inaugurate a Provisional World Cabinet at the next sessions of the Parliament. The Cabinet will be composed of continuing Cabinet Ministers and Commissions, and will be responsible for implementing, insofar as possible, the legislation of the Parliament.

The members of the Cabinet must be accredited delegates to the Parliament, and will in effect serve as a Provisional World Government, merging with the Cabinet of the eventual World Government under a ratified Constitution for the Federation of Earth.

6. WORLD CONSTITUENT ASSEMBLY: Prior to the final campaign for ratification of the Constitution for the Federation of Earth, another session of the World Constituent Assembly will be held, to go over the Earth Constitution, and make any amendments found necessary. It is proposed to hold the next session of the World Constituent Assembly when five countries have given provisional ratification to the Earth Constitution.

7. FUNDING: To carry out this total program, the wCPA seeks adequate funding of several billion dollars over the next few years, as provided under World Legislative Bill #7 for the World Government Funding Corporation.

Membership is open to individuals in all parts and countries of the world who agree to support the above objectives and programs of the World Constitution and Parliament Association.

In recent correspondence, Philip Isely (during his thirtieth year of leadership for wCPA) emphasized that although wCPA supports the following, they are independent from and not a part of the wCPA:

• The sessions of the World Constitution Convention and the World Constituent Assemblies.

• The Drafting Commission.

• The Constitution for the Federation of Earth.

• The sessions of the Provisional World Parliament.

• The legislative bills or acts of the Provisional World Parliament.

The *Calls* for a World Constitution Convention and the subsequent sessions of the World Constituent Assemblies came from those who signed the Calls, rather than from wCPA. A continuation drafting commission was authorized at the first session at Interlaken, Switzerland, and Wolfach, West Germany. As indicated above, work on the Constitution for the

Federation of Earth was begun at that time and continued in 1977 in Innsbruck, Austria, and reinforced in Colombo, Sri Lanka, in 1979.

The resulting World Constitution became the organizing agent for various activities which are carried forward in their own right. The WCPA works with and provides assistance and leadership for these activities, but as a separate worldwide membership organization.

For example, although the Provisional World Parliament was authorized by Article XIX of the Constitution for the Federation of Earth and is a separate entity from the WCPA, the latter helps to organize sessions of the Parliament at this stage of development.

Participation in the Provisional World Parliament is open to any person who adheres to the purposes of the Provisional World Parliament and who supports the Constitution for the Federation of Earth (although not necessarily in agreement with every detail).

While space limitations make it impossible to provide an adequate summary of the Constitution for the Federation of Earth in this publication, a few points of interest will be shared here. (Appendix F gives Articles XII and XIII in full. A complete copy of "A Constitution for the Federation of Earth" is available from WCPA by writing to the address shown in Appendix B.)

Article I lists the broad functions of the World Government. They are:

1. To prevent war, secure disarmament, and resolve territorial and other disputes which endanger peace and human rights.

2. To protect universal human rights, including life, liberty, security, democracy, and equal opportunities in life.

3. To obtain for all people on Earth the condition required for equitable economic and social development and for social and distributive justice.

4. To regulate world trade, communications, transportation, currency, standards, use of world resources, and other global and international processes.

5. To protect the environment and the ecological fabric of life from all sources of damage, and to control technological innovations whose effects transcend national boundaries, for the purpose of keeping Earth a safe, healthy and happy home for humanity.

6. To devise and implement solutions to all problems which are beyond the capacity of national governments, or which are now or may become of global or international concern or consequence.

Article II outlines the basic structure of the World Federation and World Government. (See chart on page 182.)

Article III outlines the specific powers granted to the World Government; and Article IV lists the organs of the World Government through which these powers will be exercised.

The next several articles go into detail on the functions and powers of the World Parliament (V); the World Executive (VI); the World Administration (VII); the Integrative Complex (VIII); the World Judiciary (IX); the Enforcement System (X); and the World Ombudsmus (XI).

Article XII provides a mandatory Bill of Rights for the Citizens of Earth; and Article XIII, Directive Principles for the World Government, provides a list of additional rights not yet universally realized or guaranteed to be considered for future legislation. (See Appendix F for full text of XII and XIII.)

Article XIV provides certain safeguards for all nations and peoples within the federation.

Article XV addresses World Federal Zones and World Capitals; and Article XVI pertains to world territories and exterior relations.

Article XVII outlines procedures for ratification and implementation; and Article XVIII provides for amendments to the World Constitution.

The final Article, XIX, outlines the operations of a Provisional World Government.

On the seventeenth anniversary of beginning work on the drafting of the Constitution for the Federation of Earth in the Town Hall of Wolfach, West Germany, a regional meeting of wcpa was held in the same Town Hall September 6-7, 1985. At this meeting was launched an Association of Cities, Towns and Communities for World Federation.

Another Regional Conference of wcpa was held in Pondicherry, India, October 11-13, 1985.

The Third Session of the Provisional World Parliament was held in Miami Beach, Florida, U.S.A., June 18-29, 1987. At this session, three additional legislative bills were adopted: Bill #9, for a World Environmental Protection Agency; Bill #10, for a World Hydrogen Energy System; and Bill #11, for a New Earth Financial Credit Corporation.

In addition, plans were developed for implementing World Legislative Bills one and six; and steps were taken to form a Provisional World Cabinet. Steps were also taken to give the Provisional World Parliament greater self-identity and continuity.

Two other events were held in conjunction with the Third Session of the Provisional World Parliament: an International Arts and Crafts Fair, and a World Problems Expo organized by the Earth Rescue Corp and the Graduate School of World Problems.

## World Peace Through Law Center

President Dwight D. Eisenhower, in his 1956 Law Day speech, warned us, "If civilization is to survive, it must choose the rule of law."

One of the important organizations in the movement to substitute world law and order for war is the World Peace Through Law Center, which was formed at a meeting in Athens, Greece, in 1963 to meet the needs of the world's legal community. Its ultimate goal is to ensure peace under law.

The WPTLC was the first worldwide venture to combine the efforts of judges, lawyers, law professors and others throughout the world into an effective, cooperative endeavor to mold a future legal order for humankind that would further world peace. It believes it can accomplish its goal by strengthening the world's legal system, both its laws and its legal institutions (such as the International Court of Justice), and by evaluating world law and developing new international machinery to provide for the peaceful settlement of disputes between nations under the rule of law.

The World Peace Through Law Center has a world president and four regional presidents for Africa, the Americas, Asia and Australia, and Europe. Members can concentrate within four sections: human rights, intellectual property, international legal education, or law and computer technology. Along with individual memberships, WPTLC includes four professional memberships: (1) the World Association of Judges, (2) the World Association of Lawyers, (3) the World Association of Law Professors, and (4) the World Association of Law Students.

The Center stages world conferences in major cities in different areas of the world every two years. Thus far, it has sponsored nine world conferences on four continents in Abidjan, Ivory Coast; Athens, Greece; Bangkok, Thailand; Belgrade, Yugoslavia; Geneva, Switzerland; Madrid, Spain; Manila, Philippines; and Washington, D.C. (twice).

The delegates (from over 100 countries each year) have compiled formal resolutions to help hasten the formation of international law. Some of the problems discussed have been hijacking, terrorism, rights of refugees, international protection of human rights, the role of the United Nations, expanding the jurisdiction of the International Court of Justice, the environment, copyrights, patents, regulation of dangerous drugs, urban development, and multinational businesses.

At four of these world conferences, the Center held demonstration trials to show the possibilities for resolving international disputes under the legal processes in the courts.

The Center has also done research on a number of projects, one of which was concerned with plans for the computerization of law internationally.

Pursuant to resolutions passed at the 1973 conference at Abidjan, the Center initiated a program seeking wider ratification and implementation of multilateral treaties and conventions. To that end, the Center's national chairpersons established a Treaty Acceptance Committee within each of their respective countries.

## American Movement for World Government

Although not incorporated until 1970, the American Movement for World Government, Inc., started to take shape in the 1950s, led by people who strongly agreed with the views of *Emery Reves* and the international leaders who endorsed his best-selling book, *The Anatomy of Peace*. This book about the causes of war and the need to build peace on a global level was written in 1945, just before the explosion of the first nuclear weapon used in war.

In his book, Reves pointed out that modern technology had made the concept of sovereign nation-states obsolete — and deadly dangerous. He believed the time had come to build a framework of international law which could be enforced by a world body. The following quotation from *The Anatomy of Peace* will help to clarify his stand:

> The question is not one of "surrendering" national sovereignty. The problem is not negative and does not involve giving up something we already have. The problem is positive — creating something we lack, something we never had, but that we imperatively need. . . .
>
> Democratic sovereignty of the people can be correctly expressed and effectively instituted only if local affairs are handled by local government, national affairs by national government, and international, world affairs, by international, world government. . . .

The AMWG seeks to educate the American public concerning the need for a democratic, federal world government created through a constitutional convention — or through a transformation of the United Nations into an effective world government. While it focuses on the need for a world federal government, it works with other peace and justice groups to establish a more just world order and to combat international anarchy.

To help accomplish its objectives, AMWG provides a speakers' bureau and educational services for peace groups, churches, and school systems. It maintains a *World Government Center,* and publishes a newspaper, *World Peace News — A World Government Report.* It also publishes booklets, monographs, fact sheets on world affairs and a bibliography on world government.

In addition, its *World Peace News* conducts annual World Government Seminars in New York City each May. Many world unity groups meet in New York in conjunction with these WPN World Government Seminars. For example, the World Government Organization Coalition plans an annual meeting in New York immediately following the seminar. (It was of interest to note that in 1984, the year the Soviets quit the Olympic games, they did send a senior advisor to the Fourteenth Annual World Government Seminar of WPN.)

An invitation to its Seventeenth Annual World Government Seminar in its January–March 1987 issue of WPN read, in part:

> Let's have a "Call to Meeting in the Case for Humanity." Let's ask wordwise folk to volunteer to be heard before a Grand Jury of the Court with Chief Justice Pierre Elliott Trudeau of Canada presiding.

Its World Government Center publishes a quarterly called *Peace Bulletin,* and its 1985 Summer issue included a short article entitled

# A DECLARATION OF
# *Interdependence*

As we survey our crowded planet—plundered, polluted, war-ravaged—we recognize the devastating effects of unbridled national sovereignty upon the "unalienable rights" of man.

The pursuit of happiness becomes ever more difficult, and international anarchy has placed the life and liberty of every man in constant jeopardy.

We, therefore, call for a new relationship among nations and for new world institutions to ensure the survival of man in a harmonious habitation of Earth. In so doing, we reaffirm the principles laid down by our founding fathers almost 200 years ago.

> "We hold these truths to be self-evident, that all men are created equal, that they are endowed by their Creator with certain unalienable Rights, that among these are Life, Liberty, and the pursuit of Happiness. — That to secure these Rights, Governments are instituted among Men deriving their just powers from the consent of the governed . . ."

**And furthermore:** That having partially secured these rights through government at the municipal, state, and national levels, it is now necessary to institute a *government for the world community to end war, to curb the lethal pollution and overpopulation of our planet, and to solve other problems affecting, to a vital degree, the rights and welfare of all mankind;*

**And that such a world government,** whether established through a transformation of the United Nations, a world constitutional convention, or other legal means, should be democratic and federal in form, thus preserving the diversity of human society and reserving, for the nations and their governments, jurisdiction over their own internal affairs.

**Toward these ends,** like our founding fathers before us, *"We mutually pledge to each other our lives, our fortunes, and our sacred honor."*

*The American Movement for World Government's "Declaration of Interdependence."*

**"Our History of Peace Building."** A direct quote from this article follows:

We have worked for over three decades to spread the idea of government on the world level, using the concepts formulated by Reves and by other writers and statespeople as the foundation of our work. As a membership organization, our intention has been to educate people to the possibilities for peace through world government, and to partake in and encourage the development of realistic and concrete proposals for construction of a world government.

We see world government as a mechanism to release power and freedom to those who are deprived of it, not as a focus of centralized control. We see it as a vehicle for the creation of international cooperation and law which would enhance and strengthen individual nation-states, and the governance of the planet in general.

This will not mean the end of identity for nations — as Golda Meir said, "Orchestras do not mean the end of violins" — it will mean their fulfillment as channels for the creative work and industries of mankind. It will mean the end of weapons spending which runs to a trillion dollars annually, and which Dwight Eisenhower called "a theft from those who hunger and are not fed, those who are cold and not clothed."

We make this point about peace.

As long as there are sovereign nations possessing great power, war is inevitable. No campaign for disarmament or for a build-up of weaponry will change that. Disarmament may well invite attack by a hostile power. And an arms build-up creates a state of hostility and instability in which any small flare-up can escalate into an all-out war. The only realistic hope for peace is in the creation of a world government, democratic and representative, which can guarantee basic freedom and liberties — including the right not to be a victim of war — to the world's citizens.

In August 1987, AMWG was one of 25 co-sponsors of an International Bicentennial Symposium on Strengthening the United Nations held in Philadelphia, Pennsylvania. At that historic event, the AMWG distributed a "Declaration of _Inter_dependence" (see page 189), and a brochure which stated:

Therefore, a federal world government must be established at the earliest possible moment by basic transformation of the UN or other reasonable means.

The brochure continued by listing ten *Essentials of a World Federal Government:*

1. A constitution with a Bill of Rights.
2. A popularly elected legislature to enact world laws.
3. A world court to interpret these laws, with compulsory jurisdiction over world disputes.
4. A civilian executive branch with the power to enforce world laws directly upon individuals.
5. A system of checks and balances to prevent the abuse of power by any branch of the world government.
6. The control of all weapons of mass destruction by the world government with the disarmament of all nations, under careful inspection, down to the level required for internal policing.
7. Carefully defined and limited power of taxation to support those

functions necessary to world peace and the solution of problems affecting, to a vital degree, the welfare of all mankind.

8. Reasonable provision for amendments to the constitution.

9. Participation in the world federal government to be open at all times to all nations without right of secession.

10. All power not expressly delegated to the world government to be reserved to the nations and their peoples, thus leaving each nation to choose its own political, social and economic system.

(See report on the World Federalist Association in this chapter for more information on the Symposium.)

## Planetary Citizens

Another organization which aims to help people acquire a global perspective is Planetary Citizens, Inc. It was formed in 1972 and incorporated in 1974 by *Norman Cousins,* former editor of *Saturday Review,* and *Dr. U Thant,* the former Secretary-General of the United Nations, as honorary Co-Chairman. It has registered several hundred thousand people from more than 60 countries as Planetary Citizens and, as indicated in the following pledge, it too supports the strengthening of the United Nations.

*Pledge of Planetary Citizenship*

I recognize my membership in the human community while I reaffirm my allegiance to my own community and nation. As a member of the planetary family, the good of the world is my first concern.

Therefore:

• I will work to end divisions and wars among people.
• I will work for realization of human rights—civil and political, economic, social, and cultural—for all people.
• I will work to bring the actions of the nations into conformity with the needs of the world community.
• I will work for the strengthening and improvement of the United Nations:
  • to give the UN the authority to act on behalf of the common will of humanity.
  • to curb the excesses of nations, and to meet the common global dangers and needs of the human family.

Under the leadership of Donald Keys, Planetary Citizens provides training for world service, intern programs, information networks via computers, a planetary "passport," public information, and opportunities for local activities.

Quoting from the Planetary Citizens' brochure:

Two great trends describe our times:

THE TREND TOWARDS A MEGA CRISIS OF GLOBAL DIMEN-
SIONS.

Deeply serious problems in areas of peace, employment and poverty,
health, environment and resources, economy and human rights are in-
teracting and reinforcing each other. They are creating a mega crisis
which threatens to peak and involve our survival in these next few years.
This trend is dangerous, obvious and visible.

THE TREND TOWARDS A GENERAL SHIFT IN CONSCIOUS-
NESS.

This trend contains the hope for a brighter future. It has inner and
outer dimensions. It involves:

• A new sense of our own deep connections to the source of life
itself, by whatever name it is known.

• An end to the sense of separateness that has dominated human
affairs.

• A shift to Planetary Consciousness and a commitment to global
community.

• A new way of relating to the living planet itself, which provides
and sustains all life-support systems.

Taken together, these two trends indicate our crisis *and* opportunity.

The *crisis* is now self-evident; it can mean the end of life on earth.

The *opportunity:*

• Involves the growing up of humanity into fully self-aware global
species assuming planetary stewardship.

• Involves the founding of the world civilization made possible and
necessary by the travel, communication and information revolutions.

• Requires a new way of cooperatively caring for the renewable and
finite resources of the planet, its plants and animals, land and water,
gases and minerals. Planetary Citizens brings to public awareness our unprecedented state of affairs, so we can respond together to the challenge.

In an open letter addressed to "Friends of peace and the planet,"
Donald Keys, President of Planetary Citizens, pointed out the folly of seeking peace by preparing for war that may indeed end all wars. He wrote
that

peace through threat creates an atmosphere of war, sowing suspicion,
distrust and fear. We expect the worst of others, they do the same, and
tensions build to an incendiary pitch. This is called a self fulfilling
prophecy.

He compares our current global situation with the lawless days of the
American Wild West. When people got tired of lawlessness they finally
established town councils, courts, judges, and sheriffs to maintain law and
order. Now it's time for law-abiding nations to insist on a global structure

to provide security and protection from nations still "trying to have their own way at the expense of others."

In commenting on the League of Nations and the United Nations, Mr. Keys wrote:

> Twice after horrible wars, nations have met and solemnly set up processes for the keeping of the peace; and twice they have failed to honor their own efforts. The League of Nations and the United Nations have been gestures rather than serious commitments where most great powers are concerned, and wistful hopes for the rest.

His letter goes on to point out that, although political leaders and generals are still thinking of national security in terms of massive armies and armaments, the advent of nuclear weapons really meant the end of national security. "No nation can ever again provide convincingly for its own security."

Planetary Citizens, Inc., announced that its major program thrust for 1985 would be the *Search for Security Alternatives,* and it listed the following basic requirements for peace and security in a global and nuclear age:

> 1. A NEW CONSCIOUSNESS. The acceptance of our planetary citizenship, of our global community. With that acceptance the unfoldment of a sense of *belonging* and identification with that community can follow — a necessary basis for our working together.
>
> 2. A NEW RECOGNITION. The recognition of the indivisibility of peace and security. They are no longer national functions. They are functions of the community as a whole. This is not theoretical: as we see daily, nations cannot do the job. No nation or group of nations is entitled to, or, as a practical matter, can play policeman for the world.
>
> 3. A NEW APPROACH TO GLOBAL PEACE AND SECURITY. A common and concerted Search for Security Alternatives by nations and their peoples is an invitation to join a mutual effort. It is not threatening. It can remove the fear and bickering surrounding the numbers game of the arms race. It can set a positive goal instead, for defining and implementing security on a global basis — the goal of creating the conditions under which disarmament and peace become thinkable and realizable, which today they are not.
>
> 4. EMPOWERING THE INSTITUTIONS OF PEACE. The United Nations is charged with "Maintenance of International Peace and Security." Yet, realistically, it lacks the means to do so. Why? Fundamentally, because nations have been unwilling to acknowledge their situation of helplessness and to join together to redefine the problem. They, particularly a few major States, reserved to themselves the right to do as they please when they designed the UN. In a unitary and nuclear world that is no longer possible without mutual destruction.
>
> These requirements are a package. They will not work separately and yet, we must also continue to respond to moment-by-moment crises.

In 1985, at the time of the United Nation's Fortieth Anniversary General Assembly, a group of experts in the fields of peacekeeping, peacemaking, military strategy, disarmament, and surveillance was called together by Donald Keys. This distinguished group, with members from several countries, decided to form an *Independent Commission on World Security* to study and discuss alternative security systems and prepare a major report in two parts: (1) The Problem of Mutual Insecurity, and (2) Alternative Approaches to Mutual Security.

After meeting again in March, July, and November of 1986, the Commission enthusiastically concluded:

> The goal of achieving world security is best thought of in terms of three staged goals, to be achieved sequentially. These are:
>
> I. *Transnational Security*. This goal recognizes that the world is not yet ready for the kind of transnational authority that could indeed result in world security, but sees within this constraint a number of policy directions that could reduce the likelihood of major war, especially nuclear war.
>
> II. *An Unarmed World*. This is the goal of mutual security, jointly designed and supported. It includes the delegitimation of preparation for armed conflict as an element of national policy, and assumes that an effective global peacekeeping can be achieved.
>
> III. *A Secure World*. This goal describes the state in which people everywhere can feel secure in that their basic human rights are consensually defined and mutually guaranteed.

The Commission also agreed upon the following phases in addressing four key tasks:

A. *Transforming the arms system:*
Shifting in defensive emphasis.
Reducing arms levels.
Implementing an effective peacekeeping function.

B. *Building trust and openness:*
Instituting accountability for security measures.
Adopting measures to insure openness.
Implementing adequate verification procedures.

C. *Building a peace structure:*
Developing appropriate norms and laws.
Growing the necessary institutions.
Implementing effective peacemaking and conflict resolution procedures.

D. *Building global community:*
Gaining consensus on, and implementing, guarantees of universal human rights.
Making progress on human and cultural development.
Developing awareness of the common heritage of all humans.
Protecting and honoring cultural diversity.
Preserving quality of environment; protecting planetary life-support processes; taking care of the Earth.

The Independent Commission completed its report entitled *Transition to World Security* in 1987, and it plans to continue working with Planetary Citizens (1) to have an expanded meeting of experts consider the *Report* in the fall of 1987; (2) to secure endorsement of the *Report* by world leaders; and (3) to provide broad public dissemination of the *Report* to the world's political leaders, to those working in the fields of peace and disarmament, to leaders of the media, and most important of all, to the public at large.

Due to the timing of its release, the Commission's report on *Transition to World Security* can be crucially important. As stated by President Keys of Planetary Citizens:

> Governments, but even more, people, need a vision and a goal. They need to see that peace is practicably realizable, and they need to understand what must be done in order to achieve it.

In August 1987, Planetary Citizens was one of 25 co-sponsors of an International Bicentennial Symposium on Strengthening the United Nations held in Philadelphia, Pennsylvania. (For more information on the symposium, see the section for The World Federalist Association in this chapter.)

## Campaign for UN Reform

The *St. Louis Post-Dispatch* of November 3, 1982, included an editorial by Eric Cox, Legislative Director of the Campaign for UN Reform. Its headline read "IT CAN BUT WON'T, UN Could Assure Peace, But Nations Disregard It." Mr. Cox reminds us that the UN Charter permits procedures which could assure a "peaceful planet." He adds, "Nations, however, ignore those provisions, frequently guided by narrow nationalistic considerations. The United States and the Soviet Union are among the worst offenders." He says the United Nations "wants to but can't" because it lacks the funding, structure, and authority to guarantee "an orderly and safe world." Large nations, including those with permanent seats on the Security Council, have prevented establishment of structures to prevent the "scourge of war."

Polls by Gallup, Roper, and others all show the electorate would like to see the United States take a leadership role in improving the United Nations to enable it to assure world peace.

Many are concerned about the future of the United Nations and are doing everything they can to keep it from "going the way of the League of Nations." One group strongly committed to saving the United Nations is the Campaign for UN Reform, founded in 1975 as an offshoot of the World Federalist Association. It proposed fourteen needed reforms. The first six were designed to remedy deficiencies in the World's legal system. They were:

1. Increase use of International Court. Broaden Court's advisory opinion powers; convince more national governments to submit to Court's jurisdiction without self-judging reservations.

2. Improve dispute settlement ability. Create professional UN Mediation Service and panels of arbitrators to make nonbinding and binding recommendations on global disputes.

3. Create an international criminal court. Bolster global law and order by creating a world criminal court to try accused violators of international treaties against hijacking, taking hostages, and crimes against diplomats.

4. Improve peacekeeping capacity of UN. Establish standing UN peace force called for by the Charter, and a strong, well-trained peacekeeping reserve composed of earmarked national contingents.

5. Create an international disarmament organization to verify, spur arms agreements. Set up UN Disarmament Organization to verify compliance with arms reduction through international satellite surveillance, on-site inspections.

6. Modify veto on enforcement of international court decisions. Make it impossible for a party to a dispute to have the right to veto in the Security Council, enforcement of an ICJ decision against that party.

The Campaign for UN Reform also recommended eight additional reforms needed to obtain world order and justice. These were:

7. Establish an international ocean authority. Avoid anarchy on the high seas by ratifying the Law of the Sea Treaty that provides a legal framework for deep seabed mining and creates an international Ocean Authority to protect the marine environment.

8. Strengthen UN environment program. Establish firm guidelines for the environment to prevent cross-border pollution and avoid conflict between nations — for example, the controversy between Canada and the United States over acid rain. Enforcement and arbitration procedures should also be set up to gain compliance and settle disputes.

9. Create UN global resources program. Promote global conservation of resources by creating a UN Global Resources Agency to monitor the depletion of nonrenewable resources and recommend guidelines for their conservation.

10. Provide more effective human rights machinery. Set up an effective system of law in order to provide justice. Oppressed individuals could be better protected if the position of UN High Commissioner for Human Rights were created to investigate complaints and help rectify conditions on an on-going basis. In addition, a Court of Human Rights, modeled after the European Court of Human Rights, should be established to render decisions when necessary.

11. Improve voting system of the general assembly. An equitable General Assembly voting structure would provide a more viable decision-making process. The admission of numerous mini-states since the UN's creation in 1945 has made the original one-nation, one-vote system in-

equitable. A weighted voting system based on population, financial contributions to the UN, and national statehood, combined with binding decision-making powers, could transform the Assembly into a more responsible body capable of coping with global problems.

12. Improve UN development program. This program can be improved by consolidating all developing activities under a single UN Development Authority, and reorganization of the work of the Economic and Social Council to ensure better coordination and more coherent research, analysis, and policy planning. It will be extremely difficult to keep the world at peace if huge disparities continue to exist between rich and poor nations. A viable world legal system will have to include a measure of economic justice for all.

13. Make trade and monetary system more effective. More effective trade and monetary systems are the keys to our planet's economic health. Today, more than ever, protectionist policies are threatening our global economy. We need an International Common Fund to moderate: (1) commodity price fluctuations, (2) implementation of UNICEF proposals for making the international trading system more responsive to the needs of less developed countries, and (3) regional monetary networks and a centralized international credit reserve system.

14. Stabilize United Nations financing. UN peacekeeping operations have faced continual financial crises because of the refusal of some countries to pay their assessments. We must not allow important UN functions to be governed by the shortsighted policies of some nations. Instead, a special commission should be set up to recommend possible sources of revenue to supplement national assessments and voluntary contributions, and a special peacekeeping fund should be created.

In 1984, Franklin Stark, President of the Campaign for UN Reform, and his wife, Carolyn Kaiser Stark, took off in their camper and traveled throughout the United States spreading their message:

> Humankind is entitled to security. In the past, war has been an effective security system and the winners got something — territory, trade markets, etc. With the advent of nuclear weapons, no one wins anything, and our national government can no longer guarantee us security. It is time to use law and order at the global level to provide the same security it now provides us at the city, state and national levels. It is time to use courts with enforcement powers to settle disputes that can no longer be settled by going to war in this nuclear age. A strengthened, restructured UN system can provide this security. Our nation should be the nation to lead the way — the people of the United States must *demand* that their elected representatives stand for global law and order.

At the 1987 National Convention of the Campaign for UN Reform held in St. Louis, Missouri, May 29–30 under the leadership of President Stark and its Executive Vice President Walter Huffman, the original fourteen-point program for reforming and restructuring the United Nations

System was reviewed and revised. Except for combining the original points eight and nine pertaining to environment and conservation under the new point ten and the addition of a new point concerning administrative reform, the basic set of reforms as outlined above has been retained. However, their headings have been clarified, they are now presented in a revised order, and the explanations for each have been expanded in more detail. The new order and headings of the revised fourteen-point program are as follows:

1. Improved General Assembly Decision-making
2. Modification of the Veto in the Security Council
3. An International Disarmament Organization
4. Better Dispute Settlement Procedures
5. Improving the U.N.'s Peacekeeping Capability
6. Adequate and Stable U.N. Revenues
7. Increasing the Use of the International Court of Justice
8. An International Criminal Court to Try Hijackers and Terrorists
9. Improving the U.N.'s Human Rights Machinery
10. Stronger U.N. Environmental and Conservation Programs
11. International Authorities for Areas Not Under National Control
12. More Effective World Trade and Monetary Systems
13. A Consolidated U.N. Development Program
14. Administrative Reform of the U.N. System

Full texts under each of the new headings, including a statement of need for change and the proposal(s) of the Campaign, may be obtained by writing to the Campaign for UN Reform at the address shown in Appendix B.

The proponents of these reforms are quick to remind us that the UN is already providing global order and coordination in many fields of endeavor through its family of international specialized agencies. (See listing in the section on the United Nations in Chapter 1.)

In reviewing materials from the World Citizens Assembly and the World Government Organization Coalition, it was of interest to note that they both recommended the establishment of a Peoples' Assembly in the United Nations with delegates elected and responsible to the peoples of the world (along with the General Assembly, which represents nations).

Although the Campaign for UN Reform has been impeded by lethargic bureaucracies and fear of losing national sovereignty, it has continued to be involved in political action in party conventions and in congress.

In August 1987, the Campaign for UN Reform was one of 25 cosponsors of an International Bicentennial Symposium on Strengthening the United Nations held in Philadelphia, Pennsylvania. (See section on the World Federalist Association in this chapter for more information on the symposium.)

# World Citizens Assembly

Many individuals and organizations have proposed giving the peoples of the world more voice in foreign affairs and in determining war and peace issues. Again quoting President Dwight D. Eisenhower:

> People in the long run are going to do more to promote peace than are governments. Indeed, I think that people want peace so much that one of these days governments are going to have to get out of their way and let them have it.

One organization which is emphasizing a grass-roots peoples' approach to world peace is the World Citizens Assembly. It was first convened in 1975 in San Francisco on the thirtieth anniversary of the United Nations. At that assembly, 500 individuals from 22 nations resolved to combine their efforts, form a movement to unite the people of the world, elect delegates to a world assembly, and help achieve permanent peace through a democratic people-to-people political system of global dimension. Regional assemblies were held the following year in Europe, Asia, and Central America. In 1977, the Second World Citizens Assembly was convened in Innsbruck, Austria, and Paris, France. The third was held in Japan in 1980, and the fourth in Los Angeles in 1984.

The 1984 World Citizens Assembly initiated a global effort to urge endorsement, in the Fortieth Assembly Preparation Committee within the UN General Assembly, of WCA's previously submitted proposal for an *Ongoing Global Ceasefire* (truce to all wars) to begin on October 24, 1985, (Fortieth Anniversary of the UN).

In June 1985, The World Citizens Assembly held its biggest public event at the Golden Gate Bandshell in San Francisco to celebrate the fortieth anniversary of the signing of the UN Charter and the tenth anniversary of the founding of the World Citizens Assembly. The celebration included a Human Rights Cantata with choir and orchestra, inspirational talks by Robert Muller, Assistant Secretary-General to the U.N., and Ed Asner of TV fame, and a children's choir singing "We Are the World," an anthem of world citizenship.

The WCA's project of creating a second "people's" house in the United Nations was begun at this 1985 meeting and has continued to be one of its major goals. Two other major thrusts are its "Let's Abolish War" (L.A.W.) Campaign and its Peace and Environment Project.

The *Let's Abolish War Campaign,* begun in 1984, is underway in cooperation with other groups of the World Government Organization Coalition to promote the acceptance of world law and order in place of war for settling disputes among nations. (See the World Government Organization Coalition in this chapter for the Let's Abolish War brochure.)

The intent of WCA's *Peace and Environment Project* is to move from the arms race (a no-win situation) to an environmental recovery race (an

## APPLICATION FOR WORLD CITIZENSHIP

I hereby apply for registration as world's citizen because I recognize my responsibility to the world community and wish to add this additional degree of citizenship to my present nationality.

NAME _____

Last                    First                    Initial

ADDRESS _____

Street                  City                     State/Country

BIRTHPLACE (optional) _____ Age (optional) _____

Enclose $8.00 as the registration fee for your world citizen identity card in English, French, German, Spanish, Esperanto (underline one). The registration fee includes a one year subscription to the *WORLD CITIZEN* newspaper. Mail to World Citizens International Registry (U.S. Center), 312 Sutter Street, Room 506, San Francisco, California 94108.

World Citizenship is a new dimension in individual responsibility which is essentially global and does not legally affect national citizenship.

all-win situation). The project is a continuation of the efforts begun by the Peace and Environment Convention Coalition of 1984, in which over 80 groups participated. The following statements appear in WCA's Peace and Environment Project brochure:

> The twin thrusts of war and environmental deterioration make it imperative to shift from the old concept of national security through a global arms race to ORGANIC SECURITY through the building of a healthy and sustainable environment. . . .
> Current data indicate that the global situation is rapidly deteriorating. Our institutions and social impulses are still dominated by violent means of conflict resolution. These obsolete methods now consume so much of our national resources and human effort that they undermine our ability to provide a vital economy, jobs, and healthy food, water, air, forests — ORGANIC SECURITY. In the words of the highly respected Worldwatch Institute:
>> The choices are between continued militarization of the economy, and [the] restoration of its environmental support systems. . . . The world does not have the financial resources and leadership time and attention to [both] militarize and to deal with these new threats to security.

The WCA has an Executive Committee of three to five people elected from each of six geographic regions: North America, South America, Europe, Africa, South Asia, and "Pacifica" (Japan to Australia).

World Citizen Centers have been located in homes, schools, offices, buildings, and estates where world citizens can come together, obtain literature and information, and with like-minded people, initiate, develop, and administer projects and programs "to build a world community." Activities are often focused on stopping the arms race, meeting basic human needs and preserving the environment, educating for world citizenship, developing people-oriented global institutions, and cooperating with other groups for human rights and world community.

Individuals are encouraged to adopt the attitude of world citizens that "We are one humanity; the earth is our home and common heritage, and we are its trustees. No wars are acceptable on our planet." They can register as world citizens (see application form on page 200), and they can then proclaim their world citizenship in various ways. They are urged to study WCA literature and programs and discuss them with friends. World Citizens are also encouraged to become involved in:

- Activities for disarmament.
- Celebrating world holidays such as Earth Day, Life Day, and Truce Day.
- Encouraging a global perspective in education at all levels.
- Promoting the development of a Peoples' Assembly at the UN, the Provisional World Parliament, the World Court at the Hague, etc.

*Opposite: The WCA application for World Citizenship.*

• Helping to provide for the next regional and world assemblies.

The World Citizens Assembly used a full-page display in its Winter 1985 issue of its newspaper, *World Citizen,* to recognize the Fortieth Anniversary of the United Nations. It read:

> The United Nations at 40! Still the best hope for humankind! In our divided and violent world, in which a myopic nationalism is so dangerously on the rise, the United Nations remains the one global symbol of hope and vision for the future. The universal membership of this world organization, in which every country on the globe is represented, is one of the great milestones in history, and the first step toward building the world community on which the future of humanity depends.
>
> The *World Citizen* urges people in every community to commemorate the 40th Anniversary of the United Nations by forming discussion and activist groups to explore the future role of this world organization, particularly the next 15 years leading to the 21st century. This would include how the United Nations can be more effectively supported, strengthened, and structured to achieve resolution of the critical global problems we face. Involvement in this next crucial step in civilization is the greatest gift any of us can give to the future.

A *World Citizens Foundation* accepts tax-deductible contributions to help fund the activities of the World Citizens Assembly.

## Federalist Caucus

The Federalist Caucus started as a special project of the World Federalist Political Education Committee in 1976; in 1980, the UN Reform Electoral Campaign Committee became a sponsor, thus making it a project of the Campaign for UN Reform. However, in 1983, the Federalist Caucus became an autonomous transnational organization that provides an ongoing political action and information service (for a nominal one-time fee) for all voters seeking a more just and humane world order. Under the leadership of Elizabeth (Betsy) Dana, it continues to serve and maintain close working relationships with the World Federalists, the Campaign for UN Reform, the Parliamentarians Global Action, and the Arms Control and Foreign Policy Caucus within the United States Congress; and it helps to keep its members in touch with these organizations.

Its brochure states that "The purpose of the Federalist Caucus is to facilitate the process of moving beyond the war system toward a system of law and global governance," and that the following methods are used to reach that goal:

• Annually conveying to congressmen in Parliamentarians GLOBAL ACTION and the Arms Control and Foreign Policy Caucus the general philosophic and political support of Caucus members.

• Annually informing each Caucus member about progress being made by these legislative groups and, if desired, by leading citizens' groups engaging in peace research, adult and curricular education on world order, related lobbying, and electoral support of like-minded candidates for Congress.

• Enhancing the peace efforts of numerous other groups, by enabling their members to become part of this political constituency without having to pay additional fees annually, or spend additional time on organizational matters at the local level.

• Suggesting ways to inject discussions of global issues into electoral campaigns at all levels, thus increasing the understanding by the general public of the nature of the problems that confront us all.

Enrollment in the Federalist Caucus is open to any person who subscribes to its Statement of Beliefs and is eligible to vote in the national elections of his or her country. The *Statement of Beliefs* follows:

I BELIEVE:
• In the essential interrelatedness of all humanity and of the Earth's environment on which we all depend.

• That the quality of life is seriously impaired, and the future of humanity gravely threatened, by the ever-increasing danger of nuclear war, pollution of the environment, depletion of natural resources, economic and social injustices, and infringements upon basic human and political rights.

• That such world-wide problems can be adequately met only through world institutions.

• That the United Nations and its related agencies have made important contributions toward the solution of such problems, but that they still lack effective means to cope with their huge tasks.

• That just and democratic world law is required to be applied to persons as well as to the governments of nation-states.

• That each nation's sovereignty with regard to its internal affairs must be respected; and

• That the people and leaders of nations with broadly representative systems of government have a special responsibility to support and promote the universality of the principles by which such freedom has been attained.

In September of 1986, the Federalist Caucus published its tenth annual report on the work of Parliamentarians Global Action, the Arms Control and Foreign Policy Caucus of the United States Congress, and the Campaign for UN Reform, including its endorsements of congressional candidates.

## World Government Organization Coalition

With over 20 organizations devoted to the creation of a "democratic federal world government," the World Government Organization Coordinating Council (wGO-CC) was formed in 1977 in order to promote cooperation and coordination of efforts toward common goals. In 1987, the name of the organization was changed to World Government Organization *Coalition* (WGOC) to better describe its evolving role.

The members of the World Government Organization Coalition are as follows:

(As of September 1, 1987)

*Headquartered within the U.S.A.*
Academy of World Studies
American Movement for World Government
Association to Unite the Democracies
Campaign for World Government
Federalist Caucus, Inc.
Globe — Lit
One World Movement
Peoples' Assembly
World Citizens Assembly
World Constitution and Parliament Association
World Federalist Association
World Peace News — newspaper

*Headquartered in Other Countries*
Canadian Peace Research Institute (Canada)
Peoples' Congress (France)
Transnational Perspectives — magazine (Switzerland)
World Association for World Federation (Netherlands)
World Federal Authority Committee (Canada)
World Federalists of Canada (Canada)
World Federalists — Indian Edition (India)

Representatives of these organizations have been meeting two or three times a year since 1977, usually in conjunction with a major world unity event. While their styles, strategies, and resources differ widely, a general agreement has been reached concerning top priorities for collective efforts. These include organized political action wherever possible; judicial action based on existing world laws prohibiting weapons of mass destruction; and outreach to peace, environment, and youth groups.

In 1984, members of the WGO-CC met together on four occasions: (1) at the World Future Society in Washington, D.C., in June; (2) at the Global Security Conference in San Francisco (before that year's Democratic Convention); (3) at La Lambertie in France during the People's Congress; and (4) at the World Citizens Assembly in Los Angeles (before the Twenty-Third Olympics).

Actions taken at these meetings included:

• The establishment of a quarterly newsletter.

• Agreement that WGO-CC members concentrate on the abolition of war as their focus. Slogans such as "Abolish War by '94," "Let's Abolish

*Opposite: A page from the Let's Abolish War (L.A.W.) brochure.*

- War is an ineffective, unjust and obsolete method of settling disputes.

- War today can cause massive, irreversible devastation to all the earth.

- The arms race alone consumes the resources needed to restore a liveable environment.

- The survival of life, liberty and all human values now depends on the total abolition of war.

- War **can** be abolished in this century just as slavery was abolished in the last.

## THIS PROJECT WILL

- promote realization of the inter-dependence of peace and environment issues and the need for **total** abolition of war,

- unite peace and environment groups in preparing platform recommendations for national political debates,

- promote development of the civilized alter-natives to war, namely, enforceable world law, courts and a democratic fedral world government.

L·A·W· — the civilized alternative

## HOW?

- By jointly using the slogan, "**Let's Abolish War.**" While variations may be employed, L.A.W. spells the constructive alternative, which has already abolished war at local and national levels.

- By reaching out to the general public through various media including publications, theatre, radio, television, billboards, etc.

- By using a working kit of materials which has been developed, including a "**Let's Abolish War**" book and buttons, posters with quotes from famous people, instructions on how to organize home meetings and a list of other resources. (See reponse form.)

- By expanding energy, organization and funding until the political clout is achieved to transfer funds from the arms race (a no-win situation) to an environmental recovery race (an all-win situation).

## WHEN?

**Right now!** The logic of taking the next step to a federal world government can be dramatized in the context of the 200th anniversary of the U.S. Constitution which changed the U.S. from a Confederacy (like the U.N. today) into a federation of states with the power to act "for the common security", which now means all humanity.

Upcoming elections — local, regional or national — offer opportunities to present a peace and environment platform.

By the year 2000. As slavery was abolished in the 19th century and other evils before it, war must now be abolished before it abolishes life on earth.

## WHO?

Abolition of war is a goal of the World Federalist movement in the U.S.A. and Canada, of the World Citizens Assembly, the Campaign for U.N. Reform and a growing number of non-governmental organizations.

It is also included in the collective platform of the Peace and Environment Coalition (of about 100 groups) for national election campaigns.

Contacts for the "**Let's Abolish War**" project are:

In U.S.A.    Dr. Lucile Green
             c/o World Citizens Assembly
             312 Sutter Street, Suite 506
             San Francisco, CA 94108

             Capt. Tom Hudgens
             43 Sunset Drive
             Englewood, Colorado 80110

In Canada    Ross Smyth
             8965 Tolhurst Street
             Montreal, Quebec H2N 1W9

In the words of General Dwight Eisenhower, "The world no longer has a choice between force and law; if civilization is to survive, it must choose the rule of law."

**L.A.W. by 2000!**

*From the Let's Abolish War (L.A.W.) brochure.*

War (L.A.W.)," and "Abolish War by the Year 2001" were suggested to reach the disarmament and "freeze" groups with the message of world law and government as the civilized substitute for war.

- Establishment of a WGO-CC Task Force to implement the Abolish War Campaign.

- Agreement to improve communications and coordination with European groups through: distribution of press bulletins, participation in each other's events by members of the World Council of Mondialized Cities, and sharing news and periodicals.

- Initiating a drive to establish a Peoples' Assembly in the United Nations (a second assembly along with the General Assembly, which represents nations). This UN Second (People's) Assembly would include non-governmental persons from many walks of life who would be charged with a global loyalty in undertaking their UN responsibilities.

• Endorsement of the platform proposed (for the Peace and Environment Coalition) to shift emphasis from the arms race to a global recovery race (from an "all-lose" to an "all-win" strategy).

In 1985, WGO leaders met for various events in Asia, Europe, and North America. (See WCPA section in this chapter re: the second session of the Provisional World Parliament held in New Delhi.)

Committees were formed to follow up on the Habicht Initiative for a constituent assembly of governments for drafting a Constitution for a World Federation, and the "Six-Nation Initiative" organized by the Parliamentarians for World Order (now Parliamentarians GLOBAL ACTION, covered in this chapter).

Along with several other agenda items, the WGO-CC made plans for observing the Fortieth Anniversary of the UN and the 1987 Two-hundredth Anniversary of the United States Constitution.

The World Federalists of Canada agreed to approach religious and other community leaders, urging them to organize a highly visible abolish-war campaign.

A suggestion received from England was to broaden the slogan to read "Abolish War and Feed the Hungry."

In her July 1985 report to members of the WGO-CC, Lucile Green stated:

> It seems to me that our movement is honing in on the most critical, life-and-death issues of our times: abolition of war and restoration of a livable environment: that these two are interdependent (the cost of restoring the environment would be roughly equivalent to the cost of the arms race by the year 2000): and that both require the replacement of anarchy by enforceable world law and global institutions representing the common good over national and other special interests.

At a "summit" meeting of WGO-CC in Milwaukee, Wisconsin, on September 12, 1986, a working draft of the proposed brochure for the "Let's Abolish War" (L.A.W.) campaign was distributed for final feedback and suggestions. (See pages 205–206.) This brochure is a good example of a joint effort coordinated by the Council. It was designed so each organization could insert its own return address.

Other business at the Milwaukee meeting included agreement that WGO-CC should co-sponsor the Bicentennial Symposium on the United States Constitution in Philadelphia, August 6–9, 1987, being planned by the World Federalist Movement and the Common Heritage Institute of Villanova University.

In a November 8, 1986, memorandum to representatives for the Council, Lucile Green recommended, "We can put our collective support behind the Federalists' legal actions in U.S.A. and Canada, behind the "Let's Abolish War" (L.A.W.) campaign, and the Second House in the UN, and think about a permanent 'world citizen' assembly of our collective memberships — plus — in New York."

In the April 1987 issue of *World Peace News,* Dr. Green called attention to four important events scheduled in 1987 for world unity groups at which informal wgoc caucuses or full meetings would be held:

• World Federalist Association national meeting in Tucson on March 13.

• The Seventeenth Annual World Government Seminar sponsored by the *World Peace News — A World Government Report,* May 9.

• The third session of the Provisional World Parliament facilitated by the World Constitution and Parliament Association in Miami Beach, June 18–28.

• United States Constitution Bicentennial events in Philadelphia sponsored by the World Federalist Movement, August 6–13.

Dr. Green further stated that she planned to propose holding annual assemblies "of all globally-minded citizens" in New York coinciding with sessions of the United Nations and with the Parliamentarians for GLOBAL ACTION. The purpose would be "to develop an agenda and priorities for people working for a democratic, federal world community." The hope is that "out of discussions would come means for increasing cooperation and, thereby, the influence of globally-minded citizens, organizations and coalitions."

## Parliamentarians GLOBAL ACTION

Parliamentarians GLOBAL ACTION (GLOBAL ACTION) is a shortened title for *Parliamentarians GLOBAL ACTION for Disarmament, Development, and World Reform.* It is an international group of legislators (members of a congress or a parliament) working together on disarmament, development, and the strengthening of global institutions.

Although a number of parliamentarian groups were formed in the mid-1940s, they languished during the 1960s and 1970s until they were brought together into a world association through the leadership of *Nicholas Dunlop.* Members of former groups were joined by parliamentarians from new nations (former colonies), and they founded the Parliamentarians for World Order (pwo) in 1980. The change to its current name was made in 1986. GLOBAL ACTION now has over 600 members from 36 countries with headquarters in New York City, where Mr. Dunlop continues to serve as its Secretary-General.

As key politicians from different political parties, its members command unique access to every level of politics and diplomacy, from the upper echelons of government to the grass-roots.

Also, as an action network of individual parliamentarians, GLOBAL ACTION has the ability to coordinate simultaneous legislative action on a global scale, such as its 1983 *Call for Global Survival,* a document endorsed by over 1,000 MPs (members of parliaments) in more than 55 countries including deputies from the U.S.S.R. That document read as follows:

### A Call for Global Survival

This statement is being circulated for signature to parliamentarians around the globe. The Call has already been signed by over a thousand parliamentarians in more than 55 national legislatures.

As members of parliament from every continent, we are speaking with one voice to convey an urgent and pressing message to the leaders of every national government.

The security of the whole planet is threatened by an arms race that knows no parallel in human history. The existence of fifty thousand nuclear weapons with the destructive power of one million Hiroshima bombs can lead only to global catastrophe. And yet the build-up of nuclear arsenals continues.

Vast resources of money and skills are diverted into disarmaments, while eight hundred million people live in absolute poverty. This situation is unjust and dangerous.

There is a widespread feeling that the world is drifting towards nuclear war, which could begin through miscalculation, accident or terrorism. We are raising our voices together to warn that humanity today is launched on a disaster course.

We therefore make this call for global survival.

We call upon the nuclear powers to seek a temporary freeze by all nations on the testing, production and deployment of nuclear weapons and delivery systems, pending a genuine reduction in nuclear arsenals. Such a freeze is a concrete, practical step which can be taken now, without delay. We believe that, with massive overkill, each side has more than enough nuclear weapons for any rational deterrence.

A nuclear freeze must be only a first step. As long as the threat of war itself continues, so will the threat of nuclear holocaust. We declare that the security of our citizens requires nothing less than general disarmament under a reliable global security system.

We therefore call for negotiations on a world treaty for simultaneous, balanced, verifiable and enforceable disarmament, which must include:

> disarmament by all nations to the level of arms required for internal security;

> an international inspection organization able to monitor disarmament, using both satellites and on-site inspection;

> a world peace force able to enforce disarmament and prevent international aggression, the members of which should be individually recruited;

> an effective system of world courts and arbitration tribunals;

> a world development fund through which a fixed proportion of the resources made available through disarmament will be devoted to development in the poorest nations.

We commit ourselves to this task.

We recognize that the chief obstacle to disarmament and development is not technical difficulty but a lack of political will. On behalf of the millions we represent, we affirm our political will.

We make this appeal on behalf of our constituents who, whatever their culture, whatever their ideology, whatever their nationality, share one desire: the desire for life.

The *Call* and a companion piece, *An Action Programme for World Security,* 1983, were presented to Soviet and American leaders at the Kremlin and the White House in personal discussions. Parliamentary resolutions based on the *Call* have been introduced by members into parliaments around the world, e.g., the United States Congress, the New Zealand Parliament, and the Parliament of Iceland.

Especially notable PWO activities in 1984 included:

• Its sponsorship of a Parliamentary Forum at the U.N. on the theme of *Global Militarization versus Economic Development.*

• Its conference in Rome on *Hunger.*

• Its sponsorship of another U.N. Forum on *The U.N. at Forty: Crisis and Opportunity.*

Another excellent example of simultaneous, joint action by Parliamentarians for World Order was the Five-Continent Peace Initiative (also known as the Six-Nation Initiative for Peace and Disarmament) organized in 1984. The parliamentarians agreed the most effective action could come from a small group of five or six leaders. In the summer of 1983, small groups of parliamentarians set out around the world to meet with key national leaders who shared a growing concern over the deteriorating relations among the nuclear weapons nations. After numerous consultations, the leaders who agreed to join together in this unique initiative were President Raul Alfonsin of Argentina, Prime Minister Indira Gandhi of India, President Miguel de La Madrid of Mexico, Prime Minister Olaf Palme of Sweden, Prime Minister Andreas Papandreou of Greece, and President Julius Nyerere of Tanzania.

In a Joint Declaration issued simultaneously from their capitals on May 22, 1984, the six vowed "to do everything in our power to facilitate agreement among the nuclear weapons states." They called for "a halt to all testing, production, and deployment of nuclear weapons and their delivery systems, to be immediately followed by substantial reduction in nuclear forces." They hoped to break the political impasse by using their combined appeal directly to the United States and the Soviet Union, as well as to the other nuclear weapons states, to put a halt to "the rush towards global suicide."

This Five-Continent Peace Initiative was formally launched when the leaders of Argentina, Greece, India, Mexico, Sweden, and Tanzania gathered for their first summit meeting in the Indian capital and issued their historic *Delhi Declaration* on January 26, 1985. (See Appendix G for text of the Delhi Declaration.) It should be noted that, due to their untimely deaths, Indira Gandhi of India and Olaf Palme of Sweden were replaced respectively by Rajiv Gandhi and Ingvar Carlsson within this leadership group.

On December 14, 1985, the leaders of the Five-Continent Peace Initiative were presented with the annual Beyond War Award for their "significant contribution toward building a world beyond war." This simultaneous presentation ceremony was made possible by a global space bridge linking the five continents together in a live satellite teleconference.

In their second annual meeting, held in Ixtapa, Mexico, the six leaders issued their *Mexico Declaration* on August 7, 1986, "to proclaim humanity's right to peace, and to reiterate our commitment to the task of protecting this right so that the human race may endure." At this second summit, they also issued their detailed document *On Verification Measures* (See Appendix H) in which they offered to provide on-site inspection and monitoring of a mutual moratorium or test ban agreed to by the U.S.A. and U.S.S.R.

More recent communication from Parliamentarians GLOBAL ACTION indicates a strong emphasis on follow-up support for the Five-Continent Peace Initiative. GLOBAL ACTION enthusiastically reports the Initiative has had positive results:

- It was largely responsible for the Soviet Union's change to a willingness to have on-site verification of nuclear weapons testing suspension by a third party.
- The Initiative has been supported by statements from Pope John Paul II, the U.N. Secretary-General, and an endorsement drafted by Carl Sagan and signed by 83 Nobel Laureates from 19 countries.
- 120 members of the United States Senate and House of Representatives signed a letter to President Reagan in support of the Initiative.
- Major peace groups such as SANE, the Nuclear Weapons Freeze Campaign, and the Physicians for Social Responsibility on both sides of the Atlantic are building public support for the Initiative.

While maintaining its efforts to help defuse the East-West conflict, GLOBAL ACTION has also devoted considerable time to the pressing issues of economic development and the improvement of North-South relations.

# 5. Developing Future Approaches

*Observations and Comments on Past and Current
Efforts to Promote Peace and Their Possible
Impact on Future Efforts Towards Peace,
Justice, and Potential Prosperity for
All the World*

Having shared the information sent by 92 respondents to our survey on positive efforts to promote peace, and having provided a historical background for current efforts, I would now like to take another look at what we have learned. Could we synthesize more effective approaches to world peace based on past experiences?

Separate reports follow in this chapter on my observations and reactions to each of the following: (1) the respondents; (2) historical approaches to world peace; (3) personal approaches to world peace; (4) instructional approaches to world peace; (5) structural approaches to world peace; and (6) combining approaches in future efforts.

Although some of my personal biases were revealed in the chapters reporting responses from the 92 peace organizations, this final chapter will share more of my personal thinking on humanity's search for peace.

Also to be found in this chapter are comments on improving peace communications; a possible world of peace, justice, and prosperity; and positive actions for readers.

## Observations Regarding Respondents

Most organizations were quick to respond to our survey. Some indicated that, due to limited staffing, they did not have time to respond in line with the suggested format (see Appendix A), but they were very generous in sending materials already on hand, such as their fact sheets, brochures, and recent newsletters. A few followed the format and sent their materials as well. All who responded seemed glad to have the opportunity to tell about their efforts for peace.

Of the 92 responses used in this compilation, 30 were examples of organizations using "personal contacts" as their primary approach, 49 were examples of those using "instruction" as their primary approach, and 13 were examples of organizations promoting peace primarily through "structural" changes.

It was of interest to note that the first two of the above categories had organizations still in operation that started early in this century, such as the World Peace Foundation (1910), the Fellowship of Reconciliation (1914), the Women's International League for Peace and Freedom (1916), and the American Friends Service Committee (1917). The Campaign for World Government (1924) was the oldest respondent of the third category.

Also of significance was the fact that a good share of the respondents were relatively young organizations, indicating an acceleration in the peace movement. Organizations in the last third of the structural change group were founded since 1972; those in the youngest third of the personal approach group were organized since 1978; and those in the latest third of the instructional group were founded since 1980.

As I was compiling the materials received from respondents to this survey, I learned of many more organizations equally worthy of inclusion in this compilation. I did add a few to the original groupings, but there came a time when I had to call a halt and "go with what I had" in order to finish the book. I sincerely apologize for serious omissions. Since this compilation is just a small sampling of the thousands of organizations actively involved in positive efforts to promote peace, it was inevitable that many effective groups would not be included. My hope is that the sampling will be sufficient to create an interest in learning more about and getting involved in the growing peace movement.

## Comments on Historical Approaches to World Peace

When making the decision to precede the reports on current efforts with historical approaches to peace in Chapter 1, I assumed such a review would be both inspiring and encouraging. However, I must admit that this initial assumption proved questionable. My reaction has been a combination of amazement and frustration. True, in looking back at where we have been, it has been an inspiration to note that ancient wise men, philosophers, and scholars have been searching for peace throughout history, looking for ways to settle differences and problems in ways other than by war, for ways of helping and supporting each other toward a better life. But the progress has been so very slow! Why has it taken humanity so long to learn and accept peace as the best way of life?

Many historians have reasoned that "peace plans" of the past failed to be implemented primarily due to the slow communications of their day. Assuming the validity of such a statement, we should be able to state the converse and be encouraged by it: that today's instantaneous communications and jet air travel have brought us to a point where we have a much better chance of succeeding in our quest for a world of justice and peace.

The historical review also disclosed a promising trend in humanity's evolution in meeting the need for reducing resorts to violence in settling differences. As larger organizational groups absorbed smaller groups and established control over them, the violence between or among the smaller units diminished. This trend and the successful implementation of the many historical peace plans by the former British colonies in the United States Constitution (followed by other federal unions) are all good cause for optimism.

Calling attention to the two-hundredth anniversary of the drafting of the United States Constitution, the theme chosen for the International Bicentennial Symposium on Strengthening the United Nations held in Philadelphia, Pennsylvania, August 6–9, 1987, was "What Has Philadelphia 1787 to Say to the World of 1987?" The three initiating sponsors, the Common Heritage Institute of Villanova University, the World Federalist Association (U.S.A.), and the World Association of World Federalists, urged world leaders to consider following the example of the American founding fathers. Many participants advocated moving the United Nations toward a world federation of nations as one way of strengthening the UN. Just as in the United States Constitution, a world federation would leave internal affairs up to the individual nation-states while filling the need for international peacekeeping and enforceable world law to cover transnational concerns. (See report on the UN in Chapter 1 for a listing of international agencies affiliated with the UN already regulating transnational relationships.)

## Observations and Comments on
## Personal Approaches to World Peace

In reviewing this sampling of organizations promoting peace primarily through friendship, positive pacifism, mutual understanding, service, and global unity, we find they can also be grouped under (1) the *religious perspective* to peacemaking, (2) *exchange programs,* and (3) *support groups.*

*The Religious Perspective.* As might be expected, a large majority of organizations in this chapter were founded by various religious groups. Whereas history has recorded many wars fought over religious differences, we were pleased to note that many religious organizations are now working together toward their common goal of world peace. For example, the World Conference on Religion and Peace has held four world assemblies, starting in 1970. It is making a deliberate effort to develop mutual understanding and respect among the major religions of the world and is finding ways in which participants can support each other in their efforts to promote peace. The WCRP operates as an NGO of the United Nations.

It is significant that along with several Christian peace fellowships within this "religious perspective" group are a Buddhist and a Jewish peace fellowship. While many of the denominational peace fellowships were initiated to support "conscientious objectors" within their respective churches, I choose to refer to them as "positive pacifists" in recognition of their constructive service to humanity.

The Center on Law and Pacifism (1978) provides legal and theological counseling for those in conflict with the law due to their religious consciences.

The Fellowship of Reconciliation (1914), one of the oldest peace fellowships, continues as an ecumenical coalition of peace fellowships from both Christian and non–Christian traditions.

Clergy and Laity Concerned (1965) is another interfaith peace organization, including Catholics, Protestants, Jews, and Muslims.

The AFSC (American Friends Service Committee) (1917) has earned respect and recognition for its efforts to be of service to war victims worldwide. Services of the Friends (Quakers) as peacemakers and mediators has also been invaluable.

Both the AFSC and the UUSC (Unitarian Universalists Service Committee, 1939) emphasize self-help health and human justice programs and work with local staffs and volunteers.

It was also of interest to note that a relatively new religion, Baha'i (1844), includes in its teachings the concepts of "the common foundation of all religions," and "universal peace upheld by world government."

These peace organizations and their religious founders have an optimistic faith that peace is possible through a global community built on love, freedom, justice, and truth.

***Exchange Programs.*** Three United States presidents sponsored three of the organizations described in Chapter 2. President Eisenhower started his People-to-People program in 1956. President Kennedy started the Peace Corps in 1961, and President Carter his Friendship Force in 1977. In addition, a group of private citizens established the Eisenhower Exchange Fellowships in 1953 in Eisenhower's honor. All four continue as viable efforts to promote peace.

The U.S. Servas Committee, Inc., is a national branch of a similar exchange program of hosts and travelers founded in Denmark in 1948. It is an open-door system of work, study, and travel.

Volunteers for Peace (1981) operates international work camps with similar goals of developing friendships, mutual understanding, and appreciation through volunteer projects.

The AFS International/Intercultural Programs have been well received and have made a real contribution toward mutual understanding among current and future world leaders.

Three of the descriptions in this grouping are examples of efforts to improve relations specifically between the United States and the Soviet Union: (1) The National Council of American-Soviet Friendship, Inc. (1943), (2) The US/USSR Church Relations Committee of the National Council of

Churches (1956), and (3) The John T. Conner Center for US/USSR Reconciliation (1979).

Two organizations included in this chapter are deeply involved in developing international friendship and understanding primarily through correspondence: the International Friendship League (1934), and World Pen Pals (1950).

All of these exchange programs are making a strong impact in intensifying citizen demand for world peace.

***Support Groups.*** Pax World Foundation (1970) provides financial support for selected programs and projects, and it gives priority to those involving beneficiaries in the planning, implementation, direction, and evaluation of their projects.

World Peacemakers (1978), of the ecumenical Church of the Savior, helps other churches take appropriate action in light of the current crises in foreign and military affairs.

The Council for International Understanding (1981) aims to develop a constituency of intelligent Americans who will be able to influence our political leaders toward sounder foreign policy formulation and execution.

The National Council of Returned Peace Corp Volunteers (1979) continues to provide a source of better understanding among Americans of other peoples.

The Center for Innovative Diplomacy (1983), along with its Citizen Diplomacy Program, now operates a Local Elected Officials Project, a Municipal Foreign Policy Program, an Alternative Security Project, and PeaceNET (a global computer network).

As I reviewed the materials from this "personal approach" group of respondents, common threads reappeared, such as:

• Forming fellowships to support conscientious objectors.

• Discovering a common goal of world peace by world's religions and denominations.

• Striving for reconciliation between man-made adversaries.

• Developing personal friendships and understanding through correspondence and personal contact among peoples of different countries.

• Involving local leaders in planning, implementing, and evaluating service projects in Third World countries.

All in all, the materials received from these peace groups made for exciting and inspiring reading. Their positive message precludes pessimism about the future of humanity and our planet Earth. With millions of dedicated people working for world peace, it will be, it must be achieved!

However, one is left with a feeling that something more is needed. The development of friendship and understanding at the grass-roots level is great, but how does it get translated into global justice and peace? How do citizens involved convince governments that they are wrong when they say that people in another country are their enemies? How do citizen demands for peace move government leaders to work more diligently for peace?

These personal approaches to peace are a very necessary component of the peace movment, but require cooperating or collaborating coalitions with other kinds of peace groups in developing structures for peace to enable them to reach their common goal of peace with justice.

## Observations and Comments on Instructional Approaches to World Peace

In reviewing the material received from 49 organizations focusing on instructional approaches to promoting peace through knowledge, research, publications and education, I was impressed by the leadership provided by women from the early years of the peace movement to the present. It was of interest to note that Jane Addams, better known for her Hull House in Chicago and her contributions as a social worker, was also the recipient of the Nobel Peace Prize for her years of leadership in the Women's International League for Peace and Freedom. Another excellent example of positive action by women has been the historic work of the League of Women Voters (now open to men). Eleanor Roosevelt's leadership in founding the National Committee for an Effective Congress and those who formed the Jane Addams Peace Association are also good examples.

This determined leadership in the peace movement from women should not be too surprising. After centuries of sacrificing their husbands and sons in battle, women finally gathered the courage and strength to do something about it. "Listen to the women for a change!" became the slogan of the WILPF.

The following statement by Julia Ward Howe written in 1870 continues to challenge women everywhere:

Arise then, women of this day!
Arise all women who have hearts,
Whether your baptism be that of water or of tears!
Say firmly:
"We will not have great questions decided by irrelevant agencies,
Our husbands shall not come to us, reeking with carnage, for caresses
    and applause.
Our sons shall not be taken from us to unlearn all that we have been able
    to teach them of charity, mercy and patience.
We women of one country
Will be too tender of those of another country
To allow our sons to be trained to injure theirs."
From the bosom of the devastated earth a voice goes up
With our own. It says, "Disarm! Disarm!"

While most of the organizations described in this section include education of the general public and those in "positions of power," they may well be sub-divided into (1) research groups; (2) educational institutions and adjuncts; (3) educators' associations and publishers of materials; (4) political action groups; (5) engineers', physicians', and scientists' groups; (6) religious groups; (7) peace education organizations of special note; and (8) coalition groups.

*Research Groups.* Research studies have contributed considerably to the peace movement. Examples of organizations sharing their findings with political and military leaders and foreign relations personnel as well as the general public include the Association for Transarmament Studies; the Center for Defense Information; the Center for War/Peace Studies; the Conference on Peace Research in History; the Fund for Peace; the Institute for Space and Security Studies; the International Peace Research Association; Physicians for Social Responsibility; Psychologists for Social Responsibility; the World Policy Institute; and the Wisconsin Institute for the Study of War, Peace, and Global Cooperation.

One of these research groups, CDI (Center for Defense Information), is operated primarily by retired military personnel under the direction of Admiral Gene R. LaRocque, U.S.N. Ret. They advocate an effective defense, but also recommend adjusting national priorities in order to stop the arms race. They believe there can be no winners in a nuclear war.

It was of special interest to note that Dr. Robert Bowman, Lt. Col. U.S.A.F. Ret. and former Director of "Star Wars," is now President of the Institute for Space and Security Studies and is making speeches throughout the nation opposing the deployment of an ABM system (SDI or Star Wars).

It was also of interest to learn that Dr. Gene Sharp of Harvard's Center for International Affairs, author of the three-volume book *The Politics of Non-Violent Action,* has founded the Association of Transarmament Studies, which advocates a planned, nonviolent, civilian-based defense as an alternative to war.

In this survey, I found that the Fund for Peace was supporting ten different projects. In addition to helping to launch four continuing programs, including the above Center for Defense Information, it is currently supporting six new projects, as described in Chapter 3.

*Educational Institutions and Adjuncts.* Whereas most peace education is being provided by concerned citizen organizations, there are several educational institutions with a strong peace emphasis in their mission. Examples include the Common Heritage Institute — Villanova University; the Institute on Global Conflict and Cooperation — University of California; the International Peace Academy; the United Nations University — headquarters in Tokyo; the United World Colleges — six campuses worldwide; the University of Peace — Costa Rica; and the Wisconsin Institute for the Study of War, Peace, and Global Cooperation — a consortium of 21 institutions of higher learning.

*Educators' Associations and Publishers of Materials.* If we want peace, we must prepare for peace. Preparation starts with the provision of teachers willing and able to integrate global perspectives and peace education with their ongoing curriculum. Likewise, they need appropriate resource materials for use in their learning activities. Examples of educators' associations and publishers of resource materials include Educators for Social Responsibility; Global Education Associates; Global Learning, Inc.; Global Perspectives in Education, Inc.; and the International Association of Educators for World Peace.

*Political Action Groups.* Some organizations have developed more skill in the political arena than others. Believing strongly in the need to work through their elected representatives in the United States Congress, they have developed networks for alerting constituents of crucial times to contact their legislators about pending legislation. They have also developed sophisticated programs for supporting their choice of candidates and monitoring their voting records on key peace issues. Examples of these groups include the Campaign for UN Reform; the Council for a Livable World (Senate); Jobs with Peace; the National Committee for an Effective Congress; the National Impact Network; National SANE; Peace PAC (House); the U.S. Committee Against Nuclear War; and the War Resisters League.

*Engineers', Physicians', and Scientists' Group.* Because of their expertise in their fields related to the threat of nuclear warfare, this group has the potential for being the most influential in reversing the arms race and removing the threat of global destruction under which we are all held hostage. Let us hope "the political powers that be" will act on their advice, the sooner the better. Examples within this group include High Technology Professionals for Peace; International Physicians for the Prevention of Nuclear War (recipient of Nobel Peace Prize); Physicians for Social Responsibility; Psychologists for Social Responsibility; and the Union of Concerned Scientists.

*Religious Groups.* Along with their personal approaches to promoting peace (See Chapter 2), many denominations and religious coalitions have developed educational materials for local study of peace and war issues. Some have broadened their curriculum through their Church and Society boards or committees to include personal peace, and peace and justice in the home, community, and nation as well as in the world. Examples of church-related peace education programs include the Baha'i (See Chapter 2); the Institute for Peace and Justice (ecumenical); the National Impact Network (an interfaith network); National Week for Peace with Justice (interfaith witness); Presbyterian Peacemaking Project; United Church of Christ's Peace Priority; United Methodist Church's Emphasis on Peace and Justice; and the Unitarian Universalist Peace Network.

*Peace Education Organizations of Special Note.* While most organizations in this chapter had an education component, six examples of citizen peace education groups were of special interest.

The Beyond War network is a "missionary-type" movement in which families have devoted a year away from home helping people in another part of the country to develop a new way of thinking: primarily that "war is obsolete" and "together we can build a world beyond war." I especially liked their materials pointing out that "forgetful of our common humanity and common mortality," the United States and the U.S.S.R. are "preparing to fight the wrong enemy with the wrong weapons." Their literature further suggests, "Are we [the United States] and our Soviet rivals not forgetting that:

• The best guarantor of one's security is the security of others, including the adversary's;

• The best guarantor of one's prosperity is the prosperity of others;

• There can be neither security nor prosperity in an overmilitarized, dehumanized, economically chaotic, and ecologically devastated world!"

Why not work together on solving world problems such as world hunger, rampant population growth, illiteracy, soil erosion, acid rain, nuclear and toxic waste disposal, and other environmental and ecological problems? As Beyond War emphasizes, these and war itself are our common enemies and problems which we could join our efforts and resources to resolve, instead of adding to the problems by preparing for a suicidal nuclear war which must never be fought.

The group SANE/FREEZE is one of the largest citizens' organizations in the United States trying to reverse the arms race. Due to its long experience in working for peace, it is a respected source of knowledge and creative thinking on how to reduce the nuclear threat and plan for economic alternatives. As its members say, "We don't just hope and plead for peace—we work for it."

Promoting Enduring Peace is a grass-roots citizens' peace organization which sends free reprints of peace-related articles and materials on a quarterly basis to anyone requesting to be on its mailing list. It is a simple but effective method of informing citizens on current peace and war issues. It is also the prime sponsor for American-Soviet peace cruises in both countries.

World Citizens, Inc., encourages the formation of World Citizen Clubs for youth, grades 5–12, to introduce a global perspective for future business, education, and government leaders through a variety of creative and fun activities, including movies, speakers, discussions, peace projects, and helping Third World students.

The World Peace Foundation was created in 1910 by turn-of-the-century business leaders such as *Edwin Ginn* and *Andrew Carnegie,* who were convinced of the need for international institutions to assure an organized world peace. Their Foundation was established to advance the cause of peace through study and public education in international relations; and more specifically, to educate the people of all nations "to a full knowledge of the waste and devastation of war; and generally, by every practical means to promote peace and good will among all mankind." The Foundation is still in operation, still working to achieve its goals more than 75 years after its inception.

The World Without War Council, an initiating, consulting/manage-

ment, coordinating, publishing, and training resource center, made exceptionally good sense to me. I strongly support its encouragement of "peace initiatives." As defined by the Council, "a peace initiative is a non-military act undertaken without prior agreement in order to induce reciprocation."
• Examples would include United States President John F. Kennedy's pledge to ban atmospheric testing of nuclear weapons which led to the 1963 Atmospheric Test Ban Treaty between the U.S. and the U.S.S.R., the 1977 initiative of Egypt's Anwar Sadat in going to Israel, and the unilateral moratorium on nuclear weapons testing by the Soviet Secretary-General Mikhail S. Gorbachev in 1985.

The Council is convinced that the central problem of the peace movement is the lack of legal and political alternatives to weapons in the resolution of international conflicts. Its goal of developing legal and political institutions *capable* of resolving inevitable conflicts between nations and its strategies for securing the cooperation of nations, including the U.S.S.R., in establishing such institutions should be taken seriously by all. (See Chapter 4 on structural approaches.)

***Coalition Groups.*** Another encouraging observation was that many of the organizations using the "instructional approach" to promoting peace were cooperating and collaborating through various coalitions and networks. Good examples of organizations working with others with common goals are High Technology Professionals for Peace; the Institute on Global Conflict and Cooperation (9 campuses of the University of California); Jobs with Peace; National Impact Network; National Mobilization for Survival; National Peace with Justice Week; National SANE; Promoting Enduring Peace; the Unitarian Universalists Peace Network; the United Nations University (28 associated institutions); the War Resisters League; and the Wisconsin Institute for the Study of War, Peace, and Global Cooperation (consortium of 21 institutions of higher learning).

I could not help being impressed by the sheer volume of time and effort contributed by thousands of dedicated volunteers involved in these various instructional approaches to promoting peace. The published findings of research on war and peace issues and other materials produced for the education of youth and adults in the general public and for our political leaders are bound to have some impact.

Common recurring ideas from this "instructional group" of respondents included:

• Need to develop a global perspective in education and politics.

• Recognition that national security can best be obtained through the development of common security for all.

• Recognition that national prosperity can best be obtained through the promotion of general global prosperity.

• Recognition of the cost of the urgent restoration of our common planetary home and saving it from ecological and environmental destruction as being approximately equal to the current cost of world armaments. We *cannot* afford both!

• Recognition of the magnitude of constructive educational, development, and social programs that are sacrificed due to military expenditures.

• Recognition that peacemaking is a mission of the church.

• Need to inform and involve citizens in foreign policy.

• Need to collaborate among peace organizations in order to increase their impact on political leaders.

Again, the question returns: How can we maximize this group's impact sufficiently to move national leaders to think and act with a global perspective in the interest of world peace? Do we need to consolidate our efforts on an all-inclusive goal acceptable to all, such as global survival, or should we join forces on one immediate goal, such as stopping the costly anti-ballistic missile program ("Star Wars") of both the U.S. and the U.S.S.R. from further development?

## Observations and Comments on Structural Approaches to World Peace

Of the three groups of responses to our survey of positive efforts to promote peace, I found the structural change or world unity group most congruent to my way of thinking. My awareness of the oneness of humanity evolved as I matured through education in public schools, Sunday school, church, and higher education; and my realization of our sharing the responsibility for our one planet was sharpened when I read Wendell Willkie's book *One World* at the end of World War II. Ever since, literature on the concept of the oneness of humanity and the need to be good stewards of our earth for future generations has caught my attention.

It was of interest to note that one of the examples, the Campaign for World Government organization, was already making plans for a world convention to draw up a constitution for a world federation of nations in the 1920s. Although its work was interrupted by World War II, it is still advocating such a federation, having been disappointed in the way the United Nations was organized around the concept of national sovereignty.

The response from the World Constitution and Parliament Association disclosed that its organization had already supported the writing of a Constitution for the Federation of Earth in 1977 and had helped organize two sessions of a Provisional World Parliament, which had already passed world legislation concerning world problems. This association, too, felt it necessary to bypass the UN due to its emphasis on protecting national sovereignty and its veto power in the Security Council blocking any attempt to amend the Charter.

Of the examples of current organizations promoting peace primarily through the development of new institutions or structures for world management:

• Some advocate continuing support for the United Nations with important modifications to make it more effective as a peacekeeping body.

• Many support the federal principle (sharing sovereignty among local, state, national, and global levels).

• Some are supportive of trying to move the UN toward a world federation of nations before establishing a federation as an alternative to the UN.

• Some advocate establishing a world federation of nations without waiting for UN reform.

• Many agree on the need for a world management system to protect both individual human rights and the well-being of individual nations.

• Some emphasize the sovereignty of the people and advocate giving them a larger role in global management, as world citizens.

• Some encourage personal registration as "world citizens."

• Some emphasize the need for the nations of the world to join together in a world management system to save their common planetary home from physical destruction.

• Some emphasize the substitution of enforceable world law for war as a means of settling disputes.

• All agree on the need for world management to prevent war and global suicide.

These are but a few examples of the constructive thinking of these organizations. They are trying to get the attention of our world's political leaders and their foreign relations and military personnel. Some may counter that their proposals are naive and too simplistic, but the "people" are tired of politicians throwing up smoke screens of complexity to avoid action. To the person on the street, it just doesn't make sense to waste our talents and money on preparing for wars none of us want. Instead, we should be using our international talents and resources to jointly tackle and solve the many global problems that impinge upon all people.

The people of the world find it impossible to understand:

• Why nations are stockpiling weapons in the hopes they will never have to use them. Why not make sure they will never be used by eliminating them? Disarm!

• Why nations are continually adding to a nuclear arsenal when they already have more than enough to destroy the planet.

• Why nations are trying to obtain peace by preparing for war instead of preparing for peace. Deterrence has never worked. The airplane and the machine gun were both supposed to make war obsolete; but both became weapons of destruction simply because they were available. We must make sure history does not repeat itself.

• Why we waste talent and money trying to develop new weapons such as for the Strategic Defense Initiative (sDI or "Star Wars") to render intercontinental nuclear missiles "impotent and obsolete." We could save billions of dollars for constructive purposes if nations would simply agree to scrap these weapons (instead of trying to make them obsolete). As an alternative to "Star Wars," the public asks, "Why not cooperate in space for the benefit of all humankind?"

Unfortunately, there appears to be a need for more communications, cooperation, and coordination among these organizations in promoting world peace through world order and justice. Perhaps peace organizations are no more immune to problems of territorial and personality conflicts than other kinds of organizations. Hopefully, the World Government Organization Coalition of San Francisco will be able to bring these groups together in working on their common goal of peace through world order.

As indicated earlier, the trend toward ever larger political units has been with us from early times. Having proved federalism to be a workable principle in the United States, in India, and in many other nations, many believe the time is ripe for a global federation of nations. While some skeptics warn such a world federation is a long way off, others remind us that other events in history have come faster than expected. Who knows? Perhaps Philip Isley's Earth Rescue Corps of the World Constitution and Parliament Association may be the catalyst to bring the nations together in a common cause to save our shared home, planet Earth, from a fatal buildup of carbon dioxide or other environmental or ecological problems that transcend national boundaries. As some have pointed out, we do not need a common enemy from outer space to unite us. We already have common enemies (environmental problems, international terrorists, and other global concerns) which can unite us. The human and monetary resources now wasted on weapons and preparation for the wars that must never be fought are needed to save our earthly home from destruction.

One big problem with institutional changes for world peace, as I see it, is to get people to take their proponents seriously. The general public too often laughs them off as impossible dreams. The political leaders are still too concerned with national sovereignty secured by military might.

Again, there appears to be a need for a broad coalition with other organizations such as environmentalists and other kinds of peace organizations.

## Combining Approaches in Future Efforts

Many organizations such as the American Friends Service Committee are already using a combined approach of service and education; various combinations can and will be utilized in future efforts to promote world peace.

As indicated at the end of comments on all three categories of peace organizations surveyed, each set of approaches to promoting peace, while essential, was still incomplete.

Those involved primarily in "personal approaches" are contributing much toward greater mutual understanding among people from different cultural, political, religious, and social backgrounds, but they lack the political force needed to move governments away from their concern for national sovereignty protected by military strength.

Those primarily in "instructional approaches" are contributing a great deal through their research, publications, and educational efforts, but these materials need more exposure to the general public (the voters) and our national leaders; and they need more emphasis on world structures to implement their findings.

The "structural approaches" can provide the needed organization lacking in the "personal" and "instructional" approaches. At the same time, those advocating structural approaches can benefit greatly from the experience of the personal approach groups and the knowledge of the instructional groups described in this compilation. Coalitions of groups from all three approaches under dynamic leadership could become very effective and influential in bringing the nations of the world together in a federal world management system.

These world peace coalitions could also gain support from world environmentalists deeply concerned about the physical future of our planet and the need to divert talents and funds from destructive military expenditures to constructive environmental and ecological programs.

Organizations already monitoring the voting records of legislators on peace and environmental issues could continue sharing their findings with other organizations and the mass media. Individuals could vote for "peace candidates" within their respective political parties. Coalitions in some nations may find it possible to form "peace parties" and nominate candidates for public office who have demonstrated their global consciousness.

As we continue the aforementioned trend toward world management, all previous positive and proven efforts in promoting world peace should be encouraged and continued. Those given responsibility for recommending and implementing changes to increase the effectiveness of the United Nations (or those having leadership responsibilities for organizing a world federation of nations) would do well to take seriously the following recommendations derived from this study of positive efforts to promote peace:

1. Follow the leadership of religious organizations such as the World Conference on Religion and Peace in seeking divine guidance in using their God-given talents in addressing their tasks.

2. Take advantage of the knowledge, understanding, and goodwill gained by those who have had experience in "personal approaches" to promoting peace.

3. Take advantage of the research and educational materials prepared by those who have been involved in the "instructional approach."

4. Develop structures within the UN or within some form of world federation which would give the people of the world a greater voice in the solution of international problems. Most people of most nations want international peace, but they usually feel helpless and are frustrated in their desires for peace and plenty by the narrow nationalism of people in political

power. To remedy this situation, some have recommended the people be allowed to elect their national representatives to the UnitedNations, and the UN could amend its Charter to include a House of Peoples with representation based on population.

5. Seriously study all other carefully prepared proposals for strengthening the United Nations, and implement those deemed most needed and feasible. According to various polls, most people believe the UN is still "the best hope of humankind."

6. Develop international law and enforcement procedures to protect human rights as defined in the UN's Universal Declaration of Human Rights. (See Appendix D.)

7. Develop international law and enforcement procedures applicable to individual offenders. We must be able to enforce decisions on individual lawbreakers rather than going to war with the lawbreaker's nation.

8. Explore computerization of international law and the development of computer-assisted conflict resolution for use in settling international disputes.

9. Develop procedures within the UN or within some form of world federation to provide universally accepted identification and travel documents.

10. Update our thinking on many terms such as sovereignty, security, citizenship, allegiance, and patriotism. Just as we hope the advent of the atom bomb made war obsolete and unthinkable, we must change our ways of thinking about the above terms. No nation can guarantee security for its people in a nuclear age. With this loss of security, no nation can claim complete sovereignty. All nations have become hostage to nuclear weapons. A great share of national sovereignty has already been turned over to specialized agencies for global affairs. Thus, it is difficult to understand why some are so concerned about loss of sovereignty when trying to strengthen the United Nations or establish some other type of world management system.

11. Extend the federal principle. As indicated earlier, nations have already found it in their best interest to turn over to specialized agencies of the UN the administration of many global affairs (e.g., the International Civil Aviation Organization and the Universal Postal Union). The experience gained in working cooperatively in these agencies provides a good foundation for joining in a federation of nations for the purpose of peacekeeping and dealing with other urgent world problems not manageable by individual nations.

## Improving Peace Communications

Many have advocated the development of a universal language as a means of improving communications and understanding among people of the world and a positive step toward world peace. One such artificial language, called "Volanuk," was invented by a German priest in 1879. The most successful attempt was called "Esperanto." Created in 1887 by a Polish doctor and scholar, Dr. L.L. Zamenhof, it was based on European languages such as English, French, German, Italian, and Spanish. Esperanto had many supporters, especially in the first third of the twentieth century, but until recently worldwide acceptance had been slow due to two primary reasons: (1) the pronunciations did not fit well with non–European languages, and (2) the teaching of English as a second language became common in a majority of developed nations.

However, the advent of the computer has given new life to Esperanto. Thanks to its basic vocabulary without ambiguity, it has proved to be an excellent translating bridge and storage language. For accurate translations, computers can now accept material typed in a given language, translate and store it in Esperanto and provide a translation when needed in another language.

Also, Chinese students who wish to learn "western" languages have found it easier to learn them if they learn Esperanto first as a bridge language.

In more recent years, many organizations promoting peace have been publishing their own newsletters, magazines, and papers to keep their members informed. One good example is the *World Peace News, a World Government Report,* published by the American Movement for World Government.

In that report's 1984 June–September issue, Professor Gonzalo Pernos of Puerto Rico estimated that "there are perhaps 20 world government organizations striving separately for more than three decades for the same cause." He makes a plea for world government advocates to "learn to speak with one voice" in convincing the man on the street that "in order to survive, the world needs a world governing body."

Granted, there may be some merit in having different organizations working on diverse approaches to achieving world peace and justice. However, there is also much to be gained by mutual support.

As I received responses to this survey, I too was concerned about the apparent lack of cooperation or collaboration. However, an article in the same issue of *World Peace News* told of a joint seminar of representatives from the Campaign for World Government, the American Movement for World Government, the World Federalists, the World Service Authority, the World Government Organizations Coordinating Council, and the World Citizens Assembly. One of the resolutions from this joint 1984 seminar (in line with the 1937 Plan of the Campaign for World Government) urged that "representatives of all national governments be encouraged to cooperate in the calling of a world constituent assembly for the purpose of drafting a constitution for democratic, federal world government." (I could not help wondering if they were planning to ignore the Constitution for the Federation of Earth, already prepared and published in 1977, or whether they were planning to borrow and build upon it as a foundation.) In the same article, the idea was advanced that "world government is needed to protect national governments."

Other articles in the same issue recommended the above constituent assembly be held in Australia by 1988, and that Tangiers in Morocco be considered as a site for a world capital.

Another article in this paper carried the headline, "Does Peace Movement Block Way to Peace?" The writer questioned the effectiveness of using fear of nuclear weapons as a tactic for selling the public on the need for a peaceful world. In reporting a speech by Ms. Edith Wynner, a veteran world governmentalist, the article pointed out that fear leads to apathy, boredom, despair, and cynicism. Fear offers no solution. Instead of this negative approach, she advocated the positive creation of a world government.

However, in another paper, John Dale of the Center for the Study and Improvement of Peace Activist Communications claims that many people are turned off by the term "world government." For many people the term "government" has a negative connotation. The term does not say who will govern whom. For most people it connotes a top-to-bottom flow of authority. Governments levy taxes, some are oppressive, and most intrude in our private lives to some extent. We do not want too much government even as a necessary evil. *World* government connotes just more of something we are not too enthusiastic about at the national level. Even if they do not object to the term, many consider the concept of a "world government" too idealistic and impracticable.

Instead of "world government," Mr. Dale recommends using "self-government at the global level" as a more palatable phrase. It is a positive statement of people having a voice in world affairs that transcend national boundaries.

This recommendation addresses a common problem of communication: Words may have different connotations for the speaker and the listener. To avoid this problem in negotiation, perhaps our ambassadors, diplomats, and negotiators should consider using a method developed by psychologist Carl Rogers. This method requires a person to refrain from responding to another's remarks without first repeating and paraphrasing his or her own understanding of those remarks, to verify that they were understood. Although this method of clarification would slow down discussions and negotiations considerably, it could very well save time and lives in the end.

Over the years, public opinion of pacifists and peace activists has changed. Before the Vietnam War, most people were proud of their patriotism: Their country, right or wrong! To question foreign policy and to advocate world peace were causes for others to doubt one's patriotism. Now it has become acceptable to question the wisdom of governmental actions. As a headline put it (in the Wisconsin AAUW's *Badger Briefs'* winter issue of 1984–85), "Peace Is Patriotic." In the heading of her article, Marge

Mueller stated, "It must become the duty of every civilian to work to prevent war."

Educational television has proved itself to be a very effective tool in its relatively short history. It was heartening to learn recently that Ted Turner and others in the broadcasting business are seriously exploring its use in educating the general public to the imperative to make decisions for peace and plenty versus war and global suicide.

Videotapes, a more recent development, have great potential as an excellent tool for peace communication and education in both school and community.

## Possible World of Peace, Justice, and Prosperity

As I understand it, the World Future Society encourages individuals and organizations to determine the kind of future they want as a goal toward which to strive (i.e., to forge their own futures).

While we can all call upon our own imaginations and envision a world free from want, hunger, malnutrition, and disease, and injustices including prejudice, discrimination, oppression, exploitation, and unemployment, I was pleased to find a short description to share with you. When a contingent of our Dane County Chapter visited the Milwaukee Chapter of WFA (World Federalist Association), they distributed a brochure entitled, "Does Our Home Have a Future?" With their permission, I would like to share the first part of the brochure below:

> Yes. We have a wonderful future — a future of peace and unbelievable prosperity.
>
> In that world, war between nations has become as unthinkable as war between Missouri and Illinois. The two billion dollars a day previously spent worldwide on the military is being used to improve the quality of life for everyone. The fear of a nuclear holocaust is gone. There are no nuclear weapons, or even large conventional weapons. There are no armies or navies. Conflicts among nations are settled without violence or threat of violence.
>
> In that world, all countries large and small determine their domestic policies without external interference. Personal liberties flourish because "national security" can no longer be used as an excuse to stifle individual freedom. Monetary, human, and natural resources are used to meet human needs rather than for wasteful armaments. Cooperative efforts control pollution and conserve natural resources. Global problems are solved by global institutions while national governments, freed from the burden of military preparedness, can devote attention to internal problems.
>
> Sound like a dream? At first, maybe yes. But this world can become a reality. It depends on what we, you and I, do.
>
> The real dreamworld is the expectation that we can just continue with our present system of international anarchy plus power politics and not have a major disaster. More nations are acquiring the capability to make

nuclear weapons. Accidental nuclear war becomes more likely as the allowable reaction time for responding to a possible attack is shortened.

History has demonstrated that local and national communities must have government to provide security for their citizens and to solve community problems. Likewise the global community must have a government to provide security for the nations of the world and to solve international problems. We won't tolerate anarchic violence in our local communities, our states, or our nation. Why suppose the world community can have peace and justice without world law?

We need a federal world government.

The United Nations is a step in the right direction, but it is not a true government. It cannot make laws. In the history of our own country, a giant step foward occurred in 1789, thirteen years after the Declaration of Independence. The existing confederation of states was changed into a federal system. A new national government was granted specified powers while the state governments retained control of all other matters. It is time for a similar forward step at the world level.

With a federal world government, nations would still govern their own internal affairs, but specific powers such as control over the production and possession of large weapons would be transferred to a world government. Disarmament could become a reality because enforcement would involve action against individuals who violate the law rather than against nations. War would be abolished because international disputes would be settled in court or in a parliament, just as now occurs within our nation. Worldwide prosperity would be the result.

The future (or goal) toward which the WFA is working is the abolition of war through the development of enforceable world law. As the World Federalists see it, achievement of this goal will require a federal world government with powers adequate to keep the peace and to assist in the promotion of a just world community.

## Positive Actions for Readers

Having reviewed the 92 examples of current peace organizations presented in this publication, it is hoped that you will have gained some enthusiasm for the wide scope, range, and variety of opportunities within the peace movement in which you could become involved; and that you will take steps to become active in one or more of the 5,700 local and national peace groups listed in the 1986 edition of the *Peace Resource Book* published by the Institute for Defense and Disarmament Studies. With so many varied groups, we can all find some of special personal interest.

To get started, you can make inquiries through local campuses, churches, or peace networks. For example, the Justice and Peace Network of Madison, Wisconsin, has over 60 area groups in its directory from which to choose. Personally, I chose to join the ESR, UNA-USA, and WFA (Educators for Social Responsibility; United Nations Association — United

States of America; and the World Federalist Association, including its affiliate, the Campaign for UN Reform).

For those already involved, it is hoped these brief descriptions of a sampling of groups within the peace movement will have provided encouragement and broadened your horizons and awareness of what others are doing. Perhaps they will help you find ways in which your group(s) and those of others can strengthen and support each other's efforts for peace.

Those of you who are attempting to provide a global perspective in your classrooms and integrate peace education with your ongoing curriculum will find this review a basic source of information to pass on to students at appropriate points in their studies.

Also, as indicated in the preface, it is hoped this abbreviated overview of the peace movement will motivate various foundations and individuals to provide financial support for peace organizations of their choice.

# Appendix A

*Survey Materials Sent to Peace Organizations*

*Here presented are the letter and the suggested response format sent to peace organizations for this survey.*

475 Presidential Lane
Madison, WI 53711

Gentlepersons:

May I introduce myself as a guest student at the University of Wisconsin involved in a research project on "Positive Efforts to Promote Peace Among Groups of Peoples from Ancient to Current Times." We need your help.

The purpose of this research is to compile and analyze descriptions of positive efforts for peace from the beginnings of time to the present, in the hopes that we can learn lessons from the past and coordinate current efforts to more effectively wage peace in today's world.

Since your organization is involved in efforts to promote peace, justice, and understanding among peoples of the world, we are eager to learn more about your activities and their results.

It would be much appreciated if you and your staff would take some time from your busy schedules to tell us about your past and present efforts. The enclosed suggested format has been prepared for your convenience in responding to our request.

We thank you for your interest and assistance.

Sincerely yours,


Robert S. Meyer


cc: Prof. J. Elder

## *Suggested Format*

For reporting: (1) Any particular peace effort(s) on which organization was
founded, and

(2) *Each* positive effort to promote peace among groups of peoples
in which your organization has been involved since its beginnings.

1. Name given to peace effort.

2. Approximate dates of effort.

3. Geographic designation of area at time of peace effort.

4. Group(s) responsible for this effort.

5. Philosophy or religion, if any, on which effort was based.

6. Brief description of effort to promote peace.

7. Summary of results, including:

   a. Findings from impact studies, if any.
   b. Reasons given for its successes.
   c. Reasons given for its shortcomings.

8. Sources of more information/details on above effort.

- - - - - - - - - -

9. Name and title of respondent.

10. Present name and address of organization represented.

11. Signature of respondent.


Please send your reports based on the above outline to:

Robert S. Meyer
475 Presidential Lane
Madison WI 53711

Thank you.

# Appendix B

*Names and Addresses of Cooperating Respondents to
Survey Concerning Positive Efforts
to Promote Peace*

Jane Addams Peace Association
777 United Nations Plaza
New York NY 10017

AFS International/Intercultural Programs
313 E. 43rd St.
New York NY 10017

All Children Together Movement
(Lagan College)
63 Church Road, Castlereagh
Belfast, Northern Ireland BT69SA

American Friends Service Committee
(AFSC)
1501 Cherry Street
Philadelphia PA 19102

American Movement for World Government
World Government Center
One World Trade Center, Suite 7967
New York NY 10048

Association for Transarmament Studies
*see* Civilian-Based Defense Association

The Baha'i National Office
of External Affairs
1606 New Hampshire Ave. NW
Washington DC 20009

Baptist Peace Fellowship of North
America

c/o First Baptist Church
Broadway and Main Street
Granville OH 43023

Beyond War
222 High Street
Palo Alto CA 94301

Buddhist Peace Fellowship
P.O. Box 4650
Berkeley CA 94704

Campaign for U.N. Reform
418 Seventh St. SE
Washington DC 20003

Campaign for World Government,
Inc.
331 Park Ave., Rm. 304
Glencoe IL 60022

Center for Defense Information
1500 Massachusetts Ave. NW
Washington DC 20005

Center for Innovative Diplomacy
17931 "F" Sky Park Circle
Irvine CA 92714

Center for War/Peace Studies
218 E. 18th St.
New York NY 10003

Center on Law and Pacifism
P.O. Box 308
Cokedale CO 81032

Children as the Peacemakers Foundation
950 Battery St., 2d floor
San Francisco CA 94111

Civilian-Based Defense Association
P.O. Box 31616
Omaha NE 68131-0916

Clergy and Laity Concerned
198 Broadway
New York NY 10038

Common Heritage Institute
Villanova University
Villanova PA 19085

Conference on Peace Research in History
c/o University College
Adelphi University
Garden City NY 11530

John T. Conner Center for US/USSR Reconciliation
320 North Street
West Lafayette IN 47906

Council for a Livable World
20 Park Plaza
Boston MA 02116

Council for International Understanding
136 E. 64th St.
New York NY 10021

Educators for Social Responsibility
23 Garden Street
Cambridge MA 02138

Eisenhower Exchange Fellowships
256 S. 16th Street
Philadelphia PA 19102

Federalist Caucus
P.O. Box 19482
Portland OR 97219

Friendship Force International
575 South Omni International
Atlanta GA 30303

Fellowship of Reconciliation
Box 271
Nyack NY 10960

Fund for Peace
345 E. 46th St.
New York NY 10017

Global Education Association
475 Riverside Drive, Suite 570
New York NY 10115

Global Learning, Inc.
40 S. Fullerton Ave.
Montclair NJ 07042

Global Perspectives in Education
45 John St.
New York NY 10038

High Technology Professionals for Peace
2001 Beacon St.
Brookline MA 02146

Institute for Peace and Justice
4144 Lindell, #122
St. Louis MO 63108

Institute for Space and Security Studies
7833 C Street
Chesapeake Beach MD 20732

Institute on Global Conflict and Cooperation
University of California–San Diego
Q-060
La Jolla CA 92093

International Association of Educators for World Peace
P.O. Box 3282, Mastin Lane Station
Huntsville AL 35810-0282

International Friendship League Pen Pals
55 Mount Vernon St.
Boston MA 02108

International Peace Academy
777 United Nations Plaza
New York NY 10017

International Peace Research Association
IUPRJ

Rua Paulino Fernandes 32
CEP 22270 Rio de Janeiro RJ
Brazil

International Physicians for the Prevention of Nuclear War
126 Rogers St.
Cambridge MA 02142

Jewish Peace Fellowship
Box 271
Nyack NY 10960

Jobs with Peace
76 Summer St.
Boston MA 02110

Lagan College (See All Children
Together Movement)

League of Women Voters of the U.S.
1730 M St. NW
Washington DC 20036

National Committee for an Effective
Congress
507 Capitol Court NE
Washington DC 20002

National Council of American-Soviet
Friendship
85 E. 4th St.
New York NY 10003

National Council of Returned Peace
Corps Volunteers
1317 F St. NW #900
Washington DC 20004

National Impact Network
100 Maryland Ave. NE
Washington DC 20002

National Mobilization for Survival
P.O. Box 871, Cooper Station
New York NY 10003

National Peace with Justice Week
475 Riverside Dr. Rm. 712
New York NY 10115

Parliamentarians GLOBAL ACTION
211 E. 43rd Street, Suite 1604
New York NY 10017

Pax World Foundation
4400 East-West Hwy, Suite 130
Bethesda MD 20814

Peace Corps
806 Connecticut Ave. NW
Washington DC 20526

Peace PAC
100 Maryland Ave. NE
Washington DC 20002

People to People International
501 E. Armour Blvd.
Kansas City MO 64109-2246

Physicians for Social Responsibility
1601 Connecticut Ave. NW, Suite 800
Washington DC 20009

Planetary Citizens
325 9th St.
San Francisco CA 94103-3898

Presbyterian Peace Fellowship
Box 271
Nyack NY 10960

Presbyterian Peacemaking Project
1201 Interchurch Center
475 Riverside Dr.
New York NY 10115

Promoting Enduring Peace
P.O. Box 5103
Woodmont CT 06460

Psychologists for Social Responsibility
1841 Columbia Rd. NW Suite 209
Washington DC 20009

SANE/FREEZE
711 G Street SE
Washington DC 20003

Ulster Project Delaware
c/o Pacem in Terris

1106 Adams Street
Wilmington DE 19801

Union of Concerned Scientists
26 Church St.
Cambridge MA 02238

Unitarian Universalist Peace Network
5808 Greene St.
Philadelphia PA 19144

Unitarian Universalist Service Committee
78 Beacon St.
Boston MA 02108

United Church of Christ's Peace
  Priority
Office of Church in Society
105 Madison Ave.
New York NY 10016

Peace with Justice
Board of Church and Society
United Methodist Church
100 Maryland Ave. NE
Washington DC 20002

United Nations Association of the
  U.S.A.
485 Fifth Ave.
New York NY 10017

United Nations University — Tokyo
Toho Seimei Building
15-1 Shibuya 2-chome,
Shibuya-ku, Tokyo 150, Japan

United States Servas Committee
11 John St., Rm 406
New York NY 10038

United World Colleges
c/o Armand Hammer United World
  College of the American West
P.O. Box 248
Montezuma NM 87731

University for Peace — Costa Rica
P.O. Box 199-1250
Escazu, Costa Rica

U.S. Committee Against Nuclear
  War
1140 19th St. NW
Washington DC 20036

US/USSR Church Relations Committee of the National Council of
  Churches
475 Riverside Dr., Rm 800
New York NY 10115

Volunteers for Peace (International
  Work Camps)
Tiffany Rd.
Belmont VT 05730

War Resisters League
339 Lafayette Street
New York NY 10012

Wisconsin Institute for the Study of
  War, Peace, and Global Cooperation
LRC, 900 Reserve St.
University of Wisconsin–Stevens
  Point
Stevens Point WI 94481

Women's International League for
  Peace and Freedom
1213 Race Street
Philadelphia PA 19107

World Citizens Assembly
2820 Van Ness Ave.
San Francisco CA 94109

World Citizens, Inc.
3721 48th Ave. S.
Minneapolis MN 55406

World Conference on Religion and
  Peace
777 United Nations Plaza
New York NY 10017

World Constitution and Parliament
  Association
1480 Hoyt St., Suite 31
Lakewood CO 80215

World Federalist Association
418 7th Street SE
Washington DC 20003

World Government of World Citizens
1012 14th St. NW
Washington DC 20005

World Government Organization Coalition
774 Colusa Ave.
El Cerrito CA 94530

World Peace Foundation
22 Batterymarch St.
Boston MA 02109

World Peacemakers
2025 Massachusetts Ave. NW
Washington DC 20036

World Peace Through Law Center
1000 Connecticut Ave. N.W. #800
Washington DC 20036

World Pen Pals
1690 Como Ave.
St. Paul MN 55108

World Policy Institute
777 United Nations Plaza
New York NY 10017

World Without War Council
1730 Martin Luther King Jr. Way
Berkeley CA 94709

# Appendix C

*Outline of the Constitution of the United States of America*

*Ratified June 21, 1788. Listing of articles, sections and amendments.*

**Preamble**
**Article I. Legislative Department.**
*Sections:*
1. Legislative power, where vested.
2. House of Representatives: how composed, eligibility, term, appointment, officers, impeachment.
3. Senate: composition, classification, eligibility, term, officers, impeachment.
4. Senators and representatives: election of, sessions of Congress.
5. Membership, quorum, rules of order, discipline and expulsion, journals, yeas and nays, adjournments.
6. Compensation, privileges, ineligibility.
7. Revenue bills, how a bill becomes law, veto.
8. Powers of Congress enumerated.
9. Limitations on power of Congress, title of nobility.
10. Limitations on power of states.

**Article II. Executive Department.**
*Sections:*
1. Executive power vested in president, term, election, eligibility, successor, compensation, oath.
2. President: Chief of army and navy, may require opinions from cabinet, grant pardons, make treaties, appoint ambassadors, judges, etc., and fill vacancies.
3. President's message. He may convene and adjourn Congress, receive foreign ministers, execute laws, commission officers.
4. Removal of president, vice president, and civic officers.

**Article III. Judicial Department.**
*Sections:*
1. Judicial power, tenure, and compensation of judges.
2. Jurisdiction, original and appellate, criminal trials, venue, jury.
3. Treason: proof and punishment.

**Article IV. State Rights.**
*Sections:*
1. Full faith and credit given to each state.
2. Citizens of each state entitled to privileges in the several states.
3. Re: territories and property of the United States and the admission of new states.

4. Protection and a republican form of government guaranteed to each state.

**Article V. Amendments.**

1. How Constitution amended.

**Article VI. Assumption of Debts and Engagements of the Confederacy.**

1. Public debt validated, supreme law defined, Constitutional oath, who to take, no religious test.

**Article VII. Ratification.**

1. Adoption of Constitution.

- - - - - - - - - -

**Ten Original Amendments (Bill of Rights — December 15, 1791).**

*Articles:*

    I. No state church; guarantees freedom of worship, of speech, of assemblage, and of petition.

    II. Right to keep and bear arms.

    III. No quartering of soldiers without consent of houseowner.

    IV. Right of regulations re: search and seizure.

    V. Rights re: prosecution, trial and punishment, private property not to be taken for public use without compensation.

    VI. Right to speedy trial, witnesses, etc.

    VII. Right of trial by jury.

    VIII. Protection from excessive bail and fines, and cruel and unusual punishment.

    IX. Rule of Constitutional construction.

    X. Right of states under Constitution.

**Additional Amendments and Years Adopted**

    XI. Judicial power construed — 1795.

    XII. Election of president and vice president — 1804.

    XIII. Slavery abolished — 1865.

    XIV. Citizenship rights not to be abridged; apportionment of representatives in Congress; power of Congress to remove disabilities of United States officials for rebellion; validation of public debts — 1868.

    XV. Suffrage granted to Negroes — 1870.

    XVI. Income taxes authorized — 1913.

    XVII. Popular election of senators, vacancies in Senate — 1913.

    XVIII. Prohibition of intoxicating beverages — 1919.

    XIX. Suffrage granted to women — 1920.

    XX. Terms of president and vice president to begin on January 20; those of senators and representatives on January 3 — 1933.

    XXI. Repeal of Eighteenth Amendment by convention in states — 1933.

    XXII. Prohibition of third term for president — 1951.

    XXIII. Citizens of District of Columbia granted the right to vote in presidential elections — 1961.

    XXIV. Poll taxes prohibited for national elections — 1964.

    XXV. Procedure to be followed in the event of the death or disability of the president — 1967.

    XXVI. Right to vote at age eighteen — 1971.

# Appendix D

*United Nations Universal Declaration of Human Rights
(December 10, 1948)*

*Preamble*

Whereas recognition of the inherent dignity and of the equal and inalienable rights of all members of the human family is the foundation of freedom, justice and peace in the world,

Whereas disregard and contempt for human rights have resulted in barbarous acts which have outraged the conscience of mankind, and the advent of a world in which human beings shall enjoy freedom of speech and belief and freedom from fear and want has been proclaimed as the highest aspiration of the common people,

Whereas it is essential, if man is not to be compelled to have recourse, as a last resort, to rebellion against tyranny and oppression, that human rights should be protected by the rule of law,

Whereas it is essential to promote the development of friendly relations between nations,

Whereas the peoples of the United Nations have in the Charter reaffirmed their faith in fundamental human rights, in the dignity and worth of the human person and in the equal rights of men and women and have determined to promote social progress and better standards of life in larger freedom,

Whereas Member States have pledged themselves to achieve, in co-operation with the United Nations, the promotion of universal respect for and observance of human rights and fundamental freedoms,

Whereas a common understanding of these rights and freedoms is of the greatest importance for the full realization of this pledge,

Now, Therefore,

*the General Assembly*

proclaims

THIS UNIVERSAL DECLARATION OF HUMAN RIGHTS as a common standard of achievement for all peoples and all nations, to the end that every individual and every organ of society, keeping this Declaration constantly in mind, shall strive

242

by teaching and education to promote respect for these rights and freedoms and by progressive measures, national and international, to secure their universal and effective recognition and observance, both among the peoples of Member States themselves and among the peoples of territories under their jurisdiction.

Article 1. All human beings are born free and equal in dignity and rights. They are endowed with reason and conscience and should act towards one another in a spirit of brotherhood.

Article 2. Everyone is entitled to all the rights and freedoms set forth in this Declaration, without distinction of any kind, such as race, colour, sex, language, religious, political or other opinion, national or social origin, property, birth or other status. Furthermore, no distinction shall be made on the basis of the political, jurisdictional or international status of the country or territory to which a person belongs, whether it be independent, trust, non–self-governing or under any other limitation of sovereignty.

Article 3. Everyone has the right to life, liberty, and security of person.

Article 4. No one shall be held in slavery or servitude; slavery and the slave trade shall be prohibited in all their forms.

Article 5. No one shall be subjected to torture or to cruel, inhuman or degrading treatment or punishment.

Article 6. Everyone has the right to recognition everywhere as a person before the law.

Article 7. All are equal before the law and are entitled without any discrimination to equal protection of the law. All are entitled to equal protection against any discrimination in violation of this Declaration and against any incitement to such discrimination.

Article 8. Everyone has the right to an effective remedy by the competent national tribunals for acts violating the fundamental rights granted him by the constitution or by law.

Article 9. No one shall be subjected to arbitrary arrest, detention or exile.

Article 10. Everyone is entitled in full equality to a fair and public hearing by an independent and impartial tribunal, in the determination of his rights and obligations and of any criminal charge against him.

Article 11. (1) Everyone charged with a penal offence has the right to be presumed innocent until proved guilty according to law in a public trial at which he has had all the guarantees necessary for his defence. (2) No one shall be held guilty of any penal offence on account of any act or omission which did not constitute a penal offence, under national or international law, at the time when it was committed. Nor shall a heavier penalty be imposed than the one that was applicable at the time the penal offence was committed.

Article 12. No one shall be subjected to arbitrary interference with his privacy, family, home, or correspondence, nor to attacks upon his honour and reputation.

Everyone has the right to the protection of the law against such interference or attacks.

Article 13. (1) Everyone has the right to freedom of movement and residence within the borders of each state. (2) Everyone has the right to leave any country including his own, and to return to his country.

Article 14. (1) Everyone has the right to seek and to enjoy in other countries asylum from persecution. (2) This right may not be invoked in the case of prosecutions genuinely arising from non-political crimes or from acts contrary to the purposes and principles of the United Nations.

Article 15. (1) Everyone has the right to a nationality. (2) No one shall be arbitrarily deprived of his nationality nor denied the right to change his nationality.

Article 16. (1) Men and women of full age, without any limitation due to race, nationality or religion, have the right to marry and to found a family. They are entitled to equal rights as to marriage, during marriage and at its disolution. (2) Marriage shall be entered into only with the free and full consent of the intending spouses. (3) The family is the natural and fundamental group unit of society and is entitled to protection by society and the State.

Article 17. (1) Everyone has the right to own property alone as well as in association with others. (2) No one shall be arbitrarily deprived of his property.

Article 18. Everyone has the right to freedom of thought, conscience and religion; this right includes freedom to change his religion or belief, and freedom, either alone or in community with others and in public or private, to manifest his religion or belief in teaching, practice, worship and observance.

Article 19. Everyone has the right to freedom of opinion and expression; this right includes freedom to hold opinions without interference and to seek, receive and impart information and ideas through any media and regardless of frontiers.

Article 20. (1) Everyone has the right to freedom of peaceful assembly and association. (2) No one may be compelled to belong to an association.

Article 21. (1) Everyone has the right to take part in the government of his country, directly or through freely chosen representatives. (2) Everyone has the right of equal access to public service in his country. (3) The will of the people shall be the basis of the authority of government; this will shall be expressed in periodic and genuine elections which shall be by universal and equal suffrage and shall be held by secret vote or by equivalent free voting procedures.

Article 22. Everyone, as a member of society has the right to social security and is entitled to realization, through national effort and international co-operation and in accordance with the organization and resources of each State, of the economic, social and cultural rights indispensable for his dignity and the free development of his personality.

Article 23. (1) Everyone has the right to work, to free choice of employment, to just and favourable conditions of work and to protection against unemployment. (2) Everyone, without any discrimination, has the right to equal pay for equal work.

(3) Everyone who works has the right to just and favourable remuneration ensuring for himself and his family an existence worthy of human dignity, and supplemented, if necessary, by other means of social protection. (4) Everyone has the right to form and to join trade unions for the protection of his interests.

Article 24. Everyone has the right to rest and leisure, including reasonable limitations of working hours and periodic holidays with pay.

Article 25. (1) Everyone has the right to a standard of living adequate for the health and well-being of himself and of his family, including food, clothing, housing and medical care and necessary social services, and the right to security in the event of unemployment, sickness, disability, widowhood, old age or other lack of livelihood in circumstances beyond his control. (2) Motherhood and childhood are entitled to special care and assistance. All children, whether born in or out of wedlock, shall enjoy the same social protection.

Article 26. (1) Everyone has the right to education. Education shall be free, at least in the elementary and fundamental stages. Elementary education shall be compulsory. Technical and professional education shall be made generally available and higher education shall be equally accessible to all on the basis of merit. (2) Education shall be directed to the full development of the human personality and to the strengthening of respect for human rights and fundamental freedoms. It shall promote understanding, tolerance and friendship among all nations, racial or religious groups, and shall further the activities of the United Nations for the maintenance of peace. (3) Parents have a prior right to choose the kind of education that shall be given to their children.

Article 27. (1) Everyone has the right freely to participate in the cultural life of the community, to enjoy the arts and to share in scientific advancement and its benefits. (2) Everyone has the right to the protection of the moral and material interests resulting from any scientific, literary or artistic production of which he is the author.

Article 28. Everyone is entitled to a social and international order in which the rights and freedoms set forth in this Declaration can be fully realized.

Article 29. (1) Everyone has duties to the community in which alone the free and full development of his personality is possible. (2) In the exercise of his rights and freedoms, everyone shall be subject only to such limitations as are determined by law solely for the purpose of securing due recognition and respect for the rights and freedoms of others and of meeting the just requirements of morality, public order and the general welfare in a democratic society. (3) These rights and freedoms may in no case be exercised contrary to the purposes and principles of the United Nations.

Article 30. Nothing in this Declaration may be interpreted as implying for any State, group or person any right to engage in any activity or to perform any act aimed at the destruction of any of the rights and freedoms set forth herein.

# Appendix E

*World Government Platform of Garry Davis as a Candidate for the Office of President of the United States*

My platform will include:
- the denunciation of the arms race as illegal as well as insane; to which denunciation, I add all national programs involving the weaponization of space surrounding our planet such as the so-called Strategic Defense Initiative;
- the legal recognition of and protection for the de facto world citizenship enjoyed by every member of the human race by virtue of the physical reality of one world and one humankind;
- the immediate calling of a world constitutional convention to elaborate a constitution for the World Government;
- the "mondialization" of all United States villages, towns, cities and states and a call to governors and mayors throughout the world to officially declare their municipalities, counties and states integral and dynamic parts of the total world community;
- by a constitutional amendment, the registration of all United States citizens as World Citizens with the World Government in conformity with the 9th and 10th amendments to the U.S. Constitution reserving sovereign rights to the people, and a call to all national citizens to so register through the World Service Authority;
- the registration of all U.S. new-borns with the World Government in accordance with the accepted legal principles jus soli and jus sanguinis and the issuance of World Birth Certificates to them via the World Service Authority. This will begin human, therefore world legitimacy at birth where it belongs;
- the call to all heads of state for a world truce so that humans conscripted as national soldiers will cease killing fellow humans and that such killing be designated as criminal under revised Nuremberg Principles;
- the call to all elected officials, mayors, governors, national legislators and executive officers to promote world government through legislative action, political platforms and education of their specific citizenry;
- the establishment of a world peace corps as an option to national military service in conformity with article 1 of the Universal Declaration of Human Rights: "All human beings are born free and equal in dignity and rights; they are endowed with reason and conscience and should act towards one another in a spirit of brotherhood";
- a call to retired military men, particularly generals and admirals, to form a command unit to be called the Sovereign Order of World Guards to super-

246

vise this world peace corps. As the Nuremberg Decisions outlawed war and its preparations, no longer can fellow man kill fellow man without the charge of criminality;

- the call to religious leaders to unite under the banner of one world, God's creation. For men of religion to kill others of a different religion is to blaspheme the Creator of the Universe. Religious leaders must condemn such practice;
- a call especially to the women of the world, the mothers, from whom humanity comes, who constitute half the human race, to support the world government to the fullest of their immense and sovereign power;
- the establishment of a World Bank one of whose missions would be to issue a stable world monetary unit gradually to replace the volatile national currencies;
- the revision of the U.S. budget with deemphasis on armaments and emphasis on basic civic needs and services;
- the further implementation of the economic strategy of democratizing equity ownership of the tools of production through E.S.O.P.s (Employee Stock Ownership Plans), G.S.O.P.s (General Stock Ownership Plans), and C.S.O.P.S. (Consumer Stock Ownership Plans).
- settlement of Third World debts through establishing a World Park as a life-support system for the tropical rain forests — a common heritage of humanity — off-setting the paper value of such monetary debts;
- a call to the myriad peace movements from every clime and of every inclination to unite under the all-encompassing banner of our common world citizenship.

# Appendix F

*Bill of Rights (Article XII) and Directive Principles*
*(Article XIII) of the Constitution for the*
*Federation of Earth*

*Article XII.*

The inhabitants and citizens of Earth who are within the Federation of Earth shall have certain inalienable rights defined hereunder. It shall be mandatory for the World Parliament, the World Executive, and all organs and agencies of the World Government to honor, implement and enforce these rights, as well as for the national governments of all member nations in the Federation of Earth to do likewise. Individuals or groups suffering violation or neglect of such rights shall have full recourse through the World Ombudsmus, the Enforcement System and the World Courts for redress of grievances. The inalienable rights shall include the following:

1. Equal rights for all citizens of the Federation of Earth, with no discrimination on grounds of race, color, casts, nationality, sex, religion, political affiliation, property, or social status.
2. Equal protection and application of world legislation and world laws for all citizens of the Federation of Earth.
3. Freedom of thought and conscience, speech, press, writing, communication, expression, publication, broadcasting, telecasting, and cinema, except as an overt part of incitement to violence, armed riot or insurrection.
4. Freedom of assembly, association, organization, petition and peaceful demonstration.
5. Freedom to vote without duress, and freedom for political organization and campaigning without censorship or recrimination.
6. Freedom to profess, practice and promote religions or religious beliefs or no religion or religious belief.
7. Freedom to profess and promote political beliefs or no political beliefs.
8. Freedom for investigating, research and reporting.
9. Freedom to travel without passport or visa or other forms of registration used to limit travel between, among or within nations.
10. Prohibition against slavery, peonage, involuntary servitude, and conscription of labor.
11. Prohibition against military conscription.
12. Safety of person from arbitrary or unreasonable arrest, detention, exile, search or seizure, requirement of warrants for searches and arrests.
13. Prohibition against physical or psychological duress or torture during any period of investigation, arrest, detention or imprisonment, and against cruel or unusual punishment.

14. Right of habeas corpus, no ex post facto laws; no double jeopardy; right to refuse self-incrimination or the incrimination of another.
15. Prohibition against private armies and paramilitary organizations as being threats to the common peace and safety.
16. Safety of property from arbitrary seizure; protection against exercise of the power of eminent domain without reasonable compensation, but consistent with principles of distributive justice.
17. Right to family planning and free public assistance to achieve family planning objectives.
18. Right of privacy of person, family and association; prohibition against surveillance as a means of political control.

*Article XIII.*

It shall be the aim of the World Government to secure certain other rights for all inhabitants within the Federation of Earth, but without immediate guarantee of universal achievement and enforcement. These rights are defined as Directive Principles, obligating the World Government to pursue every reasonable means for universal realization and implementation, and shall include the following:

1. Equal opportunity for useful employment for everyone, with wages or remuneration sufficient to assure human dignity.
2. Freedom of choice in work, occupation, employment or profession.
3. Full access to information and to the accumulated knowledge of the human race.
4. Free and adequate public health services and medical care available to everyone throughout life under conditions of free choice.
6. Equal opportunity for leisure time for everyone; better distribution of the work load of society so that every person may have equitable leisure time opportunities.
7. Equal opportunity for everyone to enjoy the benefits of scientific and technological discoveries and developments.
8. Protection for everyone against the hazards and perils of technological innovations and developments.
9. Protection of the natural environment which is the common heritage of humanity against pollution, ecological disruption or damage which could imperil life or lower the quality of life.
10. Conservation of those natural resources of Earth which are limited so that present and future generations may continue to enjoy life on the planet Earth.
11. Assurance for everyone of adequate housing, of adequate and nutritious food supplies, of safe and adequate water supplies, of pure air with protection of oxygen supplies and the ozone layer, and in general for the continuance of an environment which can sustain healthy living for all.
12. Assure to each child the right to the full realization of his or her potential.
13. Social security for everyone to relieve the hazards of unemployment, sickness, old age, family circumstance, disability, catastrophies of nature, and technological change, and to allow retirement with sufficient lifetime income for living under conditions of human dignity during older age.
14. Rapid elimination of and prohibitions against technological hazards and man-made environmental disturbances which are found to create dangers to life on Earth.
15. Implementation of intensive programs to discover, develop and institute safe

alternatives and practical substitutions for technologies which must be eliminated and prohibited because of hazards and dangers to life.

16. Encouragement for cultural diversity; encouragement for decentralized administration.

17. Freedom for peaceful self-determination for minorities, refugees and dissenters.

18. Freedom for change of residence to anywhere on Earth.

19. Prohibition against the death penalty.

# Appendix G

*Delhi Declaration*
*of the Five Continent Peace Initiative*

Issued 28 January 1985 by H.E. Mr. Raúl Alfonsín, *President of Argentina;*
H.E. Mr. Rajiv Gandhi, *Prime Minister of India;* H.E. Mr. Miguel de la Madrid,
*President of Mexico;* H.E. Mr. Julius Nyerere, *President of the United Republic*
*of Tanzania;* H.E. Mr. Olof Palme, *Prime Minister of Sweden;* H.E. Mr. Andreas
Papandreou, *Prime Minister of Greece.*

FORTY YEARS AGO, when atomic bombs were blasted over Hiroshima and
Nagasaki, the human race became aware that it could destroy itself, and horror
came to dwell among us. Forty years ago, also, the nations of the world gathered
to organise the international community, and with the United Nations hope was
born for all people.

ALMOST IMPERCEPTIBLY, over the last four decades, every nation and
every human being has lost ultimate control over their own life and death. For all
of us, it is a small group of men and machines in cities far away who can decide
our fate. Every day we remain alive is a day of grace as if mankind as a whole were
a prisoner in the death cell awaiting the uncertain moment of execution. And like
every innocent defendant, we refuse to believe that the execution will ever take
place.

WE FIND OURSELVES in this situation because the nuclear weapon states
have applied traditional doctrines of war in a world where new weapons have made
them obsolete. What is the point of nuclear "superiority" or "balance" when each
side already has enough weapons to devastate the Earth dozens of times over? If
the old doctrines are applied in the future, the holocaust will be inescapable sooner
or later. But nuclear war can be prevented if our voices are joined in a universal
demand in defence of our right to live.

AS A RESULT of recent atmospheric and biological studies, there have been
new findings which indicate that in addition to blast, heat and radiation, nuclear
war, even on a limited scale, would trigger an arctic nuclear winter which may
transform the Earth into a darkened, frozen planet posing unprecedented peril to
all nations, even those far removed from the nuclear explosions. We are convinced
that this makes it still more pressing to take preventive action to exclude forever the
use of nuclear weapons and the occurrence of a nuclear war.

IN OUR JOINT STATEMENT OF MAY 22, 1984, we called upon the nuclear
weapon states to bring their arms race to a halt. We are encouraged by the worldwide response to our appeal. The international support we received, and the

251

responses of the nuclear weapon states themselves, have been such that we deemed it our duty to meet here in New Delhi to consider ways to further our efforts.

THE NUCLEAR WEAPON STATES have a particular responsibility for the dangerous state of the arms race. We urge them to join us in the search for a new direction. We welcome the agreement in Geneva on January 8, 1985, between the Soviet Union and the United States to start bilateral negotiations on "a complex of questions concerning space and nuclear arms — both strategic and intermediate range — with all the questions considered and resolved in their inter-relationship." We attach great importance to the proclaimed objective of these negotiations: to prevent an arms race in space and to terminate it on earth, ultimately to eliminate nuclear arms everywhere. We expect the two major nuclear weapon powers to implement, in good faith, their undertaking and their negotiations to produce, at an early date, significant results. We will follow their work closely and we expect that they will keep the international community informed of its progress. We stress that the agenda for and the outcome of these negotiations is a matter of concern for all nations and all people.

WE REITERATE OUR APPEAL for an all-embracing halt to the testing, production and deployment of nuclear weapons and their delivery systems. Such a halt would greatly facilitate negotiations. Two specific steps today require special attention: the prevention of an arms race in outer space, and a comprehensive test ban treaty.

OUTER SPACE must be used for the benefit of mankind as a whole, not as a battleground of the future. We therefore call for the prohibition of the development, testing, production, deployment and use of all space weapons. An arms race in space would be enormously costly, and have grave destabilising effects. It would also endanger a number of arms limitation and disarmament agreements.

WE FURTHER URGE the nuclear weapon states to immediately halt the testing of all kinds of nuclear weapons, and to conclude, at an early date, a treaty on a nuclear weapon test ban. Such a treaty would be a major step towards ending the continuous modernisation of nuclear arsenals.

WE ARE CONVINCED that all such steps, in so far as necessary, can be accompanied by adequate and non-discriminatory measures of verification.

A HALT TO THE NUCLEAR ARMS RACE is at the present moment imperative. Only thus can it be ensured that nuclear arsenals do not grow while negotiations proceed. However, this halt should not be an end in itself. It must be immediately followed by substantial reductions in nuclear forces, leading to the complete elimination of nuclear weapons and the final goal of General and Complete Disarmament. Parallel to this process, it is urgently necessary to transfer precious resources currently wasted in military expenditure to social and economic development. The strengthening of the United Nations must also be an essential part of this endeavour.

IT IS IMPERATIVE to find a remedy to the existing situation where hundreds of billions of dollars, amounting to approximately one and a half million per minute, are spent annually on weapons. This stands in dramatic contrast to the poverty, and in some cases misery, in which two-thirds of the world population lives.

THE FUTURE OF ALL PEOPLES is at stake. As representatives from non-nuclear weapon states, we will not cease to express our legitimate concern and make known our demands. We affirm our determination to facilitate agreement among the nuclear weapon states, so that the required steps can be taken. We will seek to work together with them for the common security of mankind and for peace.

WE URGE PEOPLE, parliaments and governments the world over to lend forceful support to this appeal. Progress in disarmament can only be achieved with an informed public applying strong pressure on governments. Only then will governments summon the necessary political will to overcome the many obstacles which lie in the path of peace. The World Disarmament Campaign launched by the United Nations represents a very important element in generating that political will.

FOR CENTURIES, men and women have fought for their rights and freedoms. We now face the greatest struggle of all—for the right to live, for ourselves and for future generations.

FORTY YEARS AGO, in Hiroshima and San Francisco, the horror of nuclear war was matched by the hope for peace. We would like this year of 1985 to be the year when hope begins to prevail over terror. We dare to hope that by October 24, 1985, the Fortieth Anniversary of the United Nations, we might see the first concrete steps to avert the threat to the survival of humanity.

# Appendix H

*Document Issued at the Mexico Summit On Verification Measures (7 August 1986)*

Issued by Raúl Alfonsín, *President of Argentina;* Andreas Papandreou, *Prime Minister of Greece;* Rajiv Gandhi, *Prime Minister of India;* Miguel de la Madrid, *President of Mexico;* Ingvar Carlsson, *Prime Minister of Sweden;* and Julius Nyerere, *First President of Tanzania.*

**1.** It is the responsibility of the nuclear powers to halt nuclear testing as a significant step to curb the nuclear arms race. The USA and the USSR, being the two major nuclear powers, have a special responsibility to initiate the process of nuclear disarmament by immediately halting their nuclear testing. To facilitate such an immediate step the six nations of the Five Continent Initiative are prepared to assist in the monitoring of a mutual moratorium or a test ban.

**2.** We are prepared to participate in co-operative efforts together with the USA and the USSR and also to take certain steps on our own to facilitate the achievement of adequate verification arrangements.

**Verification of a moratorium in co-operation with the USA and the USSR**

**3.** In our view, some temporary measures could greatly enhance confidence in a USA-USSR moratorium and would constitute important steps towards the establishment of an adequate verification system for a comprehensive test ban treaty.

**Possible monitoring of test sites**

**4.** To provide assurance that the test sites, which are well equipped for nuclear testing and where the effects of nuclear explosions are well known, are not used for clandestine testing, we consider the establishment of temporary monitoring facilities at existing test sites to be an important measure.

**5.** The three test sites recently used, Nevada in the United States and Semipalatinsk and Novaya Zemlya in the Soviet Union are quite small geographically and could be monitored by a limited number of seismic stations placed in these two countries at or close to each test area.

**6.** Rapidly to establish temporary stations at the test sites, available portable seismic equipment would have to be used. Five to eight interconnected stations placed around each test area would be adequate, some of the stations at the test sites could also be equipped with instruments interchanged between the USA and the USSR to enhance mutual confidence.

**7.** In connection with a mutual halt in nuclear testing, our six nations are prepared to establish promptly and in co-operation with the USA and the USSR, temporary monitoring stations at existing test sites and to operate them for an initial period of one year. All data should be available to the six nations, the USA and the USSR. Data analysis could be a joint undertaking and preliminary analysis would be done at the sites. Monitoring of test sites by instruments installed on-site would provide an extremely high sensitivity down to small fractions of kiloton and even tons of explosives.

**8.** It is expected that a number of earthquakes would be detected at the test sites. The numbers and sizes will vary between the three sites. To reduce the risk of misinterpreting such shallow earthquakes as being nuclear explosions, a scheme of on-site inspections at the test sites could be envisioned. This would be most important during the initial period while experience is gained at the actual sites. Our six nations are prepared to participate in such inspections conducted in co-operation with the host country.

**Possible monitoring of the territories of the USA and the USSR outside the test sites**

**9.** To provide assurance that nuclear explosions are not conducted and that natural earthquakes are not misinterpreted as clandestine nuclear test explosions, events all over the USA and the USSR would have to be monitored.

**10.** There are areas of the two countries, in addition to the test sites, that might be considered to be more important to monitor than others. The possibilities of conducting unnoticed tests are, for example, increased by the availability of large cavities or unconsolidated rock which reduce the strength of the seismic signals. Other possible areas of importance are regions of shallow seismicity. It might be desirable to establish specific verification arrangements in some of these areas, and our six nations are prepared to co-operate with the USA and the USSR on this issue.

**11.** There is today a large number of seismological stations, established to record local earthquakes, both within the USA and the USSR. Some of these stations might not be equipped at present with the most modern or high sensitivity instruments and they might not be sited in an optimal way to monitor a moratorium or a CTB. They are however operational today and could initially be of great value in rapidly improving the present monitoring capability. A major question is to assure the authenticity of the measurements obtained at these stations.

**12.** This could be achieved by "internationalizing" a number of selected stations, tentatively 20–30, in each of the two countries by placing observers from our six nations at these stations. Their task would be to verify that the instruments are properly operated and that all information obtained is reported without omission. We are prepared to work out the necessary arrangements, which could be made with little delay and to contribute observers for an initial period of one year.

**13.** To replace these temporary measures with permanent arrangements, our experts are ready to co-operate with experts of the USA and the USSR in the development of an optimal network of internal stations in the USA and USSR.

### Possible inspection of large chemical explosions

**14.** To ensure that large chemical explosions conducted during a moratorium are not misinterpreted as nuclear tests, we are prepared to establish, together with the USA and the USSR, procedures for on-site inspections of large chemical explosions and to take part in such inspections.

### Activities by our six countries independently of the USA and the USSR

**15.** In order to pave the way for the establishment of efficient verification measures, our six countries will take a number of technical actions independently of the USA and the USSR. We shall be strengthening our mutual co-operation with a view to monitoring and announcing ongoing test activities. This will involve rapid exchange of data related to presumed explosions as well as informal technical consultations about the nature of observed events. Our countries will jointly publish yearly statistics on test activities in the nuclear weapon states. To this end, efforts are also being made further to improve our national verification facilities to achieve an even higher and balanced monitoring capability with regard to existing test sites.

**16.** We will also support the establishment of an international verification system by actively participating in the on-going work on such a system by the group of scientific experts at the Conference on Disarmament in Geneva. Our six nations will also consider steps by which the non-nuclear weapon states may co-operate in international verification arrangements related to future nuclear disarmament.

### Expert discussions with the USA and the USSR

**17.** We have proposed to the leaders of the USA and the USSR that experts from our six nations meet with Soviet and American experts. The purpose should be to explain in detail the proposals put forward in this document, to discuss how they could be implemented, and to explore other possible ways in which our six countries could facilitate test ban verification.

*Published by PARLIAMENTARIANS GLOBAL ACTION, 220 East 42nd Street, Suite 3301, New York, New York 10017 USA.*

# Bibliography

*The following works are recommended for further reading. In addition, many of the organizations listed in Appendix B have reading material available.*

American Friends Service Committee. *Questions and Answers on the Soviet Threat and National Security.* Philadelphia PA: AFSC, 1981.

Bowen, Catherine D. *Miracle at Philadelphia.* Boston and Toronto: Little, Brown, 1966 (reprinted 1986).

Bowman, Robert M. *Star Wars: Defense or Death Star?* Potomac MD: Institute for Space and Security Studies, 1985.

Brock, Peter. *Pioneer of the Peaceable Kingdom.* Princeton NJ: Princeton University Press, 1968.

Brown, Robert McAfee. *Making Peace in the Global Village.* Philadelphia PA: Westminster, 1981.

Clark, Grenville, and Louis Sohn. *World Peace Through World Law.* Cambridge: Harvard University Press, 1966.

Curti, Merle. *Peace or War: The American Struggle, 1636–1936.* Boston: Canner, 1959.

Davis, Garry. *My Country Is the World.* Sorrento ME: Juniper Ledge, 1961.

_____. *World Government, Ready or Not.* Sorrento ME: Juniper Ledge, 1984.

Dorner, Peter, ed. *World Without War, Political and Institutional Challenges.* Madison WI: University of Wisconsin Press, 1984.

Fadden, John. *The Great Law of Peace of the Longhouse People.* Rooseveltown NY: Akwesane Notes, Mohawk Nation, 1975.

Ferencz, Benjamin B. *A Common Sense Guide to World Peace.* New York: Oceana, 1985.

_____. *Planethood.* Coos Bay OR: Vision, 1988.

Foundazione Europea Luciane Bolis. *The Federalist, a Political Review.* Pavia, Italy: EDIF, 1984.

Galt, Tom. *Peace and War: Man-Made.* Boston: Beacon, 1962.

Glossop, Ronald J. *Confronting War.* Jefferson NC and London: McFarland, 1983.

Holland, Elizabeth Jay, ed. *Peace Is Possible.* New York: Grossman, 1966.

Hudgens, Tom A. *Let's Abolish War.* Denver CO: BILR, 1986.

Hugo, Victor. *United States of Europe* (Vol. IV, No. 6, Part II of Pamphlet Series). Boston: World Peace Foundation, 1914.

Institute for Defense and Disarmament Studies. *Peace Resource Book.* Cambridge MA: Ballinger, 1986.

Kant, Immanuel. *Perpetual Peace.* New York: Columbia University Press, 1939.

Kennedy, Moorhead. *The Ayatollah in the Cathedral: Reflections of a Hostage.* New York: Farrar, Straus, and Giroux, 1986.

Keyes, Ken, Jr. *The Great News! How to Survive the Nuclear Peril.* Booklet. Coos Bay OR: Ken Keyes College Bookroom.

_____. *The Hundredth Monkey.* Coos Bay OR: Vision, 1985.

National Conference of Catholic Bishops. *The Challenge of Peace: God's Promise and Our Response (A Pastoral Letter on War and Peace).* Washington DC: National Conference of Catholic Bishops, 1983.

Ragsdale, Jane, ed. *Wisconsin Citizen's Primer on Peacemaking.* Madison WI: University of Wisconsin Press, 1983.

Reves, Emery. *The Anatomy of Peace.* New York: Harper and Brothers, 1945.

Schell, Jonathan. *The Fate of the Earth.* New York: Alfred A. Knopf, 1982.

Sharp, Gene. *Power and Struggle* (Part I of *The Politics of Nonviolent Action).* Boston: Porter Sargent, 1973.

_____. *The Methods of Nonviolent Action* (Part II of *The Politics of Nonviolent Action).* Boston: Porter Sargent, 1973.

Stanley Foundation. *Strategy for Peace (Twenty-fourth Annual U.S. Foreign Policy Conference Report).* Muscatine IA: Stanley Foundation, 1983.

U.N. Dept. of Public Information. *Basic Facts About the United Nations.* New York: United Nations, 1983.

Van Doren, Carl. *The Great Rehearsal.* New York: Viking, 1948.

Wallace, Paul A.W. *White Roots of Peace.* Philadelphia PA: University of Pennsylvania Press, 1946.

Wallis, Jim, ed. *Peacemakers.* San Francisco: Harper and Row, 1983.

Will, Herman. *A Will for Peace.* Washington DC: General Board of Church and Society of the United Methodist Church, 1984.

Willkie, Wendell. *One World.* New York: Simon and Schuster, 1943.

Wynner, Edith, and Georgia Lloyd. *Searchlight on Peace Plans.* New York: Dutton, 1946.

# Index